NO GOD BUT GAIN

NO GOD BUT GAIN

*The Untold Story of Cuban Slavery,
the Monroe Doctrine, and the
Making of the United States*

Stephen M. Chambers

VERSO
London • New York

First published by Verso 2015
© Stephen M. Chambers 2015

1 3 5 7 9 10 8 6 4 2

Verso
UK: 6 Meard Street, London W1F 0EG
US: 20 Jay Street, Suite 1010, Brooklyn, NY 11201
www.versobooks.com

Verso is the imprint of New Left Books

ISBN-13: 978-1-78168-807-6 (HB)
eISBN-13: 978-1-78168-809-0 (UK)
eISBN-13: 978-1-78168-808-3 (US)

British Library Cataloguing in Publication Data
A catalogue record for this book is available from the British Library

Library of Congress Cataloging-in-Publication Data
A catalog record for this book is available from the Library of Congress

Typeset in Adobe Garamond Pro by MJ & N Gavan, Truro, Cornwall
Printed in the US by Maple Press

For my wife, Ceceley

"The Count was perfectly good-humored, and avowed his prejudices against the class of merchants without reserve. He says they are the cause of all these wars, without ever taking part in them or suffering from them – they fatten and grow rich upon the misery and blood of nations; that they have no country but their counting-house, no God but gain."

John Quincy Adams (St. Petersburg, Russia), May 15, 1812

Contents

The Generation of 1815

They were running out of time. James D'Wolf stomped into the secretary of state's office and, without waiting, demanded an answer: What was John Quincy Adams going to do? The British, D'Wolf told Adams, were preparing to seize the Spanish colony of Cuba.

According to Adams, "Mr D'Wolf, a Senator from Rhode-Island, came in great alarm, expecting that the British Government will within a month take possession of the Island of Cuba. I thought his apprehensions at least premature, and endeavored to reason and to laugh him out of them—not altogether successfully."[1]

It was April 1822. As secretary of state under President James Monroe, Adams was a busy man. American diplomacy remained in its infancy, and U.S. diplomats were frequently regarded as second-rate or peripheral by European powers. The United States were young. Projecting power on a global, hemispheric or continental stage remained a fantasy for many American statesmen, and each new arrival of European fleets in the Americas stirred frantic rumors of trade disruptions or even invasion. Just eight years earlier, after all, British soldiers had burned Washington to the ground.

But why should James D'Wolf, a U.S. senator from the small New England state of Rhode Island, have cared so desperately about a Spanish colony in the Caribbean? And why did John Quincy Adams likely look up at D'Wolf and smile?

The following year, James D'Wolf was back for a similar meeting.

This time, although Adams did *not* record the encounter, D'Wolf referenced his conversation in a letter posted to his brother John in Bristol, Rhode Island:

> It gives me pleasure to inform our Bristol friends, Captain John Smith and George D'Wolf in particular, that the Secretary of State, Mr. Adams, has just told me that I may be perfectly easy about the English making any attempt to get possession of Cuba. He has an official promise that no such intention exists, which to me is quite consoling, and I have no doubt it will be so to all our friends who have such *deep interest* in that island.[2]

Ten months later, in December 1823, John Quincy Adams would decisively shape the diplomatic prerogative that came to be known as the Monroe Doctrine, in which the U.S. president famously declared that Europeans were no longer welcome in the Americas: "The American continents," President James Monroe said, "by the free and independent condition which they have assumed and maintain, are henceforth not to be considered as subjects for future colonization by any European powers." Although President Monroe himself delivered the address to Congress, historians have long since concluded that John Quincy Adams was the primary architect behind it.

Since Columbus's arrival in the Americas, Europeans had carved maps of the Western Hemisphere any way they saw fit, often ignoring the realities on the ground. The influence of native populations and rival European powers was frequently ignored or deliberately marginalized in the imagination of politically minded Europeans. Empire was as much about the control of knowledge and the ability to shape a coherent vision of the world as it was about gold, sugar and slaves. In the centuries since 1492, numerous wars had been fought, casting European politics and ambitions on a new, global stage in a teetering-tottering scramble for colonial control across the Americas, Africa and Asia. By the 1820s, although much of the Americas had never actually fallen under complete European control, the influence of the Spanish, Portuguese, English and French empires resonated from the North American Great Lakes to the South American rainforests.

Now, however, these empires had come under attack from without and within, as locally born elites and a groundswell of indigenous peoples and migrants—some voluntary, many not—followed the example of the United States to declare their independence, frequently aided by European rivals. In the first decades of the nineteenth century, Europeans were losing ground. From the Seven Years' War to the Haitian Revolution, the French had suffered repeated defeats in the Americas, and although the British still clung to Canada and several important Caribbean outposts, such as Jamaica and Barbados, they too had lost the North American colonies that became the new United States. Now the Spanish and Portuguese empires had begun to pitch and burn in a string of colonial fires that raged from Mexico to Brazil. By the 1820s, the hemisphere was in turmoil. The Caribbean, in particular, was an anarchic borderland of disparate navies, revolutionaries and opportunists in which national zones of legal control often meant much less than physical violence. As the Europeans regrouped and launched counter-offensives, U.S. president James Monroe—driven by his secretary of state, John Quincy Adams—declared that the United States would no longer tolerate their interference.

This was heady talk and entirely unenforceable for a young nation with just sixteen warships. In 1823, U.S. power was almost a contradiction in terms. Although the War of 1812 had importantly shaped the United States, that conflict was a New World footnote in the Napoleonic Era for most Europeans. The war had not ended decisively for either the United States or Great Britain, and the attempted U.S. invasion of Canada had been a complete failure. Throughout much of the war, the British had been forced to contend with French forces in Europe on an unprecedented scale, and at the war's conclusion, the British government did not even send its top diplomats to the U.S. peace negotiations. More important conversations were under way at the Congress of Vienna, which redrew the map of Europe following Napoleon's 1814 defeat.

Yet despite the actual fragility of the U.S. position in 1823, the Monroe Doctrine would later be heralded as a cornerstone in U.S. diplomacy for generations and would importantly shape and justify American intervention in the hemisphere throughout the nineteenth and twentieth centuries. From nineteenth-century Latin American

trade policies, to Theodore Roosevelt's 1898 "corollary," to President
John F. Kennedy's 1962 citation of the doctrine during the Cuban
Missile Crisis, the Monroe Doctrine would be explicitly referenced as a
foundation of U.S. power in the hemisphere. By the twentieth century,
of course, the United States had become a global superpower. At the
time of the doctrine's formulation in 1823, however, matters were far
different. Only the British had the naval forces to realistically back up
the Monroe Doctrine's core provisions, and both Adams and Monroe
knew it. In fact, in the months before Monroe's 1823 speech, the British
had suggested to Adams the possibility of a joint, bilateral resolution.
Adams refused.

The next year, Adams ran for the presidency, and in February 1825,
the House of Representatives finally selected him to be the sixth president of the United States, and the first from a truly post-revolutionary
generation. Born on July 11, 1767, John Quincy Adams had been just
six years old when his father, John Adams, declared, "The second day of
July 1776, will be the most memorable epoch in the history of America."
The senior Adams had been off by two days, but now, forty-nine years
later, an aging John Adams was still alive to witness his son's rise to the
presidency. Despite his later grumblings that "no man who ever held the
office of President would congratulate a friend on obtaining it," Adams
was pleased to watch his son succeed him.[3]

James D'Wolf was happy too. The same day that Henry Clay convinced Congress to make John Quincy Adams president, James D'Wolf
wrote to his brother John: "Can go out now. The clouds disperse and
fair weather. I hope for 4 years at least."[4]

On the face of it, D'Wolf's support for Adams might seem unsurprising. Like Adams, D'Wolf was a New Englander who had been born a
decade before the American Revolution. Although John Quincy Adams
had spent much of his life in Europe and Washington, he was a native
of Massachusetts, and because James D'Wolf hailed from the Bay State's
southern neighbor of Rhode Island, he and Adams had long moved
in many of the same elite circles. The two men also had reputations
for impatience. Adams could be abrasive and cold, and throughout
his long career in European diplomatic circles he was often regarded
as decidedly undiplomatic by the more polished, aristocratic diplomats

of the old world. But if Adams was practically minded, by the 1820s James D'Wolf made him look positively frivolous by comparison. D'Wolf was a cynical, hard-nosed businessman who had little patience for Washington: "All the business of Congress could be done in two months and have full-time for deliberation and would be done," D'Wolf fumed, "if Congress[ional] wages were three dollars per day, instead of eight." In D'Wolf's estimation, Congress was packed with inept lawyers and do-nothing "country court house magpies" who made a habit of delaying legislation to collect their salaries. He was even less forgiving of the executive branch and described President James Monroe as a "timid man" with "weak nerves," whose "imbecility" made him "so feared of doing wrong that he is incapable of acting." For James D'Wolf, inaction meant loss of profit.[5]

By the time of John Quincy Adams's rise to the presidency, D'Wolf was one of the richest men in the United States. He had begun his career in shipping and became notorious for his role in the transatlantic slave trade, where he and his allies had made much of their fortune. D'Wolf was not simply a remote investor in the slave trade, as were numerous people of every stripe in the period, but a slave-ship captain himself—and a particularly notorious one at that. In fact, D'Wolf's brutality was so extreme, even by contemporary standards in the slave trade, that he had once been sued by his own crew. In the 1790s, he had been charged with murder after gagging and dumping an enslaved woman overboard his slave ship *Polly* to avoid a smallpox outbreak. Killing the enslaved woman had been a material calculation on D'Wolf's part, related to the ship's insurance policy, which, as historian Marcus Rediker notes, "would reimburse him only for the death of more than 20 percent of the enslaved, thereby creating a material incentive to kill one, save many, and profit."[6]

That the D'Wolf network allowed Bristol, Rhode Island, to remain a hub of the slave trade after its outlaw in 1808 was well known up and down the Atlantic Coast. When he was elected to the U.S. Senate in 1820, a Massachusetts paper remarked that "the Salem Gazette announces Mr. D'Wolf's election together with the conviction of two slave dealers below the Circuit Court in Boston, and adds this pointed remark—'Thus one Slave Trader goes into the United States Senate, and another into the State's Prison!'"[7] And a Pennsylvania paper similarly reflected that "*Wolf* is certainly an appropriate name for a man-stealer."[8] In Washington, too, before taking his seat D'Wolf would be chastised by Senator William Smith of South Carolina for his notorious involvement in the illegal slave trade.[9]

John Quincy Adams, on the other hand, is often celebrated by scholars for his later antislavery work in his Congressional career and for his participation in the famous *Amistad* Supreme Court decision. But that came later. Appreciating why D'Wolf and Adams remained allies in the early decades of the nineteenth century requires a reconceptualization of early U.S. development with the slave trade at its heart. In the aftermath of the American Revolution and the War of 1812, many elite members of the post-revolutionary generation of 1815 accepted that the development of the new United States would require the transatlantic slave trade. U.S. foreign policy was explicitly shaped to defend the expansion of the outlawed slave trade alongside a "liberalization" of hemispheric trade restrictions. The logic of nineteenth-century financial markets demanded both. Although historians have sometimes considered slavery to be pre-capitalist, there was, in fact, nothing so modern or necessary to the integration of nineteenth-century global markets as the expansion of slavery and the slave trade.

This book considers the role of the illegal slave trade and the slavery it made possible in the development of the United States in these crucial years of the Early Republic, from approximately the 1790s to the 1830s. These years witnessed a dramatic expansion in the size, scope and scale of the young United States. The parts of this story that are well known tend to focus on slavery within the boundaries of what would become the North American union. That is the story of how the boom in cotton production that accompanied the expansion of slavery in North America was a central driver in the formation of capital markets and industrializing cities on both sides of the Atlantic. After the War of 1812, that is also the story of how the creation of the "Old" South propelled U.S. trade with England, setting the stage for generations of interdependent, ultimately fractious economic growth that would trigger the U.S. Civil War. That is *not* the story I am concerned with in this book.

This book focuses on what I believe to be the equally important story of how slavery *outside* U.S. borders—slavery that depended on the transatlantic slave trade—impacted national U.S. development and foreign policy. From 1501 to 1867, more than 12.5 million Africans were brought to the Americas in chains, and as many as 100 million Africans died as a direct or indirect consequence of the slave trade. Of all the enslaved Africans who were carried to the Americas, fewer than 4 percent (389,000) arrived in North America. Forty-four percent (5,532,118), more than in any other region, were taken to the sugar colonies of Brazil, where the ports of Rio de Janeiro and Salvador de Bahia dominated the trade. Approximately 7 percent (889,990) of all enslaved Africans arrived in Cuba, where Havana would become a crucial center of the nineteenth-century trade.[10]

Movements to abolish the slave trade began to have an impact on public policy in the late eighteenth century: first in Denmark, which abolished the trade in 1792 (effective in 1803) and then France, where the Revolutionary Wars ended the slave trade in 1793, only to reinstate it in 1802. Legally, the U.S. Constitution guaranteed the survival of the slave trade:

> The Migration or Importation of such Persons as any of the States now existing shall think proper to admit, shall not be prohibited by the Congress prior to the Year one thousand eight hundred and eight, but a tax or duty may be imposed on such Importation, not exceeding ten dollars for each Person.

This meant that no U.S. law could outlaw the slave trade for twenty years, and it was not until March 2, 1807, that U.S. nationals were barred from participating in the slave trade. The ban would not go into effect until January 1, 1808, but later that month, Great Britain's Parliament passed "An Act for the Abolition of the Slave Trade," which also outlawed the traffic. As other nations followed suit, including the Dutch (1814), Spain (1817, effective 1820), Brazil (1826, effective 1830) and Portugal (1836), an Atlantic economic engine that had gone largely unquestioned for centuries was now suddenly under attack. The central economic engine of the Atlantic World appeared to be on the verge of extinction. But appearances can be deceiving, and the trans-atlantic slave trade would continue until at least 1867, when the last known slave ship arrived in Cuba. Slavery itself would not be abolished in these regions for another two decades; it formally ended in 1886 in Cuba and in 1888 in Brazil.

Despite the spread of antislavery sentiment and abolitionism on both sides of the Atlantic, despite numerous laws and treaties passed to curb the slave trade, and despite the dispatch of naval squadrons to patrol the coasts of Africa and the Americas, the slave trade did not end in 1808. Fully 25 percent (3.2 million) of all the enslaved Africans to arrive in the Americas were brought *after* the U.S. ban. Just as signifi-cantly, more than 85 percent (759,669) of slaves brought to Cuba and 40 percent (2.2 million) of those brought to Brazil arrived after 1807. Although the British navy would exercise significant muscle in suppress-ing the trade, many other nations that had sworn to suppress the trade did little to intervene. The United States was among them. But what some scholars have mistaken for ineptitude on the part of U.S. naval forces was often the manifestation of deliberate, indirect support for the slave trade. Where scholars have sometimes been stumped by the apparent incongruity of a U.S. foreign policy that promoted economic liberalization throughout the Americas while ignoring the expanding slave trade, I contend that these measures were entirely consistent. The pro-slavery, anti-British foreign policies of the administrations of every president from Thomas Jefferson through John Quincy Adams were for-mulated according to a theory of free trade that worked in tandem with the expansion of slavery. Moreover, because the dismantling of restric-tive mercantilist trade systems was often explicitly political—that is, anti-monarchical, anti-colonial—the fight for free trade was frequently framed as striking a blow for emancipation, even as it strengthened the slave economies of the Americas.

In North America, U.S. economic development and westward expan-sion was a direct result and driver of slavery that depended on the illegal slave trade. The U.S. banks and insurance companies that provided the agricultural loans that created the nation themselves depended on a reliable fount of specie (gold and silver), and sugar and coffee to back their notes and offset trade deficits with the financial centers of Europe.

Financial intermediaries developed in the United States, because the slave trade and the commodities produced by slave regimes provided greater access to credit and capital. Waves of turnpike, canal and manufacturing companies received corporate charters alongside new banks and marine insurance companies, which replaced private underwriters.[11] This leveraged the savings of insurance investors—including many smaller investors—into an even wider variety of credit. Capital could also be reinvested in other financial structures (primarily banks), many of which contained overlapping and familial directors.[12]

It is no coincidence that the same small cohort of elite American merchants that had made their fortunes at sea now founded the nation's banks, insurance companies, and factories, even as they rose to public office. As ship captains became merchants became bankers became senators, the personal nature of credit and the outsized wealth of individual merchants meant that lending and investment was typically a family affair.[13] And they kept their ships. Many elite merchant-bankers did *not* automatically abandon the carrying trade when they entered finance and manufacturing.[14] For decades after the U.S. ban, sugar and gold flowed north in their ships because of a steady influx of illegally transported enslaved Africans to replace the dead in the agro-industrial graveyards of the Caribbean and South America. In these years, this was the central driver of the rise of U.S. finance, market integration, and globalization. If coffee, sugar and specie unlocked the doors of European and Asian markets for U.S. capitalists, slave ships were their key. The modern system of global capitalism originated as a machine that ran on the engine of the slave trade.

This book cannot touch on every—or even most—aspects of this system. What it can do is focus on a particular, highly important node in this system to demonstrate how slavery, fed by illegal traffic, impacted the United States at this crucial moment. The point I have chosen is Cuba. To be sure, early American involvement in Cuba is not the only subject of this book. But while this book will track the relationship between power, capitalism and slavery from Boston to Washington to Russia, Cuba was a uniquely central driver of U.S. economic development and foreign policy in these early national years. Whereas the human body may not require sugar and coffee to survive, global circuits of trade certainly demanded them.[15] Once these Cuban commodities are established as central to emerging systems of global exchange, I place the slave trade at the forefront of U.S. economic and diplomatic history for years after the trade was outlawed by the United States and European powers.

For generations, scholars have debated the moral implications of ex post facto judgments with respect to slavery and the slave trade. The debate is as old as antislavery sentiment itself, and today, numerous scholars and public figures remain actively engaged in it. Twenty-first-century institutions have apologized for their participation in slavery, and the descendants of slave owners and slave traders—including those of James D'Wolf—have publicly condemned and attempted to atone for their ancestors' involvement in the enslavement of others. This book is not about that. This is not a work intended to reconcile the actions of long-dead slave traders, nor is it an effort to offer solutions to slavery's legacy in the present. This book is also not a study of the slave trade per se: Much excellent scholarship already exists, and much more is in the works by pathbreaking historians of the trade.

In many ways, the horrors of the slave trade present a challenge: The "diabolical machine," the "pool of torture," misery and loss that shaped the lives of the enslaved—and often the lives of enslavers—for the weeks and months that they spent onboard slave ships could quickly overwhelm this story.[16] The calculus of human misery of the slave trade is so staggering that I have attempted to walk a careful line between acknowledgement and avoidance. Certainly, there are moments when this book ducks into the stinking bowels of slave ships and vicious slave labor camps of the Americas, but there are many more times when it does not, simply because other fine historians have dedicated their lives to that work. This book is intended to do something different and new. It is an opening salvo in the unknown history of the slave trade's impact on U.S. development for the post-revolutionary generation of 1815, during a period that has been neglected in popular and professional historical circles alike.

The Monroe Doctrine was created to protect the illegal slave trade and the slave regimes it created. But if these were the stakes—the origins of nineteenth-century global capitalism and U.S. foreign policy—and if elite, well-known figures such as John Quincy Adams were involved, why has the role of the illicit slave trade been overlooked in early U.S. development? How have the slave trade and its beneficiaries hidden in plain sight? Part of the explanation lies in the ways that historical scholarship is conducted and subdivided by field, including the chronological benchmarks of nineteenth-century U.S. empire and the disjunction between Atlantic World studies and nineteenth-century scholarship. These are complex, methodological issues related to scholarly training and turf wars, but they are not the whole explanation. The real reason the slave trade has been overlooked is more practical: It has to do with the archive. Tracking the archival record of the illegal slave trade's impact on U.S. development is extremely difficult, in part, because many documents simply have not survived.

In many of the major hubs of the illegal slave trade, such as Cuba and Brazil, records are notoriously incomplete or difficult to access due to the local climate, archival neglect and political circumstances. In the United States, too, vast amounts of vital documents from this period were lost. In the second half of the nineteenth century, precious few documents survived to provide insight into the most powerful commercial houses from the post-revolutionary generation of 1815. By 1900, men who had once invested in fleets that dwarfed the U.S. navy were remembered only for the streets and buildings that were named in their honor. Time, accidental fire, and deliberate sabotage had conspired to swallow the evidence.

In the city of Portland, Maine, for example, whose economy was once deeply linked to the illegal slave trade, more than 1,800 buildings went up in flames in 1866. The first building to burn was a sugar warehouse, and the fire soon destroyed most of the records of the city's commercial houses, erasing all evidence that the vast majority of the sugar had come from Cuba. Today, evidence of Portland's outsized role in the trade comes from Havana, not from Maine. Six years later, ships along the Maine coast spotted a similar ominous glow in the night sky as Boston burned in 1872, and here, too, numerous records were lost.

Other fires were less random, and extraterritorial slavery's role in the development of the United States has also been overlooked, because many of its architects intended it to be that way. In March 1824, for

example, James D'Wolf ended a letter to his brother John with a for-
mality: "I hope you do not expose any of my letters," he wrote, "but
commit them to the fire when you have read them."[17] To make matters
worse, the few surviving records were often irregular, consisting of idiosyncratic, personalized methods of record-keeping.[18] Bookkeeping and
correspondence were kept out of necessity by many men who had not
been formally educated. Compared to the refined penmanship of later
generations—and of their own commercial agents—elite figures such
as James D'Wolf left a nearly illegible scrawl of commodity prices and
inscrutable missives.

This archival confusion and silence left little for subsequent generations of historians to go on when they first sat down to write the
history of this post-revolutionary era. Moreover, the first chroniclers of
the post-revolutionary generation were often direct descendants of their
subjects, and more recent scholars have often followed their predecessors'
hagiographic lead. Because many of these elite figures were successful
financially, their wealth—which has persisted even to the present in
some cases—was naturalized and given moral overtones. "Enterprising,"
"bold" and "industrious" are typical terms used to describe the "trade,"
"commerce" and "mercantile" pursuits of these "ambitious" men.
Overwhelmingly sympathetic to their subjects, generations of historians
have tended to celebrate their fortunes, leaving distant slave plantations, which often formed the bedrock of these financial empires, in the
margins. The illegal slave trade is rarely, if ever, mentioned.

The following book is the product of an interrogation of private commercial correspondence, shipping manifests, bills of lading, port records,
public diplomatic records, published state papers, foreign records of
every sort, numerous court and notarial records from both the United
States and Cuba, and periodical and print literature. Wherever possible,
I have also endeavored to overcome the absence of records by locating
new sources of data. In the cases of Boston and Havana, for example,
port records do not survive for many crucial years in the early nineteenth century. Ship entrances and clearances were published, however,
in the newspapers of both ports, and, in both cases, I have compiled a
database from these sources to demonstrate the scale and contours of
the trade. At various times, I have also leveraged traditional diplomatic

correspondence in new ways, reading consular dispatches not simply for their political overtones but also for their commercial implications. At times, *where* correspondence was sent could be as important as a document's contents in tracing how public power operated within the commercial networks of transatlantic commercial houses that made the illegal slave trade and the slave regimes it fed essential to the development of the United States. Predictably, the data source for this study is more representative than complete, but it is enough to begin the process of reconstructing what was lost.

Today, historians have (rightly, I believe) given voice to the founding members of the '76er revolutionary generation who created the United States. But when the war was won, the Constitution adopted and political succession secured, the young nation still faced many urgent and uncomfortable questions. And although some important members of this original U.S. generation survived into the early decades of the nineteenth century, their children were left with important decisions to make. None was more crucial than determining the role of slavery and the slave trade in the making of the new United States. The post-revolutionary generation, which I call the '15ers—chosen for the decisive year 1815, when members of this generation witnessed the scale and scope of what the United States might become after the War of 1812—supported the integration of both legal slavery and the illegal slave trade into U.S. development. Although many historians of U.S. foreign policy typically take 1815 as either a starting or end point, this year is better approached as 1776 is for the nation's founding generation—as a key moment in a larger arc. The generation of 1815 shaped U.S. foreign policy to protect the outlawed slave trade—primarily in Cuba—for the sake of economic development. They shelved the contentious discussion of slavery's North American future, which would ultimately lead *their* children and grandchildren to fight a bloody civil war. Two hundred years later, it is time the '15ers had their day.

ONE

Smugglers

George Morton was irritable. It was 1801, and things were not going according to plan. Havana was supposed to be a path to easy money, where the authorities could be counted on to take their share and allow the undocumented circuits of commerce to make everyone rich. But in this anarchic borderland, where national laws were often contradictory or ignored, profit depended on power and violence. Commercial success hinged on transnational connections. And Morton's contacts were in trouble.

He had been in Cuba since at least 1795, working at the cluttered desks of the U.S. consular office near the waterfront docks of Havana that looked across the crowded bay of ships and sharks to the stone fortress, El Morro, which commanded the port with heavy guns. In the centuries since Christopher Columbus had arrived in Cuba, the fortress had been the key to Spain's control of the island, and it still inspired awe in visitors. In the consular office, Morton tracked the numbers of destitute sailors who had been stranded on the island by unscrupulous American ship captains. He privately tallied the banknotes and gold and silver coins that passed in and out in bags and heavy iron boxes. Now, the boxes were light.

As Morton reflected on his troubles, a group of Americans unloaded bags in the office. They were working too slowly, wasting Morton's time, and when he shouted at them to hurry up, they answered back, mocking him. Another American merchant from New York stepped between them, but Morton had had enough. He insulted the first man, raised his cane and pulled up on the cane handle; a scabbard came away to reveal a sword blade underneath. The man saw the blade and panicked, but before Morton could lunge, the New Yorker, Seymour, pressed between them. The American workers ducked outside, while Seymour backed away from Morton.

Morton told Seymour that he was a dead man. That night Morton hired an assassin, and after three failed assassination attempts, Seymour wrote to President Thomas Jefferson of his ordeal at the hands of "a fellow citizen."[1] Although Seymour was the brother-in-law of the wealthy and influential New York merchant Nathaniel Ingraham, the president did nothing. Jefferson understood the rules of the game.

If slavery that depended on the illegal slave trade drove U.S. economic development and gave rise to nineteenth-century global capitalism, it is important to understand how and where it began. After 1808, Cuba was the first, closest, and most important point of contact with the illicit slave trade for many U.S. investors. Farther south, Americans would also play a large role in the Brazilian slave regime, beginning in the late 1820s and 1830s. By this time, North Americans had already established a de facto informal empire on the much closer Spanish island. No one had seen this coming.

In 1790, Cuba was an undeveloped backwater, important to the Spanish empire primarily as a military waypoint in the galleon trade between the Americas and Spain. By contemporary standards, there were few slaves in Cuba, and sugar and coffee production was slight compared to that of nearby French and English colonies. Soon, all of this would change. Within a generation, Cuba became the largest slave-importing colony in the Spanish empire and the center of the nineteenth-century Caribbean slave trade. It would also grow into the largest sugar producer in the world and the second-largest trade partner of the United States. By the 1820s, slavery in Cuba would become so intertwined with the U.S. economy that, as the scholar Laird Bergad has documented, "there was a positive correlation (.75) between the movement of wholesale sugar prices in the United States and prices for prime-age slaves in Cuba."[2] Before 1808, Americans made this possible, and in the years after the U.S. and British bans in 1807–8—and after the Spanish ban in 1817 (effective 1820)—U.S. citizens continued to doggedly fight to protect the illegal slave trade with the apparatus of the U.S. state for the sake of economic development.

This chapter tells the story of how this began, both because it is essential to an appreciation of what would follow and because the timeline and persistence of U.S. investment in the Cuban slave regime is simply not known. Reflecting on the field, scholars Louis Pérez and Laird Bergad make this lapse plain. By 1823, Louis Pérez suggests that "an estimated fifty North Americans owned plantations valued at more than three million dollars in Matanzas alone."[3] The areas south and southwest of Matanzas Bay attracted, in Laird Bergard's estimation, "a nucleus of U.S. citizens" along "the Canimar and Camarioca rivers" who "invested primarily in coffee cultivation." Yet, as Bergad acknowledges, "Little is known about these early U.S. investors, who were no doubt drawn to the island by the surge in U.S.–Cuban commerce."[4] Such remarks say little about the relative impact of American investment in Cuba and only hint at the chronology of U.S. participation in the Cuban slave regime.

Hugh Thomas, for example, writes that "since 1818 ... foreigners had been buying interests in Cuban sugar as well as establishing themselves as merchants. Many Americans and some Englishmen had plantations." He then proceeds to list a number of U.S. investors, including "'Don Guillermo' Stewart of Philadelphia," "Augustus Hemenway, a ship-owner from Boston," "J.W. Baker" of Philadelphia and "the North American Jenks." His roster of American merchants in Cuba includes "Frederick Freeman," "the Phinneys of Bristol," "James Burnham," "Thomas Brooks" and "Francis Adams."[5] Although Thomas begins his chronology in 1818, many of his sources date much later, and the bulk of Thomas's evidence for this U.S. expatriate community can be traced to the 1830s or even later. Louis Pérez provides a similar listing of early North American investors in the Spanish colony, which includes Moses Taylor & Co., Charles Tying & Co., Martin Knight & Co., Storey & Co., George Harris & Co., Drake Brothers & Co., Howland Brothers & Co., Dudley Selden & Co., Safford, Smith & Co., and Moreland & Co.[6] Pérez, like Thomas, groups Americans such as "Moreland" and "Knight"—who arrived in Havana in the late 1790s—with capitalists such as Moses Taylor, who did not begin to seriously invest in Cuba until the 1830s.[7] It is as if the early years of the U.S. investment—when Americans scrambled to establish a presence in a Spanish colony that had only just begun to invest in competitive sugar production—can be easily equated with a time, three decades later, when Cuba was poised to become the largest sugar producer in the world. But 1797 was not 1828.

In these early years, Northern investors and their professional corps of diplomatic-commercial agents seized a moment of opportunity that began in the 1790s to participate in one of the most ambitious development projects of the age: the transformation of Cuba from a military trading post into one of the wealthiest and most technologically driven plantation regimes in the history of New World slavery. In this period, American and European investors spent more than fifteen million pesos on the development of Cuban sugar, making it "the highest figure," according to Moreno Fraginals, "for any business of the period anywhere in the Americas."[8] While American participation in Cuba depended on longstanding trade ties and the impact of European warfare on the British and French merchant marine, the expansion of the U.S.–Cuba trade was not inevitable. U.S. investment depended on the highly contingent ingenuity and ruthlessness of American elites and their professional agents on the ground in the Spanish colony.

In these early years, Americans in Cuba often found themselves at the mercy of Spanish authorities who struggled to appease the contradictory expectations of Spanish and Creole merchants (often antagonistic to the United States) and planters (often supportive of the United States) to stave off revolutionary sensibilities among the Creole elite—that is, descendants of elite Europeans born in the Americas—in Cuba.[9] This was a halting, uncertain process, and the first American merchants and diplomats who struggled to negotiate the extreme uncertainty of the Spanish colony discovered that it was not only a vital imperial entrepôt, but also an anarchic borderland. The turbulent, often violent careers of these American expatriates helped ensure that slavery fed by illegal trade would become vital to North American economic development. Cuban sugar and coffee did not develop coincidentally with the North American cotton frontier and U.S. finance, but as a direct result and driver of both.

The expansion of the Cuban slave regime worked in tandem with the expansion of the cotton South to ensure that American merchants—and the banks and insurance companies they managed—could secure credit and banknotes from the financial centers of England.[10] Elite U.S. merchants leveraged investments in foreign and coastal trade with banking and insurance investments to grow larger fortunes. The vast majority of this wealth "was denominated in coffee and sugar shipped back from the Caribbean and sent on to Europe."[11] Dale Tomich has succinctly characterized this process of transatlantic market integration, suggesting that "merchants and bankers in New York, Boston, and Philadelphia could use the trade surplus from cotton exports to draw bills on London banks in order to finance," in part, the expansion of the slave frontier.[12] This entire economic system was premised on European demand for predictable supplies of sugar and coffee, which depended on the expansion of the slave trade.

Growing U.S. investment in Cuba also acted as a funnel for vital flows of specie into the United States. Throughout much of its history, Cuba had served as an imperial entrepôt for New World silver and gold: after 1765, for example, the staggering sum of approximately 243 million *pesos fuertes* (silver pesos worth 20 reales) was routed from New Spain through Cuba, either in an official capacity or on the account of private merchants and their clients.[13] After 1790, increasingly large amounts of this specie flowed north into the United States, helping to buttress the nascent U.S. financial infrastructure and offset U.S. trade deficits with Europe.[14] The Spanish economist Javier Cuenca Esteban has calculated that from 1790 through 1811 U.S. trade surpluses with Spanish colonies—primarily Cuba—offset 90 per cent of U.S. trade deficits with the rest of the world, which historian Linda Salvucci has suggested "went a long way toward reducing the international indebtedness of the young United States."[15] U.S. policymakers were well aware that by 1800 the U.S.–Cuba trade and slave trade also represented a significant percentage of total customs receipts, which were the lifeblood of government revenue.[16] If the national debt was the price of independence, the U.S.–Cuba trade represented an expeditious opportunity for the new nation to begin to settle its accounts.

Some of the implications of U.S. trade policy have been deliberately deferred to later chapters, and, in the service of illuminating this unexamined transnational moment in U.S. history, this chapter spends comparatively little time on the perspective of other contemporaries —most importantly, the many Spanish administrators, merchants and planters who frequently dictated the formal and informal terms on which Americans were allowed to remain in Cuba.[17] Above all, however, this chapter replaces the generalities of the early "West Indies" trade with the actions of the smugglers and thieves who created the foundations of informal American empire. They were the first foot soldiers of informal empire.

"Neither of These Gentlemen, To My Present Recollection, Considered the Undertaking Improper"

The history of the transatlantic slave trade was the history of sugar production. As Europeans had learned over their centuries of experience with the crop, sugar cultivation was backbreaking, brutal work, and the mortality rates of laborers often ran high. By the late eighteenth century, Europe had developed a sweet tooth, and demand soared. Sugar—not cotton, coffee or tobacco—was the reason more than 90 percent of all enslaved Africans were brought to the Americas: they arrived to chop cane and clear fields for the cultivation of new sugar crops, in what scholars now recognize as the "agro-industrial graveyard" of sugar production throughout the Americas. In 1790, Cuba was a small part of this system. That year, the island produced just 13,993 tons of sugar,[18] compared with almost 80,000 tons of sugar produced in both Saint Domingue and in the islands of the British Caribbean that same year.[19] More established sugar colonies, such as Barbados, had been intensively developed for years, but the land devoted to Cuba's cultivation of sugar in 1792 represented less than 2 percent of the island's total arable land.[20]

Then came the Haitian Revolution. When formerly enslaved Africans launched a bloody war for independence in the nearby French sugar colony of Saint Domingue in August 1791, European commodity markets panicked. Globally, sugar prices spiked from 12 reales per pound in 1790 to 36 reales per pound in 1795,[21] and U.S. imports of sugar from Saint Domingue plummeted.[22] When war broke out between England and the revolutionary government of France in 1793, the British and French merchant marines were suddenly cut out of the Atlantic carrying trade, and in the turmoil of chaotic British, Spanish and French regulations and requirements, American investors saw an opportunity.

In 1792, as hundreds of thousands of formerly enslaved Africans seized more territory in nearby Saint Domingue, French planters fled to Cuba, often with their slaves in tow. That year, a leading member of the Creole elite in Cuba named Francisco de Arango y Parreno articulated a new vision for the Spanish island. With the jewel of Caribbean sugar production descending into revolutionary war, he imagined a new kind of modernity and economic development, with intensive slavery at its core. Arango proposed a coherent system of commerce, in which the liberalization of trade and integration of Atlantic markets would work in tandem with the expansion of the slave trade. He called for the unrestricted, unlimited trade of African slaves, lower tariffs and more flexible credit laws: Free trade would provide the maximum number of enslaved workers.[23]

Planters were often explicit in their desire to shortcut the centuries of trial-and-error that had characterized sugar and coffee cultivation in neighboring Caribbean colonies. They were eager to replicate Saint Domingue, while avoiding the specter of Haiti with a massive militarization (and accompanying tax burden) to accompany the intensification of the slave trade.[24] In Cuba, investors had the advantage of latecomers and could immediately incorporate the most up-to-date technological advances across the vast, largely uncultivated soil.[25] Immediately after the outbreak of the Haitian Revolution, Cuban *ingenios azucareros* (sugar mills) and *cafetales* (coffee plantations) expanded at a frantic, unprecedented pace, and sugar production nearly doubled in just eight years, rising from 16,731 metric tons in 1791 to 32,586 metric tons in 1799.[26] Meanwhile, in an attempt to outmaneuver the French, Great Britain granted U.S. traders greater access to British colonial markets in the Caribbean and the U.S. re-export trade increased in value "from $8 million in 1795 to $26 million in 1796."[27] For many parts of the United States—particularly New England—a new golden age of seafaring appeared to be at hand. In the supply of slaves, too, Americans remained eager to join in, even as U.S. law—beginning in 1794 and continuing in 1800, 1803, and culminating in the 1807–8 ban—consistently restricted their participation in the slave trade.[28] In Cuba, Spanish merchants had attempted to curb the influence of U.S. merchants until Spain finally lifted restrictions on neutral shipping in 1797: then the Americans arrived en masse.[29]

After 1797, the character of U.S. investment in Cuba intensified, establishing the foundations of informal empire. This was an empire grounded not on military or political control, but on indirect economic power. Just one year later, the U.S.–Cuba trade surpassed Cuba's trade with Spain, and a number of the elite Americans who would remain influential on the island for decades arrived ready to invest.[30] The already booming U.S. re-export trade surged higher still. Hundreds of vessels began to arrive annually in the United States from Cuba, with cargoes of sugar and coffee intended for re-export. Although the U.S. economy grew just 1.08 percent in this period, as James Fichter has documented, "The re-export trade affected the U.S. economy unevenly, benefiting general economic growth less than it enriched the already well-off."[31] And the well-off benefited enormously. In the 1790s, the profits of the re-export trade quadrupled as its scale increased by a factor of fifty.[32] But attaining wealth in this anarchic borderland depended on balancing private trade and public diplomacy in a transnational territory characterized by power attained through lawbreaking and violence. Arango's vision was coming to life.

This is where the New Yorker George Morton found himself in 1801: at the center of a booming, anarchic commercial hub built on the slave trade, where the per capita income had already surpassed that of the United States (by 112 per cent).[33] Morton had watched Cuba change, and he recognized that public power and private profit were waiting to be seized. In Havana in 1795, for example, George Morton referred to himself as "acting American Consul," despite the fact that he had not been appointed to this position in the United States.[34] These were intimate, often personal matters. At the time, foreign diplomatic posts were frequently handed to the relatives and allies of wealthy U.S. merchants, who expected to receive commercial information and public protection for their foreign investments. Diplomatic agents, meanwhile, were eager to accept such posts because of the opportunities the public seal of the United States provided to increase their own commercial contacts. Vice consular positions, in particular, were more commercial than diplomatic in nature. These offices were frequently sold—either for a flat fee or for a percentage of the vice consul's commercial earnings—by the same American merchant-diplomats who had been appointed by Congress. By 1800, George Morton's brother John had received an official appointment, and they went to work in Havana on an even more ambitious scale.[35]

That summer, George Morton, with a Portuguese accomplice named Polyart and a Frenchman named Markonell, conspired to smuggle specie aboard the ship *Warren* from Vera Cruz on the account of the Spanish merchant J. Pedro de Erice, in conjunction with the Spanish intendant who ran Cuba. Using John Morton's public authority as U.S. consul in Havana, they secured "the Public Flag of the United States" for the *Warren* to make the cargo "secure against British Capture" in exchange for "a stipulated commission."[36] Unfortunately for the smugglers, when they arrived in New Spain, the officials in Vera Cruz were suspicious: "shipping money under a foreign flag was a novelty to the Mexicans which they cou'd not reconcile." The *Warren* was unable to "obtain a shipment on government account." It did, however, receive $102,000 in gold doubloons. The *Warren's* captain and crew were kept in the dark, and everything went according to plan—until disease broke out. The ship's captain and virtually all of the crew—forty-two men—perished of yellow fever, and soon the cargo was under scrutiny in Cuba.[37]

In the circuits of information that linked merchant houses in the Atlantic World, news traveled fast, and by August 1800, word of the debacle had reached the United States, likely from the correspondence of Dorchester merchant George Augustus Cushing. Cushing had received information through the commercial house of the wealthy Spanish merchant Santa Maria de la Cuesta, where Cushing did business and would soon be employed as an agent.[38] In Havana, American merchants were barred from operating independent commercial houses and could only trade in partnerships with Spanish merchants.[39] Cushing relayed information to the merchant Samuel Parkman in Boston, who told another of his associates, Thomas Amory Coffin, who, in turn, lobbied Thomas Jefferson in an attempt to replace Morton at the Havana post.[40]

This is why John Morton sailed north to Boston in 1800 to defend himself, leaving his brother George and their Portuguese and French accomplices—along with an Italian steward—in charge of the U.S. consular office in Havana.[41] In the United States, John Morton defended his actions to Secretary of State James Madison, arguing that "it had been customary for our public vessels to transport specie." Morton claimed to have described his plan to sail with the *Warren* to Vera Cruz to General Wilkinson and the commander of the *General Greene*, Captain Christopher Perry, and "neither of these gentlemen ... considered the undertaking as improper." If the now-deceased captain of the *Warren* had arranged the trip as a smuggling operation, Morton said, "it was unknown to ... me."[42]

Meanwhile, under pressure in Cuba, George Morton drew his sword cane and attempted to murder another American merchant for interfering in his business. In the aftermath, he may well have feared that the newly elected Jefferson administration might condemn and punish such violence. But that same month, the president agreed to look the other way.[43] Although Jefferson's tacit support for the corruption of the consular office may appear counterintuitive, it was consistent with republican political economy.

In the early years of the United States, two political parties dominated national public life: the Federalist party and the Democratic-Republican party. Although party politics was hardly professionalized or uniform in these early years, these two groups had very different plans for the future of the new nation—at least in theory. The pro-business Federalists were a dynamic force in national politics in the early decades of the United States and included figures such as Alexander Hamilton and John Adams. At its core, Federalism imagined a future in which a strong national government would enact trade and monetary policies designed to spur industrial growth and a deeper integration of the United States into world markets. It called for a national bank and was initially pro-British—or at least anti-French. For Hamilton, the U.S. Treasury would serve as the backbone of national development, although he later became disillusioned by the difficulties of creating a robust tax policy to run the government. In practice, the young nation ran almost exclusively on the duties collected from the carrying trade.

Federalism saw bankers, merchants and industrial entrepreneurs as the future of the United States. Unsurprisingly, many of their supporters were based in the eastern and northern urban centers, particularly in New England, where Federalist opposition to the War of 1812 would lead to genuine talks of secession at the Hartford Convention of 1814. Ironically, although Federalism was notoriously elitist, the conservatism at its core was in fact relatively accepting of minority rights, including those of women, blacks and Native Americans, so long as an educated, monied elite wielded the levers of power. Although Federalism has often received short shrift by scholars and students alike, it was a vibrant force, particularly in parts of New England, where it competed with Jeffersonian Republicanism for decades until both crumbled simultaneously in the political upheaval of the 1820s and 1830s.

Jeffersonian Republicans, the story goes, saw the world differently than their Federalist counterparts. A Republican future for the United States would be based on a more balanced allocation of rights grounded in a new kind of individual and sovereign independence. The national debt—a financial opportunity for Hamilton—was viewed as nothing less than a transatlantic chain that would condemn the new nation to perpetual dependency on European financial centers. Jefferson's famous "yeoman" farmers would settle the new nation and shape it through vibrant local and state polities. This agricultural expansion demanded land—as witnessed most famously by Jefferson's 1803 Louisiana Purchase, in which the United States acquired more than 828,000 square miles of territory west of the Mississippi River from France. But land was never the whole story. Jefferson knew that even the most remote rural community was, to some extent, already incorporated into the Atlantic economy: U.S. farmers were also Atlantic farmers.

In practice, Jeffersonian Republicanism required a healthy re-export trade and an increasingly robust foreign policy to protect it. As historian Drew McCoy makes plain, Republican congressmen from New England convinced Jefferson and Madison that the nation's agricultural development depended on the carrying trade: "American merchants exchanged domestic agricultural surpluses in the East and West Indies for tropical staples that had to be resold in Europe. If this circuitous trade was in any way obstructed, therefore, American farmers would eventually suffer the loss of valuable markets for their surpluses."[44] In fact, many of the statesmen who were most influential in convincing the administration to support the re-export trade in the early 1800s, such as Jacob Crowninshield and Harrison Gray Otis (both from Massachusetts), were either personally invested in the Cuba trade or were longtime allies of families with deep stakes in the trade. And numerous members of the most powerful elite investors in the slave trade and its products—men like James D'Wolf—were Republicans, not Federalists, precisely because they recognized that a deeper Atlantic market integration was already underway. In this wheel of exchange, the "tropical staples"—primarily sugar and coffee—that undergirded North American agricultural expansion depended on the slave trade and the expansion of American economic influence.

Both the Jefferson and Madison administrations consistently worked to protect elite U.S. merchants in Cuba who were implicated in illegal operations: what Spanish officials termed "smuggling" was the necessary prerequisite for the American economic expansion that supported Republican political economy. On December 6, 1803, for example, Secretary of State James Madison lobbied the Spanish minister in Washington to help the wealthy Baltimore merchant John Hollins in a lawsuit in Havana. The following month, he did the same with the captain-general for the U.S. merchant William Cooke, who claimed that one of his vessels had been seized in Havana on false smuggling charges.[45] Madison routinely supported such cases, despite their suspicious nature. In Cooke's claim, for example, Cooke asked for $93,000 in damages, despite the fact that the vessel and cargo were—by his own estimation—worth less than $6,000.[46] This is why George Morton could smuggle specie under a false flag and draw a sword cane with impunity in the consular office of Havana: U.S. development depended on it.

But in these borderlands, Americans were not in charge, and Americans' influence in Cuba generally advanced only with the support of their allies—primarily the slaveholding planters, who demanded a steady influx of commodities and slaves shipped by the United States. Reflecting on Adam Smith's acknowledgement that "all people attempt to employ their capital out of sight and inspection," the Spanish Consulado—the wealthy and influential merchants' guild in Havana, which included many planters—repeatedly pressured the captain-general to allow free trade on the island for U.S. merchants. Illicit trade could simply not be tracked, the Consulado argued, and if the authorities applied too much pressure, U.S. merchants would go elsewhere.[47] For these planters, the liberalization of U.S. trade was a solution to laborious Spanish imperial restrictions.

For hamstrung Spanish merchants, this was intolerable. They were often resentful of the growing influence of expert American smugglers, who frequently leveraged fake flags and forged documents to dodge customs and undercut their Spanish and Creole competitors. Writing from Boston in 1802, for example, the American merchant George Cushing described a scheme to "make a few thousand dollars" by purchasing ships in New England "to be put under Spanish colours for the Havana." Cushing suspected that the expatriate Nathaniel Fellowes's connections might allow him to obtain "compleat setts of ships papers" from the Spanish Governor. These blank documents could be shipped north and sold to New England smugglers "for seven or eight hundred dolla[r]s, & perhaps a thousand" per set. "A great number of papers," Cushing wrote, "have been procured in this way; expressly for the admission of vessels in ballast into the Havana for sale." Now, George Cushing proposed to split the profits with Fellowes and even guessed that because Fellowes had named one of his ships after the Spanish captain-general in charge of Cuba—"the '*Marques de Someruelos*'"—he might have more "influence with the Governor" in obtaining the false documents.[48]

In Philadelphia, the Spanish consul Valentín Foronda wrote in exasperation that, rather than requesting and paying for official passes for the Cuba trade (as the Spanish required), American and Spanish ship captains routinely approached him "to bid me farewell and ask if I wished to send some letters along with them," while freely advertising their departures in newspapers.[49] When rival merchants complained, American merchants frequently called on wealthy Cuban planters, who were eager to secure the flour and slaves carried in U.S. ships. In these early, turbulent years, Americans often invented excuses, typically pleading that "they cannot go for the Spaniards owe them money & they owe the Spaniards[, and] this or some such excuse satisfies the governor for awhile."[50] But this was not always enough, and occasionally the Spanish had to clamp down.

In the fall of 1801, the unrecognized U.S. consul at Santiago, Josiah Blakeley, was briefly imprisoned after the intendant at Havana accused him of being involved in an attempt by the *Prudence* of Boston to "defraud the Customs." The Spanish not only seized Blakeley's "Books & Papers," but, Blakeley wrote, "The Cash found in my house was taken away." By December 1801 Blakeley's own commerce was suffering.[51] "Few of [my contacts and friends] had sufficient courage to visit me," Blakeley complained. They feared "even to send their domestics to enquire how I was."[52] Blakely would later claim $20,000 in losses, but he, like most other Americans, was unversed in Spanish law and unable to speak fluent Spanish.[53] He didn't last long.

Fortunately for U.S. investors, men like Morton and Blakeley were soon succeeded by a cohort of commercial operatives and expatriates who quickly learned to do whatever was necessary to protect North American interests in the slave regime. Early American involvement in Cuba was violent precisely because it was fragile. In these early years, as Cuba transitioned from a second-tier outpost into one of the most intensive agro-industrial slave regimes in history, Americans knew that they might be expelled from the island at any time. Europe was engulfed in perpetual warfare, and as a steady stream of soldiers continued to arrive in the ongoing and futile fight to put down revolution in Saint Domingue, many observers feared that Cuba might be caught in the turmoil. Spain might lose the colony to France or England—or worse, to the enslaved Africans who arrived in greater numbers each year. For American investors, nothing was certain. They needed professionals.

TWO

Lawyers

Vincent Gray looked up from his desk as Spanish soldiers stepped into the doorway of his house. It was nine in the morning, Gray told them, and he was very busy. What were they doing here? Outside, in the bustle of carts and *volantes*—narrow carriages pulled by slaves and horses—he saw more soldiers approaching with swords and guns. Two Spanish officials stepped in past the soldiers: a lawyer and a notary. When the lawyer started to speak in broken English, Gray cut him off, asking in Spanish what they wanted. A U.S. ship had violated customs, the lawyer said, and there was proof of the consular office's involvement. He handed Gray a folded warrant for his arrest, with the signature and seal of the intendant, dated April 26, 1805—today. Gray should have known. In Cuba, although the captain-general ruled the island, the intendant often controlled the purse strings, and this one was reliably in the pocket of rival merchant houses. Vincent Gray closed his eyes and tried to stay calm.[1]

All of your papers are hereby seized, the lawyer told him, official and private. When the lawyer and notary had finished reading the list of charges that were being leveled against Gray, they told him that his house and the unrecognized consulate were closed. It was time to go, and a soldier gestured down the street toward the harbor. El Morro, the prison fortress: They were taking him to the cells in that stone castle across the bay. Americans who went into that prison often came out thin, pale and poor after years of wrangling with the authorities and the Spanish courts. Others never came out at all. But Vincent Gray

nodded calmly and let the soldiers take him outside into sweltering air
that tasted like saltwater. It was better than the sweaty interior of the
cramped apartments and offices that lined the old Havana streets.

El Morro loomed over the harbor like a squat stone highwayman,
with cannons ready, and when they arrived across the bay, a soldier led
Vincent Gray up worn stone steps, through gates that opened onto
narrow walkways between high walls crusted with seashells. As his cell
door clanged shut, Vincent Gray wondered, briefly, why he had ever left
Virginia. He had been born in Massachusetts, but had made a reputation in Alexandria, Virginia, and earned the contacts that brought him
to Cuba. Now, as he leaned his head against the rough stone wall, all of
that seemed to be coming to an end.

That night, Vincent Gray jolted awake and found the New Yorker
John Morton waiting for him. As they hurried out of the fortress, Morton
told Gray that every American ship in the harbor had been stopped. No
one was allowed in or out, and the Spanish had refused to grant papers
to release at least a dozen U.S. ships. The consular office was closed,
with Spanish soldiers stationed at the doors. They had taken everything,
Morton told him. And they would have kept Gray in prison if Morton
had not threatened the captain-general with war. As they returned to the
city, Vincent Gray smiled. John Morton could no more declare war on
Spain than on the moon. He wasn't a U.S. consul anymore, and besides,
the Spanish were in charge here.

A few days later, John Morton raised a toast to Vincent Gray. The
banquet hall of the Commercial Hotel in downtown Havana was
crowded with more than sixty American ship captains and merchants.
They all knew and respected Gray, and now they had gathered to show
the Spanish that a fight with one American would bring them all out.
Vincent Gray sat at the first table, with John Morton, the Bostonian
Nathaniel Fellowes and the Rhode Island captain James Perry. The room
smelled like wine, rum and cigar smoke, and now Morton raised his
glass to make the first toast. "To the United States of America," he said,
"established on old and sound principles of civil government and private
justice."

They toasted and drank, then refilled the glasses. "To the president
of the United States … to the Congress of the United States … to our

ministers, consuls, and agents resident abroad ..." At this third toast, they cheered, and several men clapped Gray on the back. By the twelfth toast, men were joking, barely listening to John Morton anymore. "To the Marquis of Someruellos," Morton said, referring to the captain-general. The room went silent. "A man of good principles—may he evince that to feel power should not be to forget justice." As Morton finished with toasts to "agriculture and yeomanry" and then to "the fair daughters of Columbia," they all laughed and cheered. Vincent Gray rose to thank them, and as dark-skinned women were brought in, they raised the American flag.

By the first decade of the nineteenth century, the scale of illicit commerce in Cuba led many American merchants and investors to turn to a new class of professional agents, who could negotiate the commercial, bureaucratic and legal routines of the Spanish state that attended the corruption and violence of U.S. trade. One of the first and most successful of these operatives was Vincent Gray. A vice consul, slave trader, commercial agent, and attorney, Gray was emblematic of the professional corps who created the foundations of the informal American empire in Cuba. By the early 1800s, Gray had leveraged a series of felicitous circumstances in his early career to establish himself as an instrumental power broker at the U.S. consular office in Havana, where he worked as both the "Provisional Commercial Agent of the United States" and as a slave trader in partnership with the wealthy Spanish merchant Antonio de Frias.[2]

While many Americans would continue to arrive on the island without the ability or willingness to learn the language, customs and procedures of the Spanish state, men like Vincent Gray made informal empire possible. For decades, he would act as a key power broker and professional intermediary in virtually every major U.S. legal dispute in Havana. Many of these disputes were a direct result of the expansion and intensification of U.S. involvement, as growing numbers of Americans transitioned from commercial houses to purchase and operate the slave plantations at the heart of the regime itself. Nathaniel Fellowes, who sat beside Vincent Gray in the Commercial Hotel in 1805, was one of them. In this more intensive stage of American intervention in Cuba, ambition and highly particular circumstances also led growing numbers of U.S. citizens to become expatriate sugar and coffee planters. Just as importantly, many of these men came from the U.S. North.

"How far the merchants here would suffer by it you well know"

By 1803, Gray was handling over $300,000 in lawsuits related to claims by U.S. merchants over American merchandise that had been seized in Havana.[3] That year, he solicited Alexander Hamilton to ask "if I can serve you or any of your friends in this quarter," enclosing "a small turtle" as "a small memento" of goodwill.[4] The turtle paid off: By 1805, he was acting as an attorney in "suits pending upwards of 280,000 Dollars on account of citizens of the United States" and another $150,000 in claims for which "no suits [had] been commenced."[5] The elite circles in which Gray moved are evident in his reception of the German nobleman Alexander von Humboldt; on Humboldt's second visit to the island for a month and a half in 1804, he was "recommended to [the] attention and protection" of James Madison by Gray.[6] But Vincent Gray's wealth and power also brought headaches.

Working as both a private commercial agent and a public diplomatic agent required him to balance the sometimes contradictory expectations of U.S. and Spanish authorities against the interests of the private merchants who paid his commission. The U.S. State Department turned to Gray, for example, when American citizens were implicated in violations of Spanish law. According to the 1795 Treaty of San Lorenzo, Americans who violated Spanish law in Spanish territory were legally subject to punishment under Spanish—not U.S.—law.[7] As the main American agent in Havana from 1802–5, Gray was also forced to confront—if only superficially—continual, rampant graft. On January 2, 1805, he claimed to have been approached by the captains of six to eight ships that he suspected were not legitimately American and had refused to issue papers and passports. "I bring down on my head," Gray wrote, "not only the hatred and resentment of those persons whom I disregard," but also the anger of established merchants accustomed to using the U.S. flag in a "disgraceful manner."[8] In fact, Vincent Gray admitted that he personally knew "some of the persons who were forgers and venders of forged American and Danish papers" in Cuba.[9]

Operating in public diplomatic offices, Spanish courts, and dock-side warehouses, professional operatives like Vincent Gray ensured that American investors profited amid contradictory restrictions in European colonial trade. In September 1805, for example, the U.S. commercial agent at Santiago, Josiah Blakely, reported that "French cruisers declare they will detain every American vessel which is not furnished with a Consular certificate of property," but "the Spanish Gov[ernment] forbid their being given." "What," he asked, "are the American Merchants to do?" Typically, they took their chances, while agents such as Blakeley struggled to make a profit through the sale of outlawed papers.[10] And when Americans officials arrived with a naive understanding of the trade, things sometimes got ugly.

When Henry Hill, the U.S. consul in Havana, threatened to fine an American captain $500 for his refusal to deposit his papers, for example, the situation quickly escalated into a fistfight.[11] Although Vincent Gray was familiar with the use of outlawed papers and false registers, Henry Hill soon found himself bloodied and bruised on the floor of the consular office. Still, Hill himself was a New York merchant and he knew enough not to press the matter, despite the obvious evidence of smuggling. Further interference on his part would not have been appropriate, Hill reflected, precisely because "it would have materially injured [the ship's] owners interests."[12] Even if he did not understand Havana, Henry Hill knew the basic rules of the game. He had arrived in Cuba to protect specific elite U.S. trade interests and had been backed by the New York Quaker merchant and founder of Tammany Hall, Jacob Barker, along with the commercial house of Bailey and Rogers.[13]

When these U.S. agents were forced to leave—Blakely departed in 1805 and Hill sailed for the United States in 1806—they left vice consuls in charge and attempted to destroy all evidence of wrongdoing.[14] In Santiago, Blakeley took "with him all his books and papers" over the objections of his vice consul.[15] In Havana, Hill was not so careful. After his 1806 departure, Vincent Gray and the consular secretary John Ramage were left to defend the U.S. accounts and records from the eyes of the Spanish intendant. "How far the merch[an]ts here wou[l]d

[suffer] by" the exposure of the documents in the consular office,"
Ramage wrote to Henry Hill in January 1807, "you well know."[16]
Hill did know. Writing to Madison about the intendant's investigation of illicit U.S. trade, Hill acknowledged the "pretty general practice
of the merchants there to make short clearances in order to save the
duty."[17] This was the routine practice whereby U.S. merchants would
declare only a fraction of their cargo or, in some cases, none at all,
and then silence the Spanish officials and guards with a bribe. U.S.
investment was still fragile, and it thrived at the margins of official
justice.

In Havana, U.S. citizens were still banned from operating independent commercial houses, and throughout the decade, there was only one
(all-male) U.S. boarding house in the city, run by an American woman
named Mrs. Scott.[18] Outside the capital, however, conditions were
sometimes more flexible. This was particularly true in the nearby port of
Matanzas, roughly sixty miles east of Havana. In the eighteenth century,
Matanzas had been a small fishing village, and now it was rapidly transforming into a busy seaport and a haven for U.S. merchants seeking a
more cost-effective depot for their goods. Here, American commission
agents openly operated commercial houses *without* Spanish partners,
and merchants often found it easier to evade Spanish customs. The
growth of Matanzas immediately attracted the attention of established
merchants in Havana, such as the unrecognized U.S. consul James
Anderson, who acknowledged that he did "not know a single soul" in
Matanzas. His solution was simple and corrupt: "I have granted to well-
known persons blank certificates with my signatures, making them take
[an] oath that the property is bona fide American property."[19]

One of the American merchants to receive these documents in
Matanzas was John Latting. In 1800, the Dorchester merchant George
Cushing had described Latting as an unscrupulous "bankrupt from
Long Island in the state of New York," who routinely boarded every
slave ship entering Havana in an attempt to procure the consignment.
Cushing complained that—in conjunction with "an outlandish Jew"
named De La Motte and a "segar maker" who had "turn'd merchant"
named Marsh—Latting had no qualms about approaching ships in
harbor and going "on board (a thing which no merchant wou'd ever

be seen to do)" to secure the consignment by claiming that "he wou'd charge but one third the customary com[m]ission &c."[20] Such commission agents routinely added additional fees later to make up the difference.[21] By 1808, Latting had lived in Matanzas for "three or four years," and Anderson described him as having "a very good reputation" before making Latting his vice consul there.[22] Latting put the influence of his appointment to immediate effect, and in 1808–10 applied to the Spanish to build a dock in Matanzas for the benefit of his commercial house in coordination with another New Englander, Zachariah Atkins, who was—in the estimation of Laird Bergad—the "progenitor of the Atkins family interests in Cuba," "an important Matanzas slave trader" and a landowner.[23]

As the wealth of Cuba blossomed, elites on the island demanded a steady flow of imported luxury goods, including items altogether foreign to the tropics. Here, North Americans were uniquely positioned to exploit their commercial connections as well as their geographical circumstances. In September 1801, the Consulado of Havana had reflected on the difficulties of life in such a hot climate and noted that recent technological innovations now allowed ice to be transported not only from New York to Charleston but also from Boston to Vera Cruz. In the fall of 1801, the Spanish commercial house of Oidor Sindico was tasked with locating a suitable provider farther north. Five years later, on March 16, 1806, the Cuban elite finally found their frosty link when Boston merchant William Savage applied to the Consulado for the exclusive right to provide the Caribbean city with ice and snow.[24] William Savage's brother, James Savage, had arranged a partnership with his cousin Frederic Tudor—the self-styled "ice king" who would later use the connection to link Walden Pond with Havana, Cuba, in a single, refrigerated circuit.[25] In March 1811, when another merchant lobbied to be allowed to supply ice shipments, members of the Consulado replied simply that they had depended on Americans for years and would continue to do so. In 1816, Cuban merchants would even acknowledge the importance of constructing refrigerated warehouses and wells to better preserve the ice,[26] and in subsequent decades ships routinely entered Havana's harbor from ports such as Boston and Bath, Maine, with cargoes of "nieve"—snow.[27]

As U.S. trade boomed, the constant push-pull between pro-American planters and anti-American merchants intensified. Although Americans won formal allowances, and Spain frequently took "the part of the Planters[,] whose Interests," as Vincent Gray wrote, "will always be respected here, and prevail against the merchants," things sometimes got ugly.[28] In 1807, for example, Vincent Gray himself was the target of an assassination plot after rumors spread that he had received "a large sum of money." A cabal of "twelve Spaniards conspired" to kill Gray and rob his offices, but after word of the plot leaked, the Spanish captain-general agreed to provide Gray with soldiers. When an assassin attacked Gray's clerk with a stiletto, the clerk shot him, and Spanish soldiers cut the man down. Five others were soon arrested.[29] Two months later, in May 1807, an American carpenter named Taylor who had lived in Havana "for more than five years" was murdered and "tied to a tree, stark naked, and covered with wounds and blood."[30] And that same year, U.S. consul James Anderson found himself "in a precarious situation"[31] and discovered than any attempt to monitor or track merchants' activities might get him killed. Anderson became convinced that any American or Spanish merchant "who thought that I stood in the way of his making a fortune" would "find an assassin" to "plunge a dagger into me at any moment of the day." "It does not require darkness," Anderson wrote, to commit murder in Havana.[32]

Then, in 1808, the stakes were raised even higher when the central driver of this entire system—the transatlantic slave trade—became illegal. That year, the United States formally outlawed American participation in the slave trade. But why should this have mattered? After all, skirting the law was nothing new; for years, Americans had been accustomed to breaking port restrictions and evading prohibitions on participation in the slave trade. Although U.S. law banned the outfitting or building of slave ships in U.S. ports in 1794 and 1800, for example, Cuban ports remained major supply points and depots for Americans involved in the slave trade.[33] In 1802, George Cushing had detailed plans to "out[fit] a Guineman at Newport" and wrote to his friend Nathaniel Fellowes that he was "confident you cou'd do better than in the Havana. Do you understand me?" Cushing wrote slyly from Boston, "I mean something about Mozambique, Zanzuebar &c &c. not forgetting the benefits to be deri'd from Rio la Plata returns to Cadiz or London."[34] As Leonardo Marques has documented, in this first decade of the nineteenth century, U.S. traders (25,000 slaves) and British traders (20,000 slaves) dominated the Cuban slave trade, transporting more than 80 percent of the total slaves that arrived at the island.[35]

Spanish authorities in Cuba were well aware of American involvement in the slave trade, and at every turn they endeavored to encourage its growth, providing explicit incentives to U.S. merchants who might be transporting other goods to supplement their cargoes with slaves. In 1802, for example, specie could only be legally exported from Cuba in slave sales, and Spanish law provided incentives to flour traders who also arrived with slaves. These regulations led many U.S. vessels—even those not bound for Africa—to supplement their cargoes with small numbers of slaves from other Caribbean islands and occasionally from North American ports.[36] The wealth of Cuba was grounded in the products of its slave regime, and in the years prior to 1807, the U.S. re-export trade (primarily sugar and coffee) expanded six times faster than the domestic trade. In these same years, growing numbers of Americans intensified the character of their participation in Cuba, rather than withdrawing from the island. At the very moment that the slave trade was under assault, U.S. citizens—including many Northerners—became expatriate sugar and coffee planters in a slave regime that fundamentally depended on the expansion of the slave trade.

Scholars have tended to distinguish elite New England merchants from slave-holding planters in this period. James Fichter, for example, has argued that elite New England merchants tended to live more conservatively—despite their fortunes—than planters, comparing the relatively modest mansion of Salem merchant Elias Derby with the extravagant lifestyle of South Carolina planter Peter Manugault, whose wealth was reportedly only one-third of Derby's. And even this, in Fichter's estimation, paled in comparison to the ostentatious lifestyles of sugar planters of the Caribbean.[37] This was no secret to contemporaries. As a small number of wealthy Americans expanded the scope of their Cuban investments, moving beyond the carrying trade and into the plantation regime itself, observers commented on the changing character of the U.S. presence in Cuba. "Some persons," U.S. consul James

Anderson wrote in 1807, "formerly citizens of the United States have settled here," and "many more begin to turn their thoughts seriously towards estates," especially "coffee plantations."[38]

Here, New Englanders were at a decided advantage: Their longstanding trade links and personal connections with the Caribbean allowed some investors to purchase ingenios and cafetales outright, becoming some of the earliest expatriate Americans on the island. At the very moment that Northern merchants were supposedly growing more distant from Southern and Caribbean planters, some elite New England merchants simultaneously *became* Caribbean planters, freely traveling from their "modest" Northern mansions to the treelined avenues of their Cuban slave plantations. Often, however, the actual series of events that contributed to the intensification of direct American involvement in the Cuban slave regime hinged on the ability of transnational actors to leverage overlapping legal authority and social power for the sake of their private interests. The Bostonian Nathaniel Fellowes was a perfect example. A friend to the Spanish captain-general and the U.S. secretary of state, Fellowes was also well known by a host of smugglers and slave traders. This was not a contradiction or a particularly unique set of circumstances. Instead, it was the unruly embodiment of the political economy, which incorporated the U.S. economy into the Atlantic World through the U.S.–Cuba trade.

In 1802, two Massachusetts men named Nathaniel Fellowes lived in Cuba. They had arrived in Cuba in the late 1790s: the elder Fellowes—born in the first half of the eighteenth century—and his nephew, born in 1780. The Fellowes family had invested in West Indies trade throughout the eighteenth century, and when Cuba opened in 1797, these two men named Nathaniel Fellowes were among the first to move south. By the 1790s, they had also formed personal and commercial alliances with many elite New England families, including the Boston Amory-Coffin family, a member of whom had married a daughter of the senior Nathaniel Fellowes. Initially, this connection paid off for Fellowes and his allies, with Fellowes acting as the Cuban hub in their networks of Atlantic trade. In 1797, for example, Thomas Amory Coffin forwarded Nathaniel Fellowes's banknote on the wealthy London merchant house of Thomas Dickason for one hundred British pounds to James Hunter

& Co.,[39] and in the years that followed Coffin invested in numerous vessels bound for Havana, such as the *George* and the *Eagle* in 1798. Members of the Fellowes family almost certainly helped to manage the Cuban consignments of such "adventures."[40]

Fellowes himself continued to participate in this trade as well. In 1801, the elder Fellowes was working in a partnership with the Bostonian and U.S. naval agent Samuel Brown and was, in the estimation of Elbridge Gerry, "a firm republican & one of the wealthiest merchants in Boston."[41] On October 13, 1802, the younger Fellowes was granted permanent residency in Cuba, and, soon after, a legal dispute in the United States led him to become one of the first true expatriate U.S. citizens on the island of Cuba.[42] As early investors in the Cuban slave regime, the Fellowes family had rapidly accumulated a small fortune: by the time of the elder Nathaniel Fellowes's death on April 23, 1806, they owned two Cuban coffee plantations, roughly "ten leagues distant" from Havana.[43] These cafetales were called the Fundador and the Reserva (the younger Fellowes would later invest in two more). Each cafetal was fourteen and a half acres in size, and their total value— including 170 enslaved African laborers—was assessed at approximately $300,000.[44]

Trouble started when the elder Fellowes died in 1806, leaving behind two wills: one in Cuba and another in the United States. The Cuban will, which was dated later than the American will, provided the nephew Nathaniel Fellowes with the bulk of the estate, whereas the Massachusetts will divided the estate more equally among the elder Fellowes's surviving descendents.[45] In October 1806, the surviving Nathaniel Fellowes arrived in Massachusetts to face his cousin's husband, the wealthy and influential Bostonian Jonathan Amory. After one of Fellowes's former overseers wrote Amory to suggest that the Cuban will was a forgery, Amory had Fellowes arrested and seized $40,000 worth of his Massachusetts property.[46] But Fellowes too had powerful friends, including Harrison Gray Otis. One of the wealthiest men in Boston, Otis had recently served as a U.S. congressman and was now finishing a term as the president of the Massachusetts Senate. Freed from prison, Fellowes offered Amory a compromise of $150,000. Amory refused, and Fellowes quickly fled to Cuba.

Here too, Fellowes had powerful allies. In 1807, amid U.S. and Cuban lawsuits and backed by influential Spanish planters, Nathaniel Fellowes successfully lobbied to become a citizen of Spain, complicating the efforts of Amory to reclaim the estate.[47] By July 1808, the suit in Massachusetts had been decided in Fellowes's favor, but Amory would continue to sue in Cuba for more than a decade, with little effect.[48] Because of his commercial connections in Cuba, Nathaniel Fellowes's ties to the U.S. government and the American foreign policy establishment ran deep. Nor was he the only member of the generation of 1815 to trade a Boston counting house for a Cuban plantation. The Jenckes family of Rhode Island—led by Sarah Updike Crawford Jenckes and "Guillermo" Scott Jenckes—had seized the opportunity to move to Cuba in the late 1790s. Like Fellowes, they were granted residency and established a coffee plantation on the eve of the U.S. ban on the slave trade.[49] In 1806, Nathaniel Fellowes had handled the consignment of the slave ship *Betsey* and the "sales of 121 negroes" in Havana for another American, the Rhode Island merchant, slave trader and politician James D'Wolf, who was also among the first to directly invest in Cuban plantations.[50] In September 1806, the Rhode Islander John Sabens, who had worked as a captain in the D'Wolf shipping empire for years, invested with the Englishman Joseph Catalogne in a cafetal "13 leagues distance" of Havana.[51] Sabens's personal stake in this investment was short-lived: In 1807, he died on a slaving voyage, leaving the care of his daughter and his estate in the hands of John D'Wolf and Charles Collins, Jr., who was the son and namesake of James D'Wolf's brother-in-law, Charles Collins, a slave trader and the customs inspector of Bristol.[52] For his part, Joseph Catalogne would also remain involved with the D'Wolf Cuban investments for years.[53] The following year, in 1808, James D'Wolf and other Rhode Island investors—including William Bowen and Charles Collins—established the Mount Hope cafetal in the Guamacaro region of Cuba, near Matanzas.[54] In the succeeding years, they would invest in at least five more.

Although every major U.S. port was involved in the U.S.–Cuba trade in the early nineteenth century, New Englanders like D'Wolf continued to command a disproportionate share of it. This was not coincidental or natural. It was the result of a concerted effort by American merchants, professional operatives and public officials to profit from the contours of the often illegal trade and to encourage the expansion of the slave trade by leveraging their ties to public power (both U.S. and Spanish) in the service of private profit. Republican political economy in the United States protected and was shaped by the actions of Americans operating behind Spanish lines. These strategies of profiteering and accommodation would intensify as the slave regime continued to expand: American investors were just getting started.

THREE

Consuls

In December 1809, John Quincy Adams had a problem. In the early morning glare of white sunlight on cold gray and blue stone, he walked the frigid streets of St. Petersburg, Russia. His wife, Louisa Catherine Adams, was at their rented quarters with their two-year-old son, Charles Francis Adams. No matter how much they bundled the boy against the cold, Louisa still complained that it was worse for him than in Boston. Now, however, Adams had other things on his mind. The crowd of ships in the harbor was already struggling against the ice, and the Russians had demanded an audience. There was a problem, they said, with the sugar. As newly arrived U.S. minister, Adams faced suspicions from officials in the Baltic that the vast amounts of sugar and coffee arriving in American vessels had come from British colonies, in violation of Napoleon's "Continental System." These accusations came at a dangerous time.

In the years since the French Revolution, French armies under the command of Napoleon Bonaparte had marched across Europe, winning a string of military victories that had brought much of the continent under their direct or indirect control. Yet the British had demonstrated that the French were far from invincible—particularly at sea. One year after the 1805 French naval defeat at the Battle of Trafalgar, Napoleon had famously endeavored to block British goods from the continent in what was termed a "Continental System" of economic warfare to counter the British blockade of the French coast by prohibiting the importation of British goods. Although the system was most effective in regions more directly controlled by the French, even ostensibly neutral nations, such as Russia, were compelled to adhere to the regulations or risk open warfare. In theory and in practice, many of the French trade restrictions designed to counter relentless British smuggling were intended to prevent colonial goods from reaching European markets via the U.S. merchant marine. The most important of these colonial goods was sugar.

Adams assured the Russians "that, with the exception perhaps of coffee, all the articles of colonial trade were produced within the United States." The sugar carried in U.S. vessels came, according to Adams, from Louisiana and Georgia or "the Spanish islands."[1] This was a lie, and Adams knew it. Not only was very little sugar produced domestically in the United States in this period, but earlier that month, Adams's secretary Alexander Everett had detailed exactly how merchants smuggled British colonial goods into Russia.[2] When he was later confronted by the French, Adams was drawn into an extended discussion of the nature of "the Havanna [sic] sugars arrived in American vessels," which he attributed to "the great increase of our trade with the island of Cuba."[3]

That year, in 1809, a series of crises hit Americans invested in the now-illegal slave trade and its products. Since 1797, American investors in the Caribbean had benefited not only from trade ties built on geographic proximity and borderland ruthlessness, but also from lack of competition, as European warfare contained the British and French merchant marines. In the networks of commerce that bound the Cuban slave frontier to North America and Europe, demand typically set the terms for supply to the extent that sugar and coffee prices in both the United States and Europe increasingly correlated with slave prices in Havana. In these early years, U.S. economic development depended on the re-export trade—that is, the system by which foreign goods and commodities landed in North American ports and were then exported once again. (Merchants typically claimed a drawback or refund of the port duties.)[4] For many U.S. ports, particularly in New England, the re-export trade was increasingly dominated by the trade in sugar and coffee carried into the U.S. and then re-exported to European markets. When these traditional European ports were shuttered to American merchants in 1809, elite U.S. investors responded, not by reducing their trade with a colony—Cuba—that was built on the slave trade, but by locating more distant sources of European demand in the Baltic. That year, when Americans looked from their New England counting houses to the docks of Havana, they envisioned St. Petersburg, Russia.[5] From 1809 to 1812, they would create a U.S. trade with Russia, with Cuba and the slave trade at its center, that would go unrivaled in scale (percentage of total U.S. exports) until World War II.

Whereas the previous chapter concentrated on the activities of the smugglers, assassins and thieves in Cuba who created this early trade, this chapter details the strategies of elite ship captains and consuls in an overlooked U.S.–Cuba–Baltic circuit (1809–12) that linked Boston with the frozen docks of St. Petersburg and the sweltering warehouses of Havana.[6] This is the story of the capital that made the Cuban slave regime possible, and the markets more than four thousand miles away that demanded slavery's products. In Massachusetts, I target the efforts of elite merchant William Gray to eliminate domestic competition through his overt support for a trade embargo, which he intended to circumvent. In the Baltic, I highlight the work of William Gray's de facto commercial agent John Quincy Adams, who leveraged the information of the diplomatic office, along with personal ties forged at Harvard University, to protect Gray's profits from French seizure. And in Cuba, I focus on the actions of the commercial agent and diplomat William Shaler, whose appreciation of Cuba's importance—more vital to U.S. "tranquility" and "independence" than New York—was coupled with his refusal to support annexation, in tacit support of the outlawed slave trade. Each of these men endeavored to incorporate public power to consolidate influence and information in the face of extreme risk in an Atlantic exchange characterized by monopolistic, increasingly clubby and insular networks.

These escalating risks had significant implications for U.S. economic development in the domestic reinvestment of their attendant profits. Key individuals involved in the creation of this U.S.–Cuba–Baltic circuit would create the foundations for their subsequent political careers and for an informal American empire premised on the slave trade. Many of the same men responsible for the more aggressively expansionist post-1815 policies that led to the Transcontinental Treaty and the Monroe Doctrine were also architects of U.S. foreign policy in these early years.[7] At the same moment that John Quincy Adams revived his political career in St. Petersburg, Russia, for example, American agents and investors in Cuba responded to growing uncertainty with moves that directly prefigured the Monroe Doctrine. In January 1811, the U.S. government adopted the famous "no-transfer principle"—in which the United States might view as a threat any transfer of territory in the Americas from one European power to another—to bar encroaching British influence in the hemisphere.[8] This was virtually the same foreign policy position that John Quincy Adams would formulate in Washington with the Monroe Doctrine, and it is no coincidence that at the moment of its initial explication, Adams was acting as an agent for U.S. investors in the products of the Cuban slave regime.

The United States had banned the slave trade, but American ships continued to bring enslaved Africans to the plantations of Cuba before carrying the sugar and coffee produced in these slave camps north to the United States and on to European markets. In 1809–11, a solid majority of U.S. vessels arriving in the Baltic hailed from New England.[9] Determining the origin of the sugar and coffee onboard these vessels depends on tracing the trade circuits of their home ports, the busiest of which was Boston. Although scholars have tended to claim ignorance of specific shipping information from Boston in this period—most records have been lost—a careful study of shipping information published in Boston newspapers is highly suggestive. A survey of 210 issues of the *Boston Gazette* from January 1, 1810, to January 2, 1812, reveals that 13 per cent of all foreign entrances (of 4,428 total entrances) and 12 percent of all foreign port clearances (of 3,771 total clearances) originated at or were bound for Cuba.[10] In Boston, Havana consistently—and often dramatically—outranked all other foreign ports, including Liverpool and Lisbon, in its share of shipping. And Boston was not alone: along the New England coast, other port records tell a similar tale about the outsized importance of the Cuba trade. Of 724 ships registered as entering Salem, Bristol/Warren, Portsmouth and Newport from foreign ports in 1810–11, 35 percent entered from Cuban ports. Whereas in Portsmouth just 4 percent arrived from Cuba, in the busier ports of Bristol/Warren

(75 percent from Cuba), Newport (41 percent) and Salem (20 percent) the extensive influence of elite American merchants created a lopsided Cuba Trade.[11] Throughout much of the region the New England "West Indies Trade" was, more accurately, a Cuba Trade. Although he had lied to the Russians, John Quincy Adams had admitted as much to the French: The sugar and coffee arriving in St. Petersburg overwhelmingly came from Havana. They were products of a regime that depended on the slave trade.

"The Measure of Their Dependents"

In the fall of 1809, Adams sailed from Boston to St. Petersburg aboard the *Horace*, a "merchant-ship laden with sugar and coffee," which was owned by the wealthy New England merchant and future lieutenant governor of Massachusetts, William Gray.[12] American merchants had visited the faraway port since at least the 1780s, and although the Russia trade could produce considerable profits if traders timed their arrivals to match market demand, it was also notoriously unpredictable. Elite investors relied on the information and personal intervention of commercial agents, including salaried members of the U.S. diplomatic corps and well-placed family members, to protect their trade networks. These agents not only worked with local commercial houses to secure sales and consignments, but also regularly reported on fluctuations in prices, tariffs and bribes. Predictably, these merchant-diplomats expected to make a profit. This was the reality of capitalism and U.S. foreign policy in the early Republic: As Peter T. Dalleo suggests, "many of those who did join the foreign service, especially the consular branch, were merchants already living abroad" who "sought consulships to enhance personal business ventures rather than to build diplomatic careers."[13] Here, at least, St. Petersburg was no different than Havana.

The network of investment that enabled the rise of the Early Republic United States hinged on the decisions of a generation of American ship captains turned merchants—men like William Gray—who were disproportionately based in the northern United States. As these men capitalized on their successes from the chaos of Atlantic commerce, they invariably traded the personal command of ships for the safety of counting houses, rising to become the directors of banks and insurance companies operated according to the dictates of their allies. In many cases, these men also used their wealth to become local and national statesmen. The profits that made this transition possible depended on access to influence and information in the face of profound transatlantic risk. Capitalizing on the weaknesses and strengths of the early U.S. state, these American investors shaped the exercise of public power across contested legal boundaries to accommodate private commerce.

Now, John Quincy Adams owed the resurrection of his political career to the products of the slave trade.[14] William Gray, the man who owned the ship that carried Adams to Russia, had been involved in this trade since at least the 1790s. While the uncertainty of geopolitics and salt-water trade may have famously driven some elite investors to withdraw from the carrying trade and reinvest in domestic industries, many more elite investors seized on the advantages of transnational public–private alliances to generate even larger profits from wartime turmoil. After all, investment in domestic manufacturing did not necessarily preclude increased involvement in the carrying trade. Like other elite members of the '15ers, William Gray had transitioned from life as a ship captain to become a highly successful merchant. By the early nineteenth century, he may even have been the wealthiest man in the United States. Tracking William Gray's efforts to manipulate and leverage U.S. law demonstrates the striking degree to which elite American merchants viewed the public powers of the new nation as open to appropriation and contestation.

Before sending Adams to Russia, William Gray had already accumulated a sizeable fortune in the carrying trade, including with both the West Indies and Asia. In 1808, William Gray, Federalist, consummate merchant, and possibly the wealthiest individual in the country, broke with his colleagues in Salem, Massachusetts, to *support* a trade embargo championed by Thomas Jefferson, despite the fact that this policy would appear to directly threaten the profits of his shipping empire.[15] Jefferson's response to the pressure of competing British and French regulations was economic isolation, with the passage of a complete (and almost entirely unsuccessful) embargo in December 1807. Initially designed to compel France and England to relax their own trade restrictions on

U.S. merchants amid European warfare, from 1807 to 1812 a series of U.S. trade laws were passed that became known as the Restrictive System.[16] Unsurprisingly, much of New England was staunchly opposed to the measures, and, indeed, on the face of it, William Gray's 1808 position makes little sense. After all, he operated an extensive world-wide shipping network employing at least 300 "hands" annually in trade that was now officially banned.[17] Yet Gray was not alone: other wealthy merchants, including the Baltimore merchant and U.S. senator Samuel Smith, whose commercial house Smith & Buchanan had long invested in the West Indies and Cuba, also supported Jefferson's trade restrictions.[18] Although contemporary supporters and twentieth-century biographers of Gray and Smith would defend their support of the embargo as acts of patriotism, their behavior was, in fact, more cynically commercial. When U.S. trade was curtailed, elite merchants with influential contacts, particularly in overseas diplomatic offices, were at a decided advantage.[19] The embargo was a means to eliminate the competition of less well-connected merchants and drive an increase in shipping profits based on escalating marine insurance premiums. Laws were sometimes made to be broken.

In Massachusetts, William Gray's significant fortune bought him diplomatic and political influence. And he was notoriously wealthy. By the end of the eighteenth century—*before* an even greater expansion of his profits—Gray's property was reportedly worth at least $900,000.[20] In the embargo years, he was likely worth even more. In September 1808, for example, it was alleged that Gray's shipping investments alone were valued at approximately $2.5 million.[21] By comparison, in the year ending September 1808, total U.S. federal receipts were $17.9 million, and disbursements were $12.6 million.[22] Gray's supporters wielded his wealth—which they reckoned to be the largest fortune in the United States, greater than that of "any other *five* men of all the New-England states" combined—as a political tool, while his critics openly accused Gray of leveraging his wealth to exploit the embargo.[23] "Mr. Gray's patriotism," his Federalist critics charged, "has procured for him the privilege of violating the non intercourse law."[24] As an anonymous editorialist explained, this was an attempt to build a personal trade monopoly, not patriotism:

William Gray may well approve the embargo ... It is well known, that vessels thus circumstanced, are carrying on a most lucrative trade. Mr. Gray, by monopolizing foreign produce, will also derive great benefit from this act.[25]

Eventually, William Gray was forced to respond to the suggestion that he was "growing rich, while others [were] suffering by the Embargo" by claiming that his "estate [had] decline[d] more than ten per cent in value." He even offered to "demonstrate" this loss "to any person."[26] Even as some of Gray's critics taunted him for his occasional shipping losses—which from April 1809 to June 1810 were estimated to be over "*one million of dollars*"—despite his "*patriot*" turn, others mocked Gray's failed smuggling attempts.[27] In November 1809, for example, Gray's critics hit on news that "two of [Gray's] vessels had been taken under Moorish colors" and chided that "we naturally suspected" that William Gray "had turned Mahometan."[28] Unsurprisingly, he never seems to have publicly opened his accounts, even as the Federalist press continued to insist that "the people who were the greatest gainers by the Embargo were the great capitalists ... Mr. Gray of Salem must have been a great gainer."[29] When Gray fought back in the press, his opponents charged that he was unfairly offering bank shares and credit to his allies, "as a reward for past and present loyalty," which they called "a species of *bribery and corruption*" to buy his political future and guarantee the survival of his fortune.[30] Yet, what Gray's opponents labeled "bribery and corruption" was, in fact, business as usual. Public diplomatic posts were big business: In 1806, for example, at a time when, as Wendell Blancke has suggested, "the dominant issues in American life were domestic rather than foreign," the United States spent $2 million—or approximately 20 percent of the total federal budget—on foreign affairs.[31]

While official U.S. records documented a dramatic drop in U.S. foreign trade in the embargo years, the reality was more complex. Those merchants who could successfully circumvent the law saw a spike in the profits in goods—which now rose to 50–100 percent over pre-embargo values—from successful smuggling voyages.[32] During the embargo years, merchants like Gray had established numerous transnational depots, such as Halifax, Montreal, and the West Indies, for many of their goods to skirt U.S. customs and trade restrictions. In Cuba, the embargo was entirely ineffective.[33] In July 1808, vice consul Vincent Gray acknowledged that in Havana, "the Embargo in consequence of its evasion, has not been felt by the People of this city."[34] And in March 1809, the captain of the U.S. naval vessel *Hornet* was shocked to discover that Havana's harbor was packed with "American vessels" that had "left the U.S. during the embargo, in direct opposition to the laws of our country."[35] Predictably, when the captain pressed the case with the consular office, U.S. consul James Anderson refused to get involved; the accused American ship captains sought protection not from U.S. authorities but from the Spanish captain-general of Cuba.[36] Yet, although U.S. merchants received support from American commercial agents and Spanish officials in Cuba, the expansion of the slave trade and U.S.–Cuba trade also depended on reliable export markets in Europe. Cuban sugar and coffee prices were premised on European demand and port access, which soon grew more tenuous.

In 1809, the French were winning, and the terms of U.S. trade with Europe shifted dramatically, as most traditional markets in continental Europe fell under direct or proxy control of the French empire. For years, French trade prohibitions had hit American merchants hard, but now, as the relentless march of French victories (with several notable exceptions, including in the Iberian Peninsula, where Portuguese ports would continue to serve as outlets for U.S. shipping) brought much of continental Europe under French control, the "Continental System" became truly continental. In the United States, the failure of the 1807 embargo to stem U.S. commerce led to the March 1809 "Non-Intercourse Bill," which barred trade with British and French possessions while officially opening it to peripheral nations, including the countries of the frozen Baltic.

This came at a time when Americans invested in the re-export trade of Cuban sugar and coffee, including William Gray, were desperate to find alternative routes into the European continent.[37] Now, with the shift in U.S. law and European circumstances in 1809, the moment for an expansion of the Baltic trade was finally at hand. But the Baltic trade was notoriously corrupt and risky. In July 1809, for example, the Philadelphia merchant and U.S. consul to St. Petersburg Levett

Harris acknowledged, "The best devised laws to restrain trade, or to [curb] the abuses … often prove inefficient." "Merchants," he wrote, "are wont to resort" to smuggling, which was "impossible to oppose."[38] In Massachusetts, William Gray needed an agent to ensure that he would not be opposed. When he moved from the Federalist stronghold of Salem to Boston, he found a ready ally in John Quincy Adams, who was now serving as a professor of rhetoric at Harvard University after being ousted from the U.S. Senate for his support of Jefferson's embargo.[39]

Both men needed each other: Adams for the revival of his political career and Gray for the protection of his profits. This was no secret at the time. In December 1809—immediately after Adams's arrival in St. Petersburg—the Federalist *Salem Gazette* charged Adams with desertion and commercial dependency to Gray: "They sacrifice without a struggle an old friend as they adopt a new one, like John Q. Adams, or, if I may be allowed to name him in the same line, William Gray—Democratic leaders must follow, not dictate, the measures of their dependents."[40]

While Adams has been applauded by scholars for his diplomatic accomplishments in St. Petersburg, in Russia he acted as a de facto private commercial agent.[41] Adams sailed for St. Petersburg in the fall of 1809 aboard William Gray's ship *Horace*, which was "laden with sugar and coffee" and cotton.[42] Gray's critics estimated that "the privileges which the ship Horace will enjoy, in consequence of conveying Mr. Adams to Russia, are worth *Forty Thousand Dollars*, besides the passage money!"[43] In succeeding years, this same ship would ferry Adams's official missives along with Gray's cargoes to and from Russia.[44] In 1810, William Gray forwarded Adams a letter of credit worth $30,000,[45] and in 1810–11, Adams not only secured the release of all of Gray's ships that had been seized in the Baltic, but he also regularly wrote to Gray with commercial advice related to the manipulation of prices by Russian merchants and customs-house bribes.[46] While the French continued to hold more than $2 million dollars' worth of American property seized in the Baltic, with Adams's help, Gray made a profit on every ship sent to Russia in 1810.[47] These profits were not incidental: In December 1810, U.S. consul Levett Harris estimated that shipments "from the U.S. to Russia" had on "average yielded a profit of at least 40 percent."[48]

The risks that made such profits possible were very real, as evidenced by fluctuating marine insurance premiums.[49]

And Adams did not go alone. Foreign secretaryships were well-known stepping-stones in the networks of commercial patronage that defined the diplomatic corps, and it is unsurprising that three of Adams's legation secretaries were members of elite families invested in the Cuba–Russia circuit. This initially included Francis Calley Gray, William Gray's son, and Alexander Everett, future U.S. agent to Spain and Cuba. In the Baltic, Everett and Gray were virtually inseparable. Like Adams, Everett also wrote "to Mr. William Gray on business" numerous times, while Gray—through his son—supplied Everett with funds; in November 1809, for example, Everett collected 500 rubles "on account of Mr. Gray."[50] Adams's own nephew, William Steuben Smith, who had participated in the failed *Leander* military expedition to Venezuela in 1806, and John Spear Smith of Baltimore, the son of West Indies merchant and U.S. senator Samuel Smith, also joined the legation.[51] Smith's mission was also primarily commercial. Reflecting on the danger to his father's commercial house from a Baltic market glutted with an "immense quantity of colonial produce," for example, John Spear Smith wrote from St. Petersburg, "May the Lord have mercy on S.S. & B. [Samuel Smith and Buchanan]."[52] Unlike Samuel Smith and William Gray, however, the Rhode Islander James D'Wolf did not send his son with Adams to St. Petersburg. Instead, in 1811, his nephew-in-law, Samuel Hazard, arrived as U.S. consul to Archangel, a position that Hazard's father hoped would lead to an "increase of lucrative business."[53]

No God But Gain

Many of these men already knew each other. While family and kinship defined the basic public-private operations of these elite trade networks, other markers of elite social respectability were often equally important. For the New Englanders who dominated the Cuba–Baltic circuit, this frequently meant an association with Harvard University and membership in the elite social entrepôt the Porcellian Club. Alexander Everett (in 1806) and Francis Calley Gray (1809), for example, were both members.[54] Typically, scholars have treated John Quincy Adams's own brief time as a member of the Harvard faculty during his tenure in the U.S. Senate and after his ouster in 1808 as either an interlude in his professional career or as a momentary lapse in momentum after his unpopular support of the embargo. This was not entirely the case. In fact, Harvard University represented a natural intersection point in the world of elite commerce that bound the U.S. Senate with Cuba and the Baltic, and it is no coincidence that between his early Senate career and his tenure in St. Petersburg, John Quincy Adams made Cambridge his home. Harvard represented a staging ground for coordinated business enterprises and familial alliances for the Northern commercial elite of the '15ers.

In the Danish port of Copenhagen, for example, fellow Harvard alum John M. Forbes worked on William Gray's account with another of William Gray's agents, Hans Rudolph Saabye. Although it was sometimes referred to as a consular office, the Copenhagen office was, in fact, unrecognized as a public diplomatic post by the U.S. government.[55] John M. Forbes and John Quincy Adams had been classmates at Harvard University, and they now continued to travel in the same elite commercial circles.[56] Even farther north, at Archangel, Francis Dana, Jr., another member of the Harvard Porcellian Club (1796), also worked on behalf of the Beverly merchant Israel Thorndike.[57] Dana, Jr. was the son of the same Francis Dana who had served as the first U.S. minister to Russia in 1780, when a fourteen-year-old John Quincy Adams had accompanied him on a largely unsuccessful mission to St. Petersburg. Now, Francis Dana, Jr. followed Adams's lead into the Baltic as a commercial agent for elite U.S. merchants. Unsurprisingly, in 1811, when Dana, Jr. asked for Adams's assistance for his client Israel Thorndike's ship, *Eliza*, which had been stopped at Archangel, Adams immediately lobbied the French on his behalf.[58]

Like Gray, Israel Thorndike brought a significant portion of his cargo from Cuba. Just two years earlier, for example, the Thorndike ship, *Hope*, had attempted to slip the embargo by logging a journey for a southern port before sailing to Havana.[59] Also like Gray, Thorndike sent his son, Nicholas Thorndike, to the Baltic, where he worked in Copenhagen with John M. Forbes and in St. Petersburg with Miers Fisher, who was the son of another wealthy Philadelphia merchant invested in Cuba.[60] In St. Petersburg, John Spear Smith shared his extensive quarters with Fisher, who regaled Alexander Everett with "his adventures in the Island of Cuba" and described how he had visited "the Intendant of the Island." Fisher claimed to have brought vital information to the Spanish administrators on the island, Everett wrote impatiently, "&c &c, of which he is very fond of talking."[61] In this clubby network, the sons of the U.S. elite drew on their old bonds from Harvard as they worked to protect the Cuban profits of their families and benefactors in the Baltic, leveraging the trade information of public office for private profit wherever possible.

U.S. consul Levett Harris was notoriously adept at turning a profit from his access to such information. While the wealthy Russian merchant Glukoff—"the agent of Mr. Gray"—made "a considerable profit" on the consignment of the goods onboard *Horace*, Levett Harris made even more. As Harris bragged in February 1810, Russian merchants were at a disadvantage, precisely because of the limitations of their information networks: "They are generally possessed of very limited correspondences abroad. This makes it easy for foreigners, who are possessed of that advantage, and who have a capital to trade on, to make large fortunes very easily." When Glukoff sold Gray's cotton shipment, Harris "knew from his correspondence that it was about to rise" and used his public office to manipulate Glukoff into selling him the cotton "as an act of friendship" and "without paying the money." Within "about fifteen days," Harris sold the cotton "at an advance of thirteen or fourteen thousand rubles."[62] In this case, Harris had no actual part in the shipment: He was not involved in the purchasing, shipping or disbursement of the goods, and he was not acting as an agent for William Gray. Instead, he simply coordinated the information networks that flowed through the consular office to purchase and immediately sell these goods at a profit and no cost. Because of his public appointment as consul, Harris had not even had to front the purchasing money; information and public power allowed him to pluck profits from thin air. And while Adams occasionally grumbled about Harris's transnational profiteering, he consistently defended Harris or looked the other way.[63]

Acknowledging the reality of this public-private overlap in diplomatic appointments, John Quincy Adams wrote to Secretary of State Robert Smith—the brother of Samuel Smith and uncle of Adams's own legation secretary—that because "consuls are merchants ... you will immediately perceive the allurements and opportunities, which the American consuls throughout Europe will have to favor and even to partake of illicit trade."[64] This was a sensibility that Adams carried with him throughout his political career, and years later he similarly reflected that "where commerce was allowed, the Consul followed of course."[65] Whether rationalized under the rubric of "trade" or "commerce," the "illicit trade" of the consular office, including bribery, corruption, the manipulation of prices, and smuggling, was as rampant in the Baltic as in Cuba.[66]

By 1809, illegal payments to customs officials to secure passage on forged American papers had become so commonplace that legitimate U.S. ships were often forced to pay as well.[67] Adams, Everett and Smith all detailed the routine "present of money or a part of their cargo" paid as bribes to "silence the officer" of Baltic customs houses.[68] Occasionally, American merchant smugglers sought the intervention of U.S. diplomats in these cases. In 1810, for example, an American merchant "accosted" John Spear Smith and demanded that Smith bring "the interference of the American Minister" to prevent being extorted for 6,000 rubles by customs house officers.[69] In fact, the involvement of U.S. officials sometimes resulted in even greater extortion. U.S. consul Levett Harris was notorious for demanding up to 24,000 rubles from entering U.S. vessels and splitting the proceeds with his Russian accomplice, the secretary of the Russian minister Count Rumiantsev.[70]

As the prevalence of smuggled cargoes increased, such bribes grew even more commonplace. "Our Regular Commerce," Harris wrote, "has suffered much the present year, principally through the suspicions which the clandestine trade carried on here from England has excited in the Commissioners." English vessels typically complemented their cargoes with American goods "to support appearances," leading to "very minute investigations" of every cargo.[71] In fact, Harris himself had routinely been involved in such evasions. In an attempt to preempt criticism of his conduct, he wrote that some forged papers varied "so materially that I have very little doubt that some were forgeries, but as they were accompanied by true Registers and the masters ... ready to make oath of their correctness," Harris claimed that he did not have the "authority to detain any of them."[72]

This is why, in 1809, John Quincy Adams faced suspicions from officials in the Baltic that the vast amounts of sugar and coffee arriving in American vessels had come from British colonies, in violation of Napoleon's Continental System. As Levett Harris detailed, "a considerable quantity of Havanna [sic] Sugar" had been imported "in American ships" before being "suspected and declared by the officers of the revenue to be refined." This sugary matter turned on wartime geopolitics and money: Refined loaf sugars were likely of English origin and therefore subject to a much higher duty than raw, predominantly Cuban sugars. Soon, under the Continental System, refined loaf sugar would be outlawed altogether. "The merchants of America and their agents," Harris wrote, had been "charge[d] of fraud against the custom[s]." When the Americans appealed to Harris, he proceeded to exchange "a very lengthy and animated correspondence" with both the Russian "Chancellor" and "Minister of Finance," defending the U.S. shipments.[73]

In practice, it was extremely difficult to determine precisely where the sugar had originated. In the Caribbean, traders could "convert" goods from one nationality to another by stopping over at neutral ports en route. As Gautham Rao suggests, the Swedish colony of St. Bart's was a haven for smugglers of every stripe, precisely because, under the vagaries of maritime law, cargoes could be "converted" from prohibited goods (British) into neutral goods (Swedish).[74] Adams's legation secretary John Spear Smith acknowledged as much in writing from Stockholm to his father, Senator Samuel Smith, about the Baltic prohibitions on British goods in early 1810. "But you can upon a pinch," he wrote, "convert your coffee into that of Java & St. Bartholemew which you know is a Swedish Island."[75]

Levett Harris chose "three persons"—Russian merchants—to "decide on the fact." At least two of these merchants promptly concluded that the sugar "had been manufactured & afterwards pulverized," meaning it had likely been smuggled from a British colony.[76] Harris was understandably disgruntled that "two merchants of respectability here,"

whom he had chosen to defend the American sugar cargoes, had confirmed the customs agents' suspicions.[77] Among the assessors was the
Russian commission merchant Mr. Cramer of the Brothers Cramer
commercial house in St. Petersburg, which did an extensive business
with Americans. Alexander Everett described "Mr. Krehmer" as "one of
the most respectable merchants" in St. Petersburg; on numerous occa-
sions, American merchants and diplomats—including Adams—dined
with and were received by him.[78] "Of all the merchants here," John
Spear Smith reflected, "he is the one that should have stood forth in
defense of the American trader."[79] Smith knew just how intimately
Cramer was tied to American merchants in the Baltic. As recently as
March 1810, for example, Cramer's service to "the American trader"
had extended to Smith himself: on March 25, 1810, John Spear Smith
drew on the Brothers Cramer for 4,000 rubles via a Dutch commercial
house, and on April 2, 1810, Smith described the Brothers Cramer as
"very attentive" Russian merchants.[80] Whether or not the sugars were
refined, American merchants expected Cramer to serve their interests
and protect their cargoes from seizure.

Ultimately Cramer's assessment proved irrelevant: After John Quincy
Adams pressured the officials involved, the ships were released, "the fact
being established that [the sugars] are raw"—that is, Cuban.[81] Levett
Harris complained to Russian officials "of the abuses" these Americans
had faced and worked "to prevent their future ocurrence [sic]."[82] Whether
the sugars were raw or refined, some damage had been done to Cramer's
reputation with American merchants. The following year, in May 1811,
Cramer pleaded with John Quincy Adams "that he had not known the
sugars to be the property of Americans," and if he had, he would have
disagreed with "the other persons consulted" in evaluating the samples.
Since that time, Cramer said, "this affair had injured him exceedingly."[83]
Yet, whatever immediate damage Cramer's miscalculation had done to
his consignment business, the reputation of the Brothers Cramer among
American merchants was not irreparably damaged. They would continue to operate in the trade for decades.

Meanwhile, the Baltic trade continued to expand, and intercon-
tinental networks of illegal trade funneled sugar and coffee from the
Baltic ports deep into the continent, in blatant violation of the French

Continental System. In July 1811, Adams estimated that "nearly two hundred American vessels" loaded with "colonial merchandise—sugar, coffee, cotton, indigo, and dye-woods" had entered St. Petersburg since the port had thawed only months earlier.[84] As trade regulations proved ineffective at curbing such rampant smuggling, these U.S.–Cuban merchants threatened to destabilize an already fragile Franco–Russian peace. When Cuban sugar and coffee infiltrated the Continental System, filtering from the ports of the Baltic into the continent, American merchants explicitly benefited from the increased demand. In 1811, for example, sugar and coffee prices were depressed throughout much of the year because of a bottleneck in European smuggling: Once the commodities began to reach farther south, in December 1811, into "the interior of Germany," the price of "Havana white sugars" rose "from 30 to 36 rubles."[85] At its height in 1811, U.S. exports to Russia amounted to $6 million worth of goods, a sum equivalent, as Alfred Crosby writes, "in value to one-tenth of the entire exports of the United States for 1811."[86] This proportion would not be reached again until World War II.

One year later, this sizeable trade would become a major pretext for the French invasion of Russia.[87] Cuban sugar and coffee—not cotton—were on Napoleon's mind when, as Russian scholar Nikolai Bolkhovitinov writes, "in a conversation with A. I. Chernyshev, [Napoleon] pointed out that in the course of the summer of 1810 American ships brought to England 'infinite profits' and 'almost completely destroyed the meaning of the continental system by inundating the whole of Europe with colonial goods.'" Napoleon Bonaparte could, in Bolkhovitinov's estimation, "destroy a whole duchy for violating the rules of the Continental blockade" but "he could not force Europe to deny itself coffee or sugar."[88] When the French invaded Russia in 1812, the Cuban trade of the American merchants who had been protected by the U.S. diplomatic corps and commercial agents in the Baltic was largely to blame.

On the eve of Napoleon's invasion, on May 15, 1812, John Quincy Adams met with Count St. Julien, a German nobleman, who irritated Adams with his aristocratic perspective:

The Count was perfectly good-humored, and avowed his prejudices against the class of merchants without reserve. He says they are the cause of all these wars, without ever taking part in them or suffering from them … they have no country but their counting-houses no God but gain … the merchants burnt and destroyed by little and little. They consumed by defrauding all sides. It was nothing to them who was victorious or who vanquished. They made their profit with equal indifference out of all.[89]

A sensible merchant, Adams wrote, could have "turned the tables" on the count by pointing out that the nobility "have vices of condition at least as odious as any that can be imputed to the merchant." But Adams did not argue. It would not have been appropriate, he reflected, precisely because Adams himself was, by his own admission, "the champion of the merchants."[90]

FOUR

Opportunists

John Joseph Chauviteau was depressed and philosophical. As he watched the harbor of Havana fill with sails and the bustle of horse-drawn carts carrying barrels and crates of sugar and coffee, he imagined extinction. Soon, all of this would be erased. The ornate buildings and gardens that lined the harbor would burn, and planters and merchants alike would be forced to scramble onto ships with whatever they could carry, as soldiers grimly watched smoke rise on the horizon. He had seen it before, but the Americans were single-minded, oblivious.

"I well know," Chauviteau wrote to his friends and commercial partners in Rhode Island, "you all care for nothing except L'argent and L'argent encore. But as I am not quite like you." He paused. It was December 1812, and what difference did it make what he wrote to John D'Wolf? They were all the same. "At best, it is all Trash," Chauviteau wrote. "We leave all behind us when we die."[1]

Chauviteau's family had been chased out of the French colony of Guadeloupe in the chaos of the late-eighteenth-century British occupations, French Revolutionary purges and local insurrections. In Guadeloupe, many of the French planters who had remained had been dispossessed or executed. By 1812, the island had changed hands numerous times and was now again occupied by the British. Chauviteau, like planters from nearby Saint Domingue, had responded to the turmoil by resettling in Cuba. He had done a regular business with Americans invested in Cuba since 1801–2, when he had toured the Atlantic coast of

North America and made connections with powerful commercial houses from Charleston to Boston.[2] Now, at the end of 1812, a second transition appeared to be at hand. Since the Anglo–U.S. war had begun, commercial houses and slave traders operating in the Caribbean and South America found that their links with North America had been cut. As more American vessels were "intercepted," traders feared that "the spirit of Speculation" was rapidly being undermined by British seizures, which might lead to the complete extinction of North American investments and the strangulation of the trade.[3] The survival of Cuban slavery and the slave trade depended on U.S. capital, protection and participation. The British were on the move. The end, Chauviteau thought, was near.

Two years earlier, William Shaler arrived as the new U.S. agent to Havana with $1,000 in gold and a letter of credit from the elite New York merchant Nathaniel Ingraham, whom he provided with regular updates.[4] In this period, many leading New England merchants either relocated farther south to New York or expanded their operations to include a New York office.[5] Like other U.S. agents in Cuba, Shaler had been dispatched based on his commercial contacts, rather than his diplomatic abilities. This was most obvious in linguistics: William Shaler spoke French but was not fluent in Spanish. In Cuba, this lack of fluency forced him to depend on other Americans who were already established on the island, such as Vincent Gray and Nathaniel Fellowes. Shortly after Shaler's arrival, for example, Fellowes, the "very great proprietor," provided him with information about the pro-U.S. "sentiment [that] is very general among" the planters.[6] Shaler was much more suspicious of Vincent Gray.[7]

Immediately after Shaler's arrival, he was welcomed by Antonio de Valle Hernandez, a secretary to the Spanish Consulado who had been born to Spanish parents in Russia and who worked for Shaler as an "expeditious translator."[8] Hernandez, however, had motives of his own. The Cuban Creole elite resented Spanish trade regulations and sought greater access to foreign markets. Since 1791, Cuba's elite had seen their wealth grow exponentially with the expansion of the slave regime, and now—as the Spanish empire began to fracture and disintegrate around them—they quietly considered alternatives to Spanish rule. As early as October

1810, some of the wealthiest families in Cuba plotted independence,[9] and then, when news arrived in 1811 that a Mexican representative at the Cortes (the Spanish assembly) in Cadiz had proposed abolishing slavery throughout the Spanish empire, planters and merchants panicked.[10] Terrified that rumors of liberation might circulate among the enslaved population and encourage an insurrection, the Creole elite recommended that the governor immediately organize "the arming and organizing of the white citizens."[11] The planters were right to worry.

In June 1811, Shaler was approached by Joseph de Arango—the cousin of Francisco de Arango, who had sailed for Spain to defend the Cuban planters—who saw only "one course for us" (the "wealthy landed proprietors" in Cuba) should Spain attempt to abolish Cuban slavery and the slave trade: "to solicit a union with you [the United States], and become one of your confederate states." The only stumbling block, according to Joseph de Arango, was the issue "of religion," which he "hope[d] and believe[d] may be reconciled." The alternative Arango envisioned—in which Cuba was dragged into the center of European warfare—might decimate U.S.–Cuba trade or worse. Arango's proposal provided an ideal opening for Shaler to advise the secretary of state to annex the island. Yet, as he had been instructed to do by Secretary Robert Smith, Shaler told Arango only that the United States would always be interested in what happened in the Spanish colony.[12] This was classic understatement. Because Britain had also abolished the slave trade and might attempt to eliminate the expanding illegal trade into Cuba if it acquired the colony, the elite Creole planters of Cuba looked north "to their brothers," Shaler wrote, "as they stile the inhabitants of the United States."[13] What both parties left unsaid was that, since the United States had followed Great Britain in formally abolishing the slave trade in 1808, U.S. annexation of Cuba might be just as ruinous to the expansion of the slave frontier as British occupation. The slave trade depended on lax Spanish administration.

As rumors circulated that a French naval force in Holland was being outfitted to attack Cuba, and as the British pressured Spain to allow British naval garrisons in both Puerto Rico and Cuba, Cuban planters found themselves pinned between three hostile powers. Spain had entertained abolitionist discussions; Britain was already actively attempting to curb the slave trade; and France had not only mismanaged Saint Domingue, but had also declared war on Spain.[14] Shaler recognized that Cuba was both militarily strategic as a naval depot in the Caribbean and economically essential. By 1811, the U.S.–Cuba trade provided lucrative exports of sugar, coffee, and Latin American specie, while also serving as the key foreign destination for U.S. flour. In the spring of 1810, for example, approximately $3 million in specie was reportedly exported from Philadelphia alone to Canton and Calcutta.[15] Much of this specie had no doubt been routed north through Philadelphia's trade with Havana. By taking Cuba, the British could not only choke off the Cuban slave trade and thereby cut the expansion of the sugar-and-coffee frontier, throttling U.S.–Cuba trade, but they could also use the island as a naval base to control the future of Mexico and the North American gulf coast. In Shaler's estimation, Cuba was the military and commercial key to the hemisphere. "It appears to me," Shaler reflected in July 1811, "that the occupation of New York by the British, would not be more dangerous to our tranquility, and even our independence than that of this Island."[16]

As Anglo–U.S. war loomed at the end of 1811, Shaler's translator, Antonio de Valle Hernandez, suggested that if hostilities broke out, "a preliminary measure on the part of England would be, the occupation of Havana [and] its dependencies." Where, Hernandez asked, would the United States stand? Shaler promised that if the planters resisted a British occupation they could "rely with confidence on the American people."[17] The Creole elite were unconvinced. They worried that "Great Britain previous to a formal declaration of war against the United States will take measures to assure herself of the Port of Havana & others of the Island of Cuba under the pretext of defending them from foreign invasion." Worse, beset by French armies, Spain might even be forced to go along with such a move, and, for all of Shaler's talk, the Creole elite in Cuba had little faith in the United States. "The government of the American Union," they wrote, "is too feeble."[18] There was little Shaler could do to assure them, and—although he recognized the obvious importance of Cuba to the economy and national security of the United States—his approach to annexation was more reactionary than pro-active. The survival of the Cuban slave trade and the expansion of the slave regime depended on the status quo.

In 1808, after the United States's abolition of the slave trade, Thomas Jefferson had made this status quo policy explicit: "we shall be well satisfied to see Cuba & Mexico remain in their present dependence," he wrote, "but very unwilling to see them in that of either France or England, politically or commercially." Jefferson then went one step further, establishing the foreign policy framework that would become the basis of the 1823 Monroe Doctrine. "We consider [Cuban and Mexican] interests & ours as the same," Jefferson wrote, "and that the object of both must be to exclude all European influence from this hemisphere."[19] Often referred to as the "No-Transfer Principle of 1811,"[20] this hemispheric policy, which had been initially explicated just months after the outlaw of the transatlantic slave trade, centered on Cuban monoculture and the influx of enslaved African laborers that made its growth possible. After the Haitian Revolution and the rise of British abolitionism, only Spain seemed capable of holding the line. Although American statesmen—Jefferson included—may have harbored fantasies of Cuban annexation, they understood that Spanish and American "interests" did not necessarily preclude statehood. The creation of an informal American empire in Cuba depended on the simultaneous survival of the Spanish empire.

Moreover, in late 1811, American influence in Cuba appeared to be under real threat: in successive dispatches from Cadiz and Havana, rumors spread that the Spanish Cortes was negotiating a loan with the British government that might involve a much greater British intervention in the dissolving Spanish American empire.[21] The rumors were not far from the truth: In June 1811, the Spanish Cortes agreed to cede trade rights in Spanish America to Great Britain in exchange for British assistance in coercing the rebellious former colonies to do "their duty" to Spain. News of an Anglo-Spanish deal was published in England and later, on October 31, 1811, in the *National Intelligencer*.[22] As Spain and Great Britain both outfitted expeditions ostensibly intended to quell rebellions in Central and South America, the Creole elite and Americans invested in the island suspected that the forces might actually be intended for Cuba.[23] By November 17, 1811, James Madison fretted that Spain had been manipulated into inviting powerful British naval forces into her dominions. A single miscalculation might cost her the island of Cuba. "The game [Spain] will play with Cuba, may more readily be conjectured," he wrote. "But like most of her others it may in the end be a losing one."[24] Balancing threats of foreign intervention was dangerous, particularly given the risks it might pose to the slave trade and the fragility of the slave regime itself.

Tellingly, amid this geopolitical turmoil—as the Cuban Creole elite plotted revolution and the Spanish and British prepared expeditionary forces across the Atlantic—the immediate cause of William Shaler's expulsion in 1811–12 was *not* his discussion of Arango's annexationist proposal. Instead, Shaler was punished for placing commerce above diplomacy: from October to November 1811, Shaler took an unauthorized leave from Havana to visit Nathaniel Fellowes's Fundador slave plantation, where he stayed for approximately one month.[25] After being seized by "three armed men" in November 1811, Shaler returned to Havana to defend his absence for "three quarters of an hour" entirely "in French," which the captain-general could understand but had difficulty speaking.[26] The Spanish captain-general of Cuba, Someruelos—who Shaler later dismissed as "thick and clumsy, with a large [nose], short legs, [and] a waddling gait"[27]—suggested that he was well aware of "the views of [the U.S.] government respecting this country." Shaler replied that the United States government only wished "that Cuba should remain in the possession of its present owners."[28]

This was more than tact; it had the benefit of being largely true. Americans invested in the island had no interest in anything that might upset the balance of slave and flour imports and sugar, coffee and specie exports. The ties linking the Cuban Creole elite with American investors placed Someruelos in a difficult position, however, precisely because foreign influence appeared to be everywhere. On November 9, 1811, at the very moment that Shaler scrambled to defend his position in Havana, a cargo of seventeen English-language books arrived in Havana onboard the *Boston* from the United States. They had departed the Massachusetts capital one month earlier direct for Antonio Frias—the same elite merchant/slave trader with whom Vincent Gray regularly worked. As Shaler wrote desperate missives to the secretary of state, Shaler's translator and contact—the secretary of the Consulado Antonio del Valle Hernandez—was tasked with reviewing the American volumes before depositing them in the elite Society's library.[29] Predictably—after Someruelos was accused by the Spanish archbishop in Cuba of harboring pro-French sympathies[30] during the French occupation of Spain—William Shaler soon found himself on a boat to New Orleans.[31]

After Shaler's departure, the Creole elite's aspirations for independence were cut short by the outbreak of the Aponte Slave Rebellion of 1812. The Kongolese leaders of the slave insurrection alluded to both their freedom—which they believed had been granted by the English king—and the legacy of the Haitian Revolution.[32] But the Spanish were well armed, and after the African warriors had been executed, the aspirations of the Creole elite faded under the necessity of Spain's heavily militarized slave regime and levity toward the slave trade.[33] American investment in Cuba continued to encourage and enable this expansion, while the many Northerners on the island remained comfortable with the continuance of the slave trade into Cuba and undisturbed by its implications. In 1809–10, for example, the wife of Boston merchant John C. Howard accompanied her husband to Cuba for his health. After staying on Nathaniel Fellowes's plantations for more than a week, she complained about the tedium of Cuban slavery, not its morality.[34]

"The conversation in most companies," she wrote, "consists of the going price of slaves, such a day a fine cargo of negroes arrived from the coast of Guinea, have you been to see them, they are fine looking felons what will they sell for." "This," she added, "is the conversation with which I am frequently entertained." In Havana, rather than criticize Fellowes for operating Cuban plantations or profiting from the outlawed slave trade, she complained of the employment by the Spanish of African wet nurses, which, she suspected, was "probably the reason why the Spaniards of this island degenerate so much & are such a growling set of people ... more black than white." The problems of Cuban slavery and the slave trade, from Howard's perspective, were rooted in its effect on the "whiteness" of the Spanish population.[35] American involvement was wholly incidental. By March 1810, her husband added an addendum to one of her letters, quipping, "This wife of mine has given but a gloomy account," but "upon the whole," he wrote, "we laugh a good deal more than we cry."[36] Like many New Englanders among the Cuban plantations, the Howards found time to laugh.

By 1812, however, there was less reason for merriment. As slave

insurrections swept Cuba, French armies advanced into Russia and the
United States declared war on Great Britain. The threads of trade that
public officials and commercial agents had endeavored to profit from
and protect—from Boston to Havana to St. Petersburg—seemed ready
to snap. The United States had been drawn into a war in which the
Cuban Creole elite believed they would be entirely outmatched. After
the war, they feared, the bulk of the Caribbean trade might readily be
strangled by the antislavery British navy, which had just been granted
authorization from Spain to meddle in colonial affairs. As the United
States readied for war, Congress sought to restrict the export of key
commodities from the nation, including specie, and American merchants who had invested in the slave regimes of the Caribbean and
South America began to panic.[37] In Russia, matters were even worse:
The French invasion had thrown trade into total disarray.[38] Everything
that men like William Gray, John Quincy Adams and William Shaler
had worked to build—a deeper integration of markets built on intensive
slavery—was now at risk.

The War of 1812 remains a contradictory conflict in U.S. history. It
was ostensibly caused by trade restrictions that had hamstrung U.S.
merchants, by the British impressment of American sailors into the
Royal Navy, and by continued British meddling in issues impacting
North American expansion, including support for anti-U.S. Native
American tribes. The conflict began at the height of the Napoleonic
Wars, as French armies gathered for the invasion of Russia; it began
as the Spanish Cortes passed one of the most liberal constitutions to
date, which triggered intensive debate about the future of slavery, the
slave trade and colonial representation in Cuba. Across the Atlantic,
the French still occupied much of Spain—as they had since 1808—and
were now bogged down in the relentless guerrilla warfare that devastated the country and broke the Spanish empire as well. Independence
movements—some instigated to resist French rule, others to oppose
Spanish or any European control—spread through Spain's colonies.
Although the liberal Spanish constitution of 1812 would ultimately be
tossed out in 1814 when the Spanish king Ferdinand VII returned to
power, its colonial impact was more immediate.

Revolutionary uprisings in Cuba (1812), the Philippines (1813) and Peru (1814) were direct reactions to the document, and the Cuban Creole elite were quieted only by the outbreak of a widespread slave rebellion. The 1812 Aponte Rebellion followed on the heels of the 1811 "German Coast" slave revolt in Louisiana, which has been dubbed "America's largest slave revolt."[39] If the Creole elite in Cuba were inspired by the example of Simón Bolívar in nearby Venezuela to protest the 1812 constitution, enslaved revolutionaries in the American Mediterranean saw the promise of Haiti. Within just two years, members of the '15ers would also consider the possibilities of revolution much farther north, in Hartford, Connecticut. When global capitalism stuttered—as warfare on both sides of the ocean obstructed market access and transatlantic transit, the drivers of demand—the Age of Revolutions intensified.

By 1812, European warfare had rattled the U.S. shipping trade and contributed to increased profits for U.S. elites; now, the Europeans were bringing the fight to the Americas, as the Spanish struggled to put down revolutionary movements and the British invaded the United States. Trade to many markets was thrown into complete disarray. As the War of 1812 intensified, merchants continued to "regret the continuance of the unhappy war between the two countries,"[40] while others spoke of secession. In New England, the war was so unpopular that in its closing weeks, from December 1814 to January 1815, elite Federalists gathered for the Hartford Convention to outline a list of grievances, which some attendees feared—and others hoped—might lead to civil war.[41] It is hardly surprising that amid such uncertain commercial prospects and secessionist rhetoric, one New England merchant remarked that American interwar trade restrictions did "indeed look to me more a hostility to New England than Old England."[42]

If the British strangled U.S. shipping, where would the sugar and coffee come from to feed European demand? What would North Americans be able to leverage into shipments of Spanish gold and silver to support the expansion of Asian trade and the rise of the fragile financial infrastructure of the United States? The integration of world markets depended on slaves: Anything that brought the British into the hemisphere was dangerous. In 1814, Vincent Gray knew where they were headed: New Orleans.

"The Most Quiet Spot Upon the Globe"

Vincent Gray had information. It was late 1814, and the war between the United States and Great Britain had not gone as expected. The British, it seemed, were not invincible. British forces did not occupy Havana, and although they had burned the American capital, they had lost battles too. Americans had fractured pro-British Native American forces and turned back British armies at New York and Baltimore (the last of which inspired Francis Scott Key's famous "Star Spangled Banner"). Even U.S. shipping had not died completely. Although Gray himself had fretted in the summer of 1813 that "war with England throws the carrying trade into [British] hands … in every quarter of the globe,"[43] many American merchants did not give up.

Despite the risks of maintaining trade channels in the face of a hostile British navy, a number of American merchants continued to invest, even in the Cuba–Baltic circuit, counting on the enormous profits they could make when their vessels got through. After all, the risks of seizure, although they had certainly escalated with the formal declaration of war, were nothing new.[44] During the war, the New Yorker Jacob Barker seems to have overcome his reservations about the Baltic trade, and in January 1813, he even managed to coordinate shipments of "Russia goods" in England. "I am glad," Thomas Hazard wrote from New Bedford, "that so many of thy vessels had reached England from Russia, they will probably make thee a handsome profit."[45] Unsurprisingly, William Gray also refused to fold and continued to dispatch ships loaded with colonial produce for the Baltic. On July 11, 1812—after the declaration of war—Thomas Hazard wrote Gray that he would accept Gray's "kind offer when I was last at thy house, of forwarding a letter to my son at Archangel, by thy ship, now on the point of sailing for that place."[46]

There was also money to be made in the privatization of war. Just twelve days after the formal declaration of war, the U.S. Congress authorized the issuing of letters of marque, prizes and prize goods for any investor who chose to refit his merchant vessels with cannons and guns.[47] This patriotic authorization to plunder was nothing new; state-sponsored piracy had provided the bedrock for the fortunes of a number of these American elites during the Revolutionary period. In 1812, however, unlike during the Revolution, many '15ers were too risk averse or disgruntled with the war's impact on trade to court British animosity, and fewer official licenses were granted. During the War of 1812, for example, the British issued over 1,300 privateering licenses, while the United States issued just 500.[48] After all, it cost money to invest in privateers: By some estimates, the going rate was approximately $40,000 to outfit and launch a ship from Baltimore. But many of the same elite men who had risked the Baltic refused to watch their shipping investments idle. In July 1812, for example—immediately after receiving Congressional authorization—James D'Wolf's vessel, the *Yankee*, captured four British ships off the coast of Newfoundland.[49] William Gray also joined in, and Gray and D'Wolf would even jointly invest in another privateer, the *Brutus*.[50]

Farther south, however, American privateers hauling British prize ships into Cuban ports ran into trouble with Spanish authorities, who struggled to stay out of the conflict and away from any potential British occupation.[51] As they tried to quell the revolutionary African population throughout the island, Spanish merchants and planters determined to stay out of the fight farther north. On August 15, 1812, for example, Havana merchants hurriedly assembled "for the purpose of adopting such measures" as would allow them to do whatever "'neutrality requires, during the war between Britain and America.'"[52] The Spanish recognized that British merchants resented the inferiority in their trade with Cuba, which may have occupied less than one-tenth the volume of the U.S. trade. As Americans saw it, the Cuban Creole elite remained "favourable to the English, not from affection but fear."[53] If Spanish merchants or planters appeared to pick one side in the conflict, the other might retaliate, and if the British arrived, the slave trade would end.

Overall, the effect of the War of 1812 on U.S. Atlantic investments was not entirely dissimilar to that of the quasi-war with France that U.S. traders had endured a decade earlier. It hit trade networks disproportionately. Whereas marine insurance premiums to Cuba ticked up by just 2 percent, rates to the European markets—the traditional outlets for sugar and coffee—climbed by 50 percent or higher.[54] And, because European demand and market access routinely set the terms of Cuban commodity prices, the Havana commercial house of Packard &

Gowen noted in 1814 that "the prices of Sugar & Coffee, which have continued to decline" were due to drop into "a still further depression" unless "prospects mend in Europe."[55] The New England–Cuba trade was particularly hard-hit. In Santiago, Cuba, for example, just fourteen American ships entered port in the six months from January to July 1814, and only one of these vessels arrived from New England.[56] There were, however, other ways to get supplies through.

Across the Gulf of Mexico in New Orleans, the U.S. merchant David Morgan explained succinctly what this meant: "Smuggling goes on brisk, as usual," he wrote in January 1814. "[H]e that can run the most goods in, is the most respectable."[57] New Englanders in particular freely moved their goods in Cuba via American, English or mercenary vessels under the eyes of complicit Spanish authorities.[58] Cuba was a safe haven, and as early as September 1813 even Vincent Gray was forced to admit that Cuba might in fact be "the most quiet spot upon the globe." Looking out on the Havana docks from the windows of a commercial house, Gray reflected that no one would ever know "that the Spanish nation was engaged in a war."[59] Cuba remained the calm eye of a storm that whipped and threatened the flow of trade all around her. The slave trade was safe—for the moment.

Vincent Gray was well aware that this could change at any time due to the sheer power of the British navy. In January 1813, James Madison had issued a report to the U.S. Senate that suggested the fragility of U.S. security along the entire Atlantic seaboard and the Gulf Coast. Great Britain was now "under the necessity of sending troops to Halifax, the West Indies and other parts of America," Madison wrote. "It will be easy for her to disguise the destination of any particular embarkation, until it reaches our coast."[60] As became quickly evident in the course of the war, Britain's naval superiority rendered all of the United States potentially vulnerable to invasion. Maritime intelligence was crucial. If the British sailed farther south into the Caribbean, they could potentially sever the contraband market that linked Cuba with the Gulf Coast and play a more active role in the Spanish colony. The loss of American influence would be Britain's gain, which would translate into a direct attack on the slave trade.

In 1814, Vincent Gray held a letter in his hand from a Liverpool

cotton broker who offered to cut Gray in on a deal related to the antici-
pated opening of North American markets to British trade. The British
navy was planning a surprise attack on New Orleans; after their expected
victory, the broker hoped to coordinate with Gray to make a sizeable
profit. Although Vincent Gray likely looked to his network of spies and
informants for confirmation of the intelligence, British sailors openly
volunteered the information. They were so confident of British victory
in Louisiana that there was no need for secrecy. On the docks of Havana,
Gray thought about it. He was an American from Massachusetts, but
he had lived in Cuba for more than a decade and had acclimated to the
ruthlessness of the Spanish island. Many of the elite American merchants who arrived expecting easy profits from an eager supplicant left
disappointed and suspicious of Gray. Vincent Gray understood Cuba;
he had survived assassination attempts and imprisonment, and he routinely broke consular seals—both in and out of Havana—to read the
missives sent by the secretary of state, consuls and other investors. Gray
was always on the lookout for a profit, and the one thing he knew, as he
walked away from the busy harbor, was that the British would be bad
for business.[61] Although he was a U.S. citizen and public diplomatic
official, Vincent Gray was also a dedicated slave trader.

Shortly after receiving his letter from Liverpool, Gray coordinated
with a merchant contact in Mobile named James Innerarity, who was
working with James Forbes at the Mobile branch of an Indian trading
company. Gray told Innerarity what he had learned from Liverpool,
and Innerarity duly passed Gray's intelligence on to the U.S. army officials. When the news reached General Andrew Jackson, he left for New
Orleans in time to draw additional forces and ready the defenses. The
maneuver led to Jackson's 1815 victory at the Battle of New Orleans and
launched Jackson's own dominating career. In Havana, Vincent Gray
had made this possible—all in order to protect the slave trade.[62]

The Battle of New Orleans famously ended the War of 1812 in early
1815—shortly *after* peace had been declared in Europe. Although the
war ended in more of a stalemate than a victory for either side, it did alter
the character of both U.S. and British involvement in North America,
ending the British presence in the west and curtailing American ambitions to annex Canada. Farther south, Americans invested in the slave

trade were eager to return to their pre-war positions, and Vincent Gray remarked that the "renewal of friendly intercourse between the United States and Great Britain" would allow him to return his full attention to where it belonged: making money.[63]

By the closing days of the war, even Vincent Gray's neighbor in Havana, John Joseph Chauviteau—who had waxed philosophical just a few years before—claimed that he "never doubted the success of the American cause, notwithstanding the hardships to individuals and the increase of the public debt." By December 1814, inspired by American resistance and successful smuggling operations, Chauviteau wrote: "I hope the war will last a couple years more, and [when] this time expires you will have some allies."[64] The next year, James D'Wolf's brother John told Chauviteau that the war "has gone off in a blaze of glory to this country, and I believe in future our late enemy will be very cautious how they deliver their insults and aggressions." The British had been put in their place, and now the Federalists' days were numbered. "I hope you see the day yet," John D'Wolf wrote, "that the Eastern State will be governed by Americans and not by traitors."[65]

In the United States, New Englanders who had threatened secession only a year earlier were eager to capitalize on the restoration of a liberal-izing carrying trade. Soon, many of these elite merchants would grow even more ambitious, and in the years ahead, the same men who had incorporated the public diplomatic apparatus of the United States into their private trade networks would rise to national public office, ready to wield the U.S. navy for the protection of their profits. Ultimately crafting a pro-slavery U.S. foreign policy to protect the slave trade, they would establish the precedent for the promulgation of informal American empire throughout the Americas. But without soldiers, "empire" is meaningless, and none of their dreams would have been possible without the acumen and brutality of the men who captained the slave ships and negotiated with customs house officers on behalf of their elite employers. As William Gray, James D'Wolf and John Quincy Adams assumed public office, it was this class of "commercial agents" on the ground who made their rise possible.

FIVE

Slavemongers

It was Christmas Eve, 1816, and Benjamin Bosworth felt good. He was drinking rum and thinking about sex, money and the funny way men's feet kicked and twirled when they were hanged by the neck. Bristol, Rhode Island, was a small, freezing port dominated by a handful of families who owned the ships that crowded the harbor. New buildings—banks and commercial houses—were going up in town along the main road that had been laid with stones carried by enslaved Africans a generation before. The wharf was crowded now with massive warehouses, distilleries and stables. It was boom time, and Bosworth was content. "We live upon the fat of the land," he wrote to his friend Edward Spalding. "Christmas comes dancing out—to introduce young Eighteen hundred *seventeen*. Swing time is out!!!—so goes the world."[1] It was a violent pun, intended to mock the dance of a hanging man's feet as he strangled to death on the gallows. With arrogance, irreverence, and—sometimes—humor, men like Benjamin Bosworth and Edward Spalding were determined to profit from this Atlantic World, in which there was perpetual conflict between legal boundaries, cultural norms and the scope of power attained through violence.[2] They regarded the outlawed slave trade with the cynicism and wit of profiteers.

In his work on the antebellum domestic slave trade in the United States, historian Edward Baptist has noted similarly lurid fetishism by "slavemongers" of enslaved African Americans who were transported and sold from Chesapeake plantations to New Orleans and Natchez. Similar to the slavers in Baptist's study, these commercial agents also

culturally translated their newfound economic and social power into fet-
ishized sexuality. This suggests that the highly sexual commodification
of human beings that Baptist identifies in the U.S. South may perhaps
be best understood as an effect of individual social transitions related to
economic opportunity built on violence. Spalding, Bosworth and Rhode
Islanders Joseph Torrey (Spalding's cousin) and Golden Dearth were
self-identified members of "the Bachelors club residing in Bristol, R.I."[3]
In 1816, when Edward Spalding sailed on the *Eliza Ann* for Havana,
Benjamin Bosworth penned missives from Bristol that were loaded
with sexual innuendo and private jokes, signed "Kiah Butterworth."
Bosworth wrote of "a certain longing after what! *A wife!!!* … a wife per-
chance a Devil" and joked that he needed "a long human gun" to make
his "hair (don't misconstrue my meaning) stand as stiff as poker Viz.
whose been F—."[4] Satirizing typical rules of correspondence, Bosworth
called Spalding the "Duke of Limbs and principal Antiquarian" and
chided him for "misconstruing" his meaning "as nothing immodest or
indelicate ought to be laid to the charge of Kiah Butterworth."[5] Many
of the sexual references in the "club's" subsequent correspondence were
expressions of power that were as related to New England courtship and
marriage as to slavery.

The same banks and insurance companies that provided the credit
for the expansion of the North American plantation frontier relied on
a steady inflow of specie into their vaults and a steady outflow of sugar,
coffee and cotton to European markets to offset persistent U.S. trade
deficits. The merchants who shipped the goods were invariably affili-
ated with these same financial institutions. Baptist suggests that "British
and northern bankers and merchants also provided the credit necessary for frontier planters to purchase" slaves and plantation goods. In
this system, "money and credit rotated in a wheel of international scale,
while plantation products such as cotton and sugar—or slaves—circled
in geared opposition." The slave traders who drove "the circulation of
capital and commodities" in this North American circuit reconciled
their extensive network knowledge and outsized profits with a deliberate
fetishization and commodification of the enslaved couched in cynically
violent language.[6] In the Atlantic wing of this same economic circuit,
Spalding and Bosworth were veritable brothers-in-arms.

By now, the United States was changing. After 1815, the young nation had demonstrated that it could resist—if with only ambiguous consequences—European military power. Just as importantly, many investors viewed the return of peace as a signal that the boom times had returned. The years after 1815—and particularly after 1817 in Cuba—witnessed an expansion in both the scale and profits of the slave trade. A new generation of commercial agents—the striving professional class of the '15ers—was eager to work this system and exploit it on behalf of their elite employers. Although I have selected 1815 as a decisive year in shaping the post-revolutionary generation, choosing one year on which to anchor the arc of history is always somewhat arbitrary and problematic. And while some years—1776, 1815 and 1861, for example have marked particularly significant events in the history of the United States, it was the consistency in the rise of the slave trade with respect to U.S. development that shaped the nation.

This period is also sometimes termed "the Era of Good Feelings," a moment of supposed political harmony in national politics in which the United States would ride the momentum of the 1815 victory into North American territorial expansion. It was also the era of slave regimes that depended on the expansion of the slave trade. As enslaved Africans cleared the jungles of Brazil and Cuba to make way for new, more innovative networks of sugar and coffee plantations, enslaved people in North America chopped trees and cleared the brush to create the cotton South. In the tropical plantations farther south, the life expectancy of enslaved Africans routinely hovered in the single digits: Men, women and children were often worked to death in the course of five to eight years, only to be replaced by new arrivals. The economic calculus of sugar and coffee continued to incentivize planters to break their enslaved laborers and purchase new, illegally transported slaves rather than alter the labor regime to keep them alive.

In North America, a dramatic internal U.S. slave trade would relocate millions of enslaved people to the south and west from the established plantations of the east. Speculation gripped the hemisphere, and during the economic Panic of 1819—a complex agricultural and financial bubble—land values in some areas collapsed while credit became hard to come by. Meanwhile, John Quincy Adams rose to the position of

secretary of state under President James Monroe, determined to continue his work on behalf of his elite allies and benefactors. In 1819,
Adams engineered the Transcontinental Treaty with Spain, which
gave the United States eastern Florida and potential access to the rest
of the western continent. The Treaty, like the later Monroe Doctrine,
was shaped to benefit Adams's elite Northern allies, who were also
deeply implicated in the profits of slavery farther south. For planters and non-slaveholding investors alike, new territories meant land
for the cultivation of the same commodities that had fed Atlantic
demand for decades: sugar, cotton and coffee. More and more, it
became clear that the present and future development of the United
States hinged on the expansion of slavery, both in North America
and abroad.

When the question of Missouri statehood arose in 1820, the divisive
debate that ensued was so vitriolic that many observers feared it might
split the Union. Although the Kentucky congressman Henry Clay would
famously engineer a compromise to admit Maine as a free state and ban
new slave states north of the latitude 36°30', it became clear that this
was not simply a U.S. matter. Amid the controversy, antislavery activists
concerned with "the introduction of slavery into any State or Territory
that may hereafter be admitted into the Union" explicitly linked the
expansion of the transatlantic slave trade with the expansion of North
American slavery. In a memorial submitted in January 1820, a group of
antislavery Rhode Islanders acknowledged their region's own complicity
in the trade as a token of legitimacy in their current condemnation of
slavery's expansion. The expansion of the illegal slave trade and North
American slavery, they wrote, were explicitly interdependent, binding
the fate of Cuba with Missouri:

> The northern colonies participated in [the slave trade] equally with
> the southern, and the navigation of the New England ports ... was
> employed continually on the African coast... There can be no reproach,
> therefore, cast upon our southern brethren for the introduction of this
> evil... But it will be in vain that Congress shall prohibit the traffic in
> slaves ... if an immense market is to be opened in the Territories of
> the west... The inevitable result of such a course of proceedings must

be ... to increase the temptations to introduce them illegally ... in the vicinity of Cuba [where there is] a great depot and slave market.[7]

By the end of the decade, when Americans looked west to Missouri, they envisioned Havana and the booming illegal slave trade that supported it.

In 1820, the United States condemned the slave trade as an act of piracy, making participation in the human traffic punishable by death. Under British pressure, a Spanish treaty outlawing the trade into Cuba went into effect that same year. American investors were terrified. Despite the outcome of the War of 1812, British machinations and British ships were everywhere. The British navy was free to patrol the Atlantic in earnest, and now even the slave trade appeared to be at risk. As men like John Quincy Adams and James D'Wolf leveraged their wealth and power into national public office, others such as Edward Spalding and Benjamin Bosworth sailed south on the fault lines of this chaotic economic boom as agents of commerce, slavery and empire.

I Do Not Wish You to Correspond With Our House on the Subject

In 1816, months before his Christmas Eve missive, Benjamin Bosworth wanted to make a bet. The terms were simple:

> If on the 1st January 1821 or at any period before that day, it can be made to appear that Edward Spalding is in possession of a net capital of *three thousand dollars* then he the said Spalding agrees to pay unto Benjamin M. Bosworth a suit of clothes complete of the winner's choice.
>
> But in case it is not made to appear that the said Spalding within the time aforesaid shall be possessed of such net capital, then the said B.M. Bosworth agrees to pay unto Edward Spalding a suit of clothes complete as aforesaid—It is also mutually agreed by the parties that the winner on receipt of the bet, shall treat with a Bottle of *Good Old Madeira Dam, ye Jo.*[8]

Arrogant and contented, Bosworth was even more certain of their future prospects than his friend Edward Spalding. What's more, Bosworth was no stranger to the lawbreaking, extreme violence and exploitation of the Atlantic system. Just weeks after the January 1, 1808, U.S. ban on the slave trade, for example, he had served as "Master, now bound from the Port of Bristol to Africa" aboard the *Concord.* His triangular course was typical: Rhode Island to Africa to Havana and back again.[9] And he knew his employers, the D'Wolfs. "I've written you once already by that Satan Frank DWolf," Bosworth joked. Despite the divine punishments they might expect from their commerce, "we have had no tornadoes, whirlwinds, thunder gusts, volcanoes, Earthquakes, floods or fiery eruptions—'the Pestilence that walkeeth in Darkness,'" Bosworth wrote, "has forborne to omite."[10]

Like Baptist's callous North American slave traders, the American agents who made the Caribbean wing of this system possible reconciled their newfound power with cynical irreverence. The documents that survive to demonstrate the arrogance of American commercial agents operating in the Atlantic World as ship captains, supercargoes, commercial agents, and attorneys offer a rare glimpse into how this professional class understood the violence and economic opportunity of emergent global capitalism. And after the resumption of commerce post-1815, business was good. In Cuba, investors were similarly eager to celebrate "the return of peace between the United States & England" and fantasize about the possibilities of "having once more unfettered American Enterprise & the commerce of this Island in your vessels."[11]

Open European markets translated into increased demand, which directly fueled a rise in sugar and coffee prices. Whereas Cuban coffee prices had been depressed at four dollars per quintal from 1812 to 1815, demand and prices soared following the transatlantic peace: coffee prices jumped from four dollars per quintal to twelve to twenty-five, before finally peaking at thirty dollars per quintal.[12] Rising prices also contributed to pressure to expand the slave frontier, which led to rampant land speculation.[13] In 1802 there had been 800 ingenios in Cuba; by 1817 there were more than 1,300, and they were rapidly modernizing.[14] Planters in Cuba had the benefit of latecomers; unlike in nearby Haiti, Barbados and Jamaica, where agricultural productivity was now lagging, Cuba's planters could skip stages of trial, error and agricultural degradation to immediately adopt the most economically effective cultivation techniques available. They benefited from the French experiences at Saint Domingue and attempted to replicate and improve on French production on an even more massive scale, while encouraging "white" immigration and transforming the island into one of the most heavily militarized geographies on the planet.

Americans profited from this expansion without footing the imperial bill, while the Spanish attempted to leverage spiking revenues into the perpetuation of the regime by appeasing the Creole elite, who continued to resent Spanish taxes and control and sought greater access to foreign markets and cheaper foreign imports. As Roger Betancourt makes plain, the years immediately after 1815 (following the restoration of absolutist Spanish rule in 1814) were crucial to the aspirations for civil liberties and the democratization of economic opportunities of the Cuban creole elite. This included a broadening of resource extraction rights (particularly in timber), the elimination of the Crown's tobacco monopoly, liberalization of trade, and a recognition of property rights on numerous fronts.[15] Trade policies principally designed to placate the Creole elite also had the effect of intensifying U.S. investment in the carrying trade and the plantation regime itself.

From 1794 to 1817, Cuban revenue from duties on foreign trade rose 75 percent overall, and in the U.S.-dominated port of Matanzas revenue grew by an astounding 4,000 percent.[16] This entire system ran on the slave trade, and when the U.S. commercial agent John Mason wrote from Santiago, Cuba, that "many citizens of the United States are indirectly and indeed almost directly engaged in the slave trade," he had men such as Edward Spalding and Benjamin Bosworth in mind.[17] Then, in 1817, things got more complicated. That year, the Spanish monarch Ferdinand VII authorized the captain-general of Cuba to naturalize white immigrants, and Cuban ports were opened to unrestricted foreign trade.[18] Yet, at the same moment that the Spanish encouraged American immigration and the liberalization of trade, they finally relented to British pressure and agreed to an 1817 Anglo-Spanish treaty, which purported to ban the slave trade into Cuba in 1820.

If the future was suddenly unclear, the commercial impact of the antislave trade treaty was immediate. In Havana, average slave prices spiked from $150 to $500, and slave imports surged. In 1817 alone, between 25,000 and 32,000 enslaved Africans arrived in Cuba, and more than 50,000 were carried to Brazil to meet the demands of anxious planters. In Cuba, the five-year period from 1815 to 1819 witnessed the highest percentage increase in slave imports to date. And as the uncertainties and risks of the slave trade contributed to a rise in slave sale prices in the Americas, purchase prices plummeted in Africa; investors realized exponential gains, even as they openly protested and won formal allowances to continue the trade.[19] In April 1820, the commander of the U.S. naval ship *Cyane*, off the coast of Sierra Leone, wrote, "The slave trade is carried on to a very great extent. There are not less than three hundred vessels on the coast engaged in that traffic, each having two or three sets of papers."[20] The governor of Sierra Leone, too, noted that a "greater number of vessels [were now] employed in that traffic [the slave trade] than at any former period." Portugal had agreed to British demands to curb slave trading north of the equator, but the United States refused to commit more than one vessel to monitor the illegal slave trade.[21]

By the end of the 1810s, Americans like Benjamin Bosworth and Edward Spalding remained deeply involved in the illegal slave trade. In December 1819, for example, a curious New Englander wandered the harbor of Havana to inspect "a Guineaman" that had "arrived with 341 slaves," remarking that the "poor negroes" were "more comfortably situated than I expected."[22] The New Englander's guide to the slave ship may, in fact, have been none other than U.S. vice consul Vincent Gray. After marrying the sister of a Spanish merchant in Havana, Gray had used the relaxation of trade and investment regulations to open his own commercial house, where his business routinely included slaves—even after the formal 1820 Spanish ban.[23]

In these years, while continuing to serve as a U.S. vice consul in Havana, Vincent Gray regularly advertised the arrival of slave ships that were consigned to his commercial house. On December 14, 1820, for example, *El Diario de la Habana* published news of the arrival of the *Antonio* in Havana with a cargo of 203 "negros bozales" consigned to "Gray & Fernandez." Three days later, news of a similar slave ship consignment was published.[24] Anyone interested in determining whether or not American agents were involved in the slave trade could simply read the newspaper. After 1808, however, most American participants in the slave trade had adopted new codes of silence, avoiding correspondence whenever possible and routinely destroying their records. Predictably, this has complicated efforts to chronicle the precise contours of the illicit trade. Some scholars have even taken the absence of a documentary record as evidence of the withdrawal of Americans—particularly New Englanders—from the slave trade in the decade after 1808, mistaking vigilance on the part of slave traders as proof of abstinence. Leonardo Marques has recently suggested, for example, that the D'Wolfs' "involvement in slave-trading activities, however, could not be sustained for long, and their disappearance from the documents after the late 1810s seems to indicate their complete withdrawal from the business."[25] This was simply not true. There is ample evidence that New Englanders such as D'Wolf and his agent Edward Spalding remained active in the slave trade into the 1820s.

Like most Americans involved in illicit trade, Spalding was often careful to avoid leaving any record that could be used against him. However, due to the vagaries of the historical record, sufficient portions of his correspondence and personal papers have survived to demonstrate that he remained active in the trade on behalf of his employers—even after it became a hanging crime in the United States in 1820. Moreover, the timing of the involvement also proves that at the same moment that James D'Wolf launched a successful bid for the U.S. Senate, he also actively invested in numerous slave ships. In 1820, as the Spanish ban on the slave trade went into effect, for example, Spalding ran into difficulty with the slave ship *Cintra*. The *Cintra* was the alias used for the American ship *Margaret*. When the vessel's first mate absconded with nine of the slaves, Edward Spalding was forced to commit pen to paper. Writing to a Spanish attorney in Havana of the incident, Spalding acknowledged that "our house is materially interested" in the stolen slaves, before adding, "I do not wish you to correspond with our house on the subject, as the interception of such a letter might be injurious."[26]

At that moment in early 1820, Spalding's backers were also invested in at least two more slave ships—the *Rambler* (owned by James D'Wolf and Charles Collins) and her tender, the *Exchange* (owned by William

Raymond, also of Bristol)—which had just been spotted on the West African coast.[27] This exposure came at a dangerous time for D'Wolf and had the potential to upset the fortunes of the entire clan. In Bristol, James D'Wolf had just watched one of his antislavery opponents, Barnabas Bates, rise to the position of port collector. Determined to replace Bates with an ally, D'Wolf was now in the process of launching a bid for the U.S. Senate and had come under fire for his well-known participation in the slave trade. On the floor of the Rhode Island legislature, he denounced the charges and swore that his involvement in the transatlantic slave trade had long since ended:

> I make this declaration, Sir, In consequence of the many unmerited accusations which have been circulated against me, in relation to a business, *in which I was formerly engaged.*—But, Sir, for several years past, I have been as much *uncontaminated by any share in it as any citizen of the State!*[28]

Meanwhile, in Cuba, Spalding dutifully noted the balance due from the *Cintra* in his pocket memorandum book: $4,500. This was exactly the market value of the nine stolen slaves on the Cuban slave market.[29] While it is unclear if the slaves were ever recovered, Spalding continued to work for D'Wolf and others to ensure that the flow of slaves to their Cuban plantations continued unabated.[30] Across the entire island, the outlawed slave trade thrived. At the eastern port of Santiago, the American agent Daniel Giraud remarked in 1822 that, "relative to the slave trade, it is with much regret that I have to say, that it still continues to be carried to this Island."[31] Similarly, in 1824, Giraud's successor James Wright acknowledged, "I have nothing to add to my former observations on the Subject of the Slave Trade—possitive [sic] prohibitions continue in force against [this] traffic, nevertheless it is a subject of notoriety that frequent evasions of the Edict take place, on those parts of the coast that are remote from the Eye and Arm of the Law."[32] Avoiding the law often meant lingering on the coast of Africa, Cuba or Brazil for days to avoid patrols or unloading captives in the dead of night far away from the ports. It also meant dumping enslaved men, women and children over the side of the ship to avoid capture. As the dangers of the slave trade escalated, potential profits increased, and the trade itself took on a new, even more ruthless character.

In April 1817, the Rhode Island slave trader Caleb Miller had written to Edward Spalding of his hopes for a successful slaving trip and the risks involved. Miller wrote "that the Mortality on board of the African vessels has been great of late" due to lack of clean air, and he asked Spalding to help him find "a vessel of a considerable size" so that "there should not be more Deaths than there would probably be in the same number in the Island of Cuba."[33] Such deaths in the human trade were as horrific as they were commonplace, and the catastrophic death rates associated with the middle passage to Cuba could rise as high as 25 to 33 percent. Over the life of the slave trade, longer transit times from Africa to plantations in the Americas typically contributed to an increase in the mortality rates of enslaved Africans onboard slave ships. But the length of a journey did not always correlate neatly with distance.

From 1776 to 1864, the average length of a slave voyage to Cuba was between fifty and fifty-nine days, and mortality rates hovered at approximately 18 to 19 percent (compared with 8 percent in the British Caribbean prior to 1807). After the Spanish outlaw of the trade in 1820, mortality rates escalated even further as conditions worsened. Farther south, the major slave trading regions of Brazil had long since carried on a varied and altogether separate slave trade. Although students of the transatlantic slave trade are well versed in the "triangular trade" that characterized the North Atlantic, following—as David Brion Davis suggests—a "northern clockwise circle [that] connected Europe, the Caribbean, and African sources of labor north of the equator," Brazil was different. For much of the trade, "a southern counterclockwise current or circle connected southwest Africa and Portuguese Brazil," which was by far the closest point in the Americas to the African continent. In this system, slave voyages to Brazil were "40 percent shorter than the Middle Passage to the Caribbean," and although mortality rates declined in the seventeenth and eighteenth centuries, when Brazil finally outlawed the trade in 1830 this contributed to an immediate spike in death rates "because captives were held longer on the coast to avoid anti-slave-trade patrols and were disembarked under hazardous conditions." The outlaw of the slave trade created perverse incentives for traders that led to the death of nearly one in five of the Africans embarked for Cuba and Brazil.[34]

These percentages played havoc with the calculations of the U.S. commercial agents and captains involved in the trade. In 1818, for example, the slave ship *Abaellino*, in which the D'Wolfs had an interest, ran into difficulty. As the captain Thomas Russell wrote to Edward Spalding, the ship had gone "to Loango" and "bonny" to purchase "a fine cargo of 320" slaves. It had then sailed toward Trinidad, Cuba, "with an Intention to smuggle the cargo on shore," before smallpox broke out. "The small pox," Russell wrote, "had attacked my crew & cargo," and he had been forced to stop in Fort Royal on November 24. As the Africans died in the lower deck, Russell scrambled to sell "the remaining 230" for an average price of $150—far below the $400–$500 prices now current in Cuba. "When they were first taken on board," Russell swore that the Africans were "as fine a cargo as ever was shipped." But now, "the poor wretches" were lucky to be sold at any price. In the aftermath of the debacle, Captain Russell urged his New Englander backers "not [to] be discouraged ... for I think there is a prospect yet if I can get a cargo here healthy."[35]

For the '15ers, the tropical gulags of the Americas drove commodity exchange on a new scale while exacting a devastating toll on the lives of the enslaved. In the nineteenth century, after the ending of the slave trade into the United States, the North American slave population tripled. To be sure, the conditions of North American slave plantations were, in many ways, every bit as brutal as conditions farther south. The labor regimes, however, were different. In the United States, enslaved people had children and families, many of whom were torn from them, sold and relocated in the massive migration of the internal slave trade of westward expansion. But their overall numbers increased; enslaved African Americans reproduced threefold in this period. Farther south, matters were different, and the catastrophic mortality rates associated with tropical sugar and coffee labor regimes of the Caribbean and South America made the slave trade absolutely vital to increased commodity production. From 1780 to 1830, although the population of enslaved people in the Caribbean doubled, twice as many people were brought to the region as slaves—meaning that the natural rate of reproduction was effectively stagnant. The slave trade represented a cornerstone of economic development: the dead could always be replaced.

SIX

Assassins

S omeone shouted his name. Robert Goodwin was well dressed in a dark coat and hat and leaning on a stiff cane. As he looked down the crowded Manhattan street to the corner of Broadway and Courtlandt, Goodwin saw him: that damned Portuguese consul Thomas Stoughton. Stoughton smirked, waiting. What had Stoughton's son James once called Goodwin—a pirate? Goodwin's family mattered, and his own brother was a naval captain. In 1819, the word "pirate" meant subversion by the worst class of people. It evoked images of murder, kidnapping, theft and rape by the same sorts of men—black, mixed, even low whites—who had turned Saint Domingue upside down. But it was also more complicated than that, and what made a man a "pirate" depended on the future of empire and individual liberty in places where revolution and profit often came hand in hand. Goodwin was a gentleman, but he was also, like many men of his generation, an occasional revolutionary. More than once, he had sailed south for the sake of ideals or money—and often both—and had been intimately involved in complex smuggling operations in the borderlands of the Caribbean, where the distinctions between piracy, warfare and pure opportunism were often confused and contradictory. Stoughton, however, had seen it differently, and the Portuguese merchants he represented wanted their cargo back.

Goodwin advanced on Stoughton, hand tight on his cane, and as they came together Stoughton slapped him hard. The shock knocked Goodwin down—but only for a moment. He lunged, and, as the two men lost their hats in a twisting fight across the sidewalk, a crowd gathered. The men staggered apart again. Someone tried to pull Goodwin away.

People were shouting for them to stop. Goodwin attacked again, and this time, when Stoughton grabbed him, Goodwin twisted the top off his cane to reveal a dagger and stabbed Stoughton in the left side. Stoughton stumbled backwards and fell. Goodwin was shaking. He reached for his hat, picked it up. Stoughton looked pale, and there was a small patch of blood on his shirt where the cane's blade had gone in. Goodwin realized that he was holding the wrong hat. Someone told him that it hardly mattered now, and as he walked away, the crowd parted around him. A serious man in a dark coat came to his side and told him that they had to get away—right now. Goodwin recognized him: Churchill C. Cambreleng. One of the wealthiest men in New York and a founding director of the Farmer's Fire Insurance and Loan Company, Cambreleng moved in the circles of Astor and D'Wolf; now, he helped Goodwin escape. Stoughton would be dead soon, but it hardly mattered. Goodwin was well connected, and his trial the following year would end in a hung jury.[1]

When Goodwin killed Stoughton in December 1819, the transnational commercial concerns and extralegal violence of the Atlantic World appeared to be spilling over into the midday streets of downtown Manhattan. Greater numbers of U.S. citizens were now freely traveling—and permanently relocating—from the United States to the turbulent borderlands of the Caribbean and South America. By the end of the second decade of the nineteenth century, the Caribbean appeared to be descending into anarchy. As revolutions shook the Spanish empire, a rise in trade was accompanied by a spike in opportunism and "piracy." By 1823, U.S. newspapers would document more than three thousand incidents of pirate attacks since 1815.[2] The unrecorded, illegal contours of commerce, particularly between the United States and Cuba, made it uniquely vulnerable to assault.[3] In August 1817, a Havana merchant wrote to his New England contacts of "the distressed state of their Commerce in these Seas, in consequence of the numerous Privateers."[4]

Breathless missives and published accounts described near-constant attacks by communities of pirates, who flourished in Cuba under the informal supervision of Spanish authorities.[5] Amid the boom in Cuban agro-industry and successive New World revolutions, Spanish officials encouraged piracy as a means to harass trade with their former colonies, and revolutionary governments responded in kind.[6] Privateers —including many North Americans—flocked to Latin America with revolutionary authorization to harass Spanish shipping. Many American merchants resented European arrogance and bristled at port restrictions that put them at a disadvantage. Latin American revolutionaries were often seen as kindred spirits—Simón Bolívar as a version of George Washington. Predictably, however, this Atlantic opportunism sometimes degenerated into indiscriminate violence and plunder. In Havana, the Spanish administration and merchants were so overwhelmed by the chaos of revolutionary, imperial, foreign and anarchic piratical interests that they were forced to hire private shipowners—including U.S. naval commanders—to hunt pirates and revolutionary privateers.[7]

Although filibustering and privateer expeditions launched by U.S. citizens against Spanish possessions were nothing new, neither the Madison nor Monroe administrations condoned such attacks, nor did they support them as an instrument of foreign policy.[8] Now, however, North American involvement in privateering expeditions grew more commonplace. American diplomatic agents to the revolutionary governments used their commercial networks to route letters of marque back to trading offices in American ports, particularly Baltimore, for privateering Americans.[9] American support for the revolutionary Americas was more than ideological; it was also material. In 1817, for example, the revolutionary government of Chile contracted with New Yorkers to build two warships, and two more were subcontracted to shipbuilders in Philadelphia and Baltimore.

Spanish authorities in Cuba were well aware of the direct and indirect U.S. involvement in this transnational colonial fight, even as they recruited other U.S. citizens to fight back.[10] Throughout the late 1810s, Spanish officials in the United States documented the regular outfitting of American privateering vessels up and down the U.S. coast. Borderland ports at the crossroads of Spanish, North American and revolutionary interests—such as New Orleans, Barrataria and Amelia Island—became centers for smuggling, slave trading and private wars that crisscrossed the Atlantic.[11] In July–August 1816, for example, dispatches arrived in Havana from the Spanish agent Luis Onis in Philadelphia, detailing the outfitting of the frigate *Caledonia* in Baltimore by a motley transatlantic crew. Months earlier, the son of a Spanish general had traveled to England to meet secretly with members of the British House of Commons and representatives of the revolutionary Mexican government. With British financing, he had then joined a party of British, French and Spanish mercenary revolutionaries—many of whom had been prisoners captured at the Battle of Waterloo—and had sailed the *Caledonia* from Liverpool to Baltimore. Armed with eighteen canons, hundreds of rifles, and letters of credit drawn on Baltimore commercial houses, the revolutionary expedition planned to rendezvous with Simón Bolívar farther south, before infighting among the crew led to its discovery by the Spanish consul.[12]

The hemispheric history of U.S. expansion in this period often targets those regions that would later become states, territories or military rivals of the North American union. In the march to Manifest Destiny, the North American West and borderlands of the expanding slave South—including Florida and Mexico—are typically where scholars have concentrated their attention. Farther south, in the tumult of Latin American revolutions, Cuba has featured peripherally in stories of transnational privateers, filibusters and opportunists. Nevertheless, contemporaries were well aware of the island's importance. In September 1816, General Jessup, a high-profile officer hailed for his recent military service, advised soon-to-be president James Monroe that "Cuba is, therefore, the key to all Western America, whether we consider it in a military, a commercial or a political point of view."[13]

For many observers, the Spanish island was the key to the hemisphere, and, as U.S. investors and their agents continued to promote the slave trade, business boomed. By the 1820s, the Cuban economy had grown enormously. In October 1821, the *Daily National Intelligencer* newspaper (published in the U.S. capital of Washington) estimated that the value of Cuba's exported produce "from 1815 to 1819" was as high as "$81,244,808" and that, "since the year 1796, when the trade with the United States opened, the Havana has been a support, and not an expence [sic] to the Spanish government and provinces," with much of this prosperity advancing "in the space of 28 years, and more particularly in 12."[14]

The post-Haiti speculative sugar boom had died down, and, as the older sugar colonies of the British Caribbean peaked and lagged, Cuban sugar and coffee production surged further. In 1815, the island had produced 43,396 metric tons of sugar; by 1827 this would rise to 76,669 metric tons.[15] This was a slave regime that depended on the slave trade, and Americans were active in every facet of its growth. As Spanish authorities worked to minimize taxes on expatriate planters and investors, Americans pushed for even more.[16] U.S. merchants began to successfully press for equal trade rights on a variety of fronts from the historically cumbersome Spanish colonial state. In May 1819, for example, the U.S. merchant Gerald Pendergrast received permission to transport five thousand live pigs from North America to Cuba at the same tax rate levied on local Spanish pig breeders. Because of the importance of pork as a food staple for "the poorer classes of society" and the economic logic of the Caribbean slave regime—which depended on regular food imports—such allowances were far from trivial.[17]

In 1820–1, Cuba supplied more than 60 percent of the sugar, 40 percent of the coffee, and 90 percent of the cigars imported into the United States.[18] In this same period, Cuba had grown into an immense market for U.S. exports, on which the Caribbean slave regime depended. These exports included flour (16 percent of total U.S. exports), beef (18 percent), pork (31 percent), fish (13 percent), wood (19 percent), tallow candles (49 percent), soap (14 percent), nails (74 percent), gunpowder (33 percent), medicinal drugs (39 percent), and spermaceti oil (61 percent).[19] From the candles and oil used to light ingenios and cafetales at night to the guns, nails and provisions necessary to coerce and feed enslaved laborers, American exports intensified their participation in the expansion of the Cuban slave regime. Here, the rise of informal empire depended on illicit trade and violence at the margins of overlapping legal regimes.

"The Powers of the Assassins in the Dark"

Although official Spanish accounts and the U.S. press celebrated the revenue that was rapidly accumulating in Cuba, this income represented just a fraction of the actual wealth flowing to and from the island. In Havana, Spanish administrators still refused to recognized U.S. diplomats, while American merchants exploited this reality to ignore, cajole and harass U.S. officials to evade customs at every leg of their journey. In December 1819, the unrecognized U.S. consul Michael Hogan estimated that "not above two thirds of the sugars carried from Cuba pay our Import Duties."[20] The Spanish, too, had difficulty collecting revenue. In 1819, Spanish revenue returns from Havana had topped $5,000,000, and Hogan estimated that an additional $2,000,000 could have been taxed "if the Revenue was collected honestly agreeable to their tarriff [sic]."[21] When Hogan determined to reform revenue collection, however, he discovered the precariousness of his position and wrote that a number of American merchants were "anxious for the suspension of my present employ" due to his "rigid adherence to the letter of the Law."[22] His attempts to collect five dollars from each American shipmaster entering Havana led to death threats.[23]

Just months before the murder of Robert Stoughton in New York, Hogan described a situation in which "captains," "Merchants" and "Managers from the United States" routinely dismissed him as having "no Authority." "But," Hogan said, "neither the fear of complaints from such people nor the powers of the assassins in the dark, which only cost a dobloon [sic] here to finish life shall deter me."[24] This was not hyperbole: As another American noted in December 1819, "Several murders [had been] committed in the streets, some supposed for plunder, others for private pique, murderers escaped." Typically, there were no witnesses: "In cases of alarm, instead of running to the assistance of the victim, everyone tries to avoid him" for fear of prison or retribution. Stories circulated in which whole families had been executed for sheltering "the intended victim of an assassin."[25]

As it had for decades, smuggling defined the expansion of American investment that continued to be shaped by violence and extralegal activities at the margins of U.S. and Spanish state power. And as trade surged, smuggling techniques that had developed in past decades became even more routine. By 1820, graft was so commonplace that Edward Spalding could chronicle precisely how it worked in particular markets. In his pocket memorandum book, Spalding explained the importance of bribery in Trinidad, Cuba: "Be very particular to be in good standing with the guards or custom house officers," Spalding wrote, "by these you shall be able to save a considerable part of the Duties." More specifically, Spalding noted that "one of them, Raphael Sacramente purchases a great quantity of goods on board and land[s] them at his own risq." Similarly, the officers in charge could be paid "once for every vessel" and "be sat-isfyd." "When you agree with any custom house officers to land flour for your acct," Spalding wrote, "you pay them on[e] Dollar and half per barrel" and "for any other article you pay them" a bribe of "about 25 pr ct of the Duty you should had paid at the custom house." It was also commonplace to "declare a very small part" in exchange for "a small gratification to the guarde and some times nothing." The specific import bribes could vary, Spalding noted, according to the officers in charge and could rise as high as five dollars per barrel of flour and one-half of the custom duty. Export duties could be avoided by declaring only a part of the cargo, as, for example, "the brig cashier is known to be a vessel of 300 Hhds at which 200 are manifested and [one] hundred pay half Duty." Other exports, such as honey, could be smuggled out with a simple payment of two hundred dollars to the custom house guard.[26] Notably, Spalding did not transmit any similar comments in his corre-spondence: These notes on smuggling were made in the private scrawl of his small memorandum book, which he likely kept with him at all times and did not intend to share or preserve for posterity.

By 1820, smuggling practices were so well established that Edward Spalding could list in precise detail how they operated according to the items and people involved. In the calculus of the trade, wealth bred stability in practices that were technically outside legal boundaries. Smuggling techniques outlined by the Dorchester merchant George Cushing two decades earlier—of embarking U.S. vessels under foreign (often Spanish) flags and papers to save on Spanish port duties—remained commonplace into the 1820s. While it is unclear to what extent American vessels operated under Spanish flags in both the slave trade and for the purposes of avoiding foreign import tariffs, in 1819 Edward Spalding explained that an American vessel was "to be dispatched from here under American papers for Tenerife, where she will be regularly documented as a Spanish vessel, dispatched thence for the coasts, & thence to Trinidad, Cuba—the vessel will also be dispatched by the Spanish Consul as a Spanish vessel, merely to save duties."[27] Commercial operatives like Spalding frequently claimed that these types of smuggling techniques were necessary to turn a profit in the face of onerous Spanish duties, while Spanish authorities simply raised duties higher, often factoring in revenue lost to smuggling when developing their policies.[28]

American success in the Cuba trade depended on familiarity with the culture of this graft—how much flour could be smuggled in exchange for customs house bribes—and possession of the funds necessary to pay. "One may do almost anything," an American captain wrote in 1820, "with the assistance of money."[29] For his part, Spalding made a respectable percentage at each leg of this Atlantic circuit. In handling shipments aboard the *Mount Pleasant* from Cuba to Russia in 1822, for example, Spalding agreed to "3p% on the amount of invoices at Matanzas 8p% on the gross sales at St Petersburg, and 4 p% on the amt. of invoices at St Petersburg."[30] For Spalding, his ability to navigate the violence and graft endemic to the U.S.–Cuba trade not only translated into thousands of dollars earned for every voyage, but also strengthened the foundations of the informal American empire based on the illegal slave trade.

Although smuggling techniques have complicated efforts to quantify the relative volume of U.S. trade with Cuba, contemporary accounts do provide a general sense of the scale of American investment. By 1820–1, the value of U.S. imports from Cuba was second only to the value of English imports,[31] and U.S. trade with Cuba occupied the third-largest volume of American tonnage, after the U.S. trade with England and the British North American colonies. Just as New Englanders controlled a disproportionately large one-third of this U.S. shipping generally, Northerners similarly dominated the trade.[32] In the 1810s and 1820s, observers routinely noted that approximately half of the vessels entering Havana were American.[33] In a port that logged more than one thousand foreign clearances each year, this represented a vast U.S. investment. In the early 1820s, Alexander von Humboldt calculated a total of 4,923 "embarkations" (clearances) from the Cuban capital (1,305 in 1820, 1,268 in 1821, 1,182 in 1822, and 1,168 in 1823), but he did not identify the nationality of the vessels or their listed ports of destination.[34] Although Cuban archival port records are notoriously incomplete, a selection of periodical materials provides a suggestive illustration of the trends of U.S.–Cuba trade to Havana in these crucial years.

A review of shipping information published in *El Diario de la Habana* in the years 1820–3 from the holdings of the Rare Books Library at the University of Havana (Havana, Cuba) included 2,588 entrances and 2,495 clearances. Approximately 50 percent of these ships were listed as American, matching contemporary accounts. Of these U.S. ships entering Havana, approximately 29 percent originated in New England ports and 27 percent were bound for New England on the way out. Half of all the American ships entering Havana from the United States sailed from New England, and approximately 37 percent of all the U.S. ships sailing for North America listed ports of destination in those same northern states. The region was dominated by Boston and by Portland, Maine, where all records related to the once-thriving trade would later be destroyed by fire.[35]

It was no wonder that by February 1820, a Rhode Island visitor to Matanzas remarked that "the country around resembles the hills of New England."[36] By the 1820s, New Englanders imagined the Caribbean landscape in their own image—particularly in Matanzas, which was now dominated by three American-run commercial houses: Latting, Adams & Stewart; Zacharia Atkins; and Simpson Tryon & Co.[37] From Havana to Matanzas to Trinidad and Santiago, elite U.S. investors eager to take advantage of liberalizations in Spanish trade policy relied on a professional class of commercial agents to navigate this transnational space and to ensure that the slave trade continued unabated. Although Americans began to look farther south to the largest slave market in the hemisphere, Brazil, in these early years, it was Cuba—not Brazil—that figured most prominently in the imaginations and activities of the '15ers.

Although scholars have rightly noted the formation of a coherent imagined community of slavery and slaveholding that linked North America with Cuba and Brazil, many of these transnational ties were far from imaginary. In the "American Mediterranean," U.S. citizens not only looked south for solidarity and inspiration, they also frequently *sailed* south for profit. This was particularly true of a disproportionate number of Northerners, and by the late 1810s the character of U.S. investment in Cuba intensified as the first wave of expatriate planters were now joined by a second wave of North American immigrants. These U.S. citizens—numerous Northerners among them—eagerly complicated their religious and national identities for the opportunity to own a piece of a slave regime built on the outlawed slave trade.

In 1818, the Spanish had coupled the liberalization of trade laws with a new decree that was explicitly designed to encourage "white" immigration to Cuba. The purpose was twofold: to attract investment in Cuban agro-industry and to attempt to offset the island's increasing African demography. In March 1818, the U.S. commercial agent at Santiago, Thomas Willock, noted that "the late Decree of Ferdinand VII allowing Foreigners to settle in this Island" had caused a rise in land values "& many new Plantations are settling."[38] On August 26, 1818, the Spanish consul in Bristol, Rhode Island—which remained almost wholly dependent on the foreign trade of Cuba—wrote of the need to encourage white immigration to more minor ports, such as Nuevitas, Cuba.[39] What had happened in Matanzas, the Spanish believed, could happen elsewhere if more Americans sailed for a deeper south.

And immigrate they did. From New England to New Orleans, larger numbers of North Americans sailed south, intent to own a part of the slave regime for themselves. In 1818, for example, Boston native William Hoskins applied to Spanish authorities to move from New Orleans to Cuba, along with his wife, a French woman from Burdeos named "Maria Cowrijales," their son "Juan José" and two daughters who lived in France named "Juana Carolina" and "Maria Habriela Laura." To satisfy the Spanish authorities in Cuba, Hoskins was required to prove that he was Catholic and to provide character references, along with evidence of his wealth, which, including property and assets, totaled more than twenty-four thousand pesos.[40] The Spanish were almost certainly more interested in Hoskins's wealth than his religion.

Many elite U.S. investors were often willing to adopt whatever cultural conventions were required of them by the Spanish regime for the sake of transnational legal power and profit. Historian Louis Pérez has rightly suggested that American immigration to Cuba coaxed "a predominantly Catholic society" to open "to a Protestant migration."[41]

As it had since the origins of U.S. investment in Cuba, American success frequently depended on a careful negotiation of the Spanish legal system. Nowhere was this more explicit than in the case of James D'Wolf. By the mid-1810s, D'Wolf, a prominent member of the Rhode Island legislature and of the Congregational Church in Bristol, Rhode Island, was also a "naturalized landowner" in the Spanish colony of Cuba—a status he would soon attempt to capitalize on.

In 1816, D'Wolf had been owed over five thousand dollars by the Baltimorean George Stevenson when Stevenson's commercial house collapsed. Stevenson was well connected and had successfully appealed to a patronage network that included Thomas Jefferson and Samuel Smith to avoid repayment of his debts via the General Assembly of Maryland. By 1817, Stevenson was looking for a fresh start, and—with Jefferson's help—secured the consular post in Havana, where he worked alongside Vincent Gray with the slave-trading house of Antonio de Frias. When James D'Wolf learned that Stevenson was in Havana, he saw an opportunity. Drawing on his standing as a "haciendo naturalizado," D'Wolf brought a lawsuit against Stevenson in Spanish court in an attempt to recover what he had been owed in Maryland.[42] Although his status as a naturalized landowner meant that James D'Wolf—a Protestant member of the Rhode Island legislature—was technically a Catholic citizen of Spain, Spanish administrators were content to overlook false piety and citizenship for real pesos.

Nor was D'Wolf the only U.S. citizen to attempt such transnational legal maneuvers: In 1815, for example, the American Jacob King died in Havana, leaving behind his one-fourth share in La Amistad coffee plantation. King had resided in Cuba since at least 1809. When he died, his relatives in Montgomery County, Pennsylvania, including his mother "Margarita" King/Prats and her husband, Valentin Prats, dispatched the U.S. attorney John Brown, Jr. from Philadelphia—certified by a U.S., not Spanish, notary—to Havana to supervise the claim. After settling a fifty-one peso medical bill that had been charged on Jacob King's deathbed, Brown placed another American living in the San Carlos district of Matanzas, William Plin Lawrence, in charge.[43] From Boston to Philadelphia to New Orleans, Americans were well aware of the value, longevity and potential tenuousness of their Cuban investments, and they jockeyed to protect it within the Spanish legal system as freely as they would have within the United States.[44]

As Americans became intimately involved in every aspect of the Cuban slave regime—including the slave trade—they routed the profits north to back the development of the financial infrastructure of the United States and fund western expansion. One of the most provocative case studies in the reinvestment of profits from Cuban slavery and the slave trade in U.S. finance occurred in New York in the 1820s. In 1822, elite '15ers invested in the Cuba trade founded the Farmers' Fire Insurance and Loan Company in New York. This included James D'Wolf's son, James D'Wolf, Jr., whose taxable wealth had risen from $15,000 in 1820 to $50,000 in 1822, and U.S. congressman from New York Churchill C. Cambreleng.[45] Cambreleng had the notorious distinction of helping Robert Goodwin escape from the scene of the murder of James Stoughton in 1819.[46] This insurance company—which has typically gone unnoticed in the annals of modern corporate governance—was the first corporation to be granted, by its 1822 charter, the power to hold property in trust. This concept may have been a reworking of commercial operations in India by the company's first president, John T. Champlin, who operated the firm (Benjamin) Minturn & Champlin.[47] Predictably, Champlin also invested in Cuba and was well connected in the U.S. government.

During the Napoleonic Wars, Minturn and Champlin had been involved in the Cuba–Baltic circuit. They had dispatched a ship from New York to Gottenburg in 1812 "for the purpose," in the estimation of John Quincy Adams, "of securing their property there and here [in St. Petersburg] from British capture." For his part, Adams had been happy to help and dined with their agent.[48] In 1812, Champlin's partner, Benjamin Minturn, had even lived on the same block of Broadway as the Cuba trader and former New Englander John Howland.[49] This cadre of New York investors included many members of the Northern elite, who were now migrating or expanding their operations down the Atlantic seaboard, as power shifted from Boston to New York.[50] As in Boston, much of the capital that made the New York Farmers' Fire Insurance and Loan Company possible in 1822—via "clubby" networks of kinship and credit—had originated in the slave fields of Cuba and the slave trade.[51]

Beginning with start-up capital of $500,000, the Farmers' Fire Insurance and Loan Company opened at 34 Wall Street, "from 9 o'clock A.M. to sunset."[52] Because New York banks were prohibited from making agricultural loans, insurance companies like the Farmers' Fire Insurance Company stepped into the breach, encouraging the rapid expansion (particularly beginning in the 1830s) of the American near-West and South. By 1827, when the New York Chamber of Commerce building was opened at a cost of $230,000—"considered the finest business structure in town"—the Farmers' Fire Insurance Company moved in. They would soon handle the first international bank transaction in the United States: a loan of £200,000 with the English merchant bank Barings in London. By 1833, the company's capital had grown to $1 million. After the New York fire of 1835, the company stopped issuing fire insurance, but it continued to turn a profit. By 1836 it hit $2 million, and during the panic of 1837 the company recorded its strongest year ever, with over $4.3 million in resources and a surplus of $96,000.[53] The company—like American investments in Cuba—would endure into the twentieth century.[54] Although the origins of the wealth that created the insurance company—and others like it—would later be obscured or forgotten, contemporary Americans were well aware that U.S. investment in transnational slavery and the slave trade had helped to create it.

And while American professional agents, revolutionaries and expatriates scrambled to profit from the expansion of the slave trade and the Cuban slave regime, elite investors in the slave regime now walked the halls of the U.S. Congress, determined to do whatever they could to leverage public power for private gain. Their ships were paying the duties, which funded the U.S. government, and, they reasoned, it seemed only fair that the powers of the state be directed to protecting their profits. In practice this meant the deployment of U.S. naval forces to protect the illegal slave trade. For the generation of 1815, this was slavery's navy.

SEVEN

Merchant-Statesmen

James D'Wolf rose to speak. The island of Cuba, he told the U.S. Senate, was under attack by pirates. "Five or six additional small vessels," D'Wolf said, "were certainly very much wanted to protect the commerce of the nation on the coast of Cuba." Although he had spent years in the Rhode Island state legislature, D'Wolf had never been a politician. Now, in 1822, his attempt to sound honest and sincere came across awkwardly, and several members of the Senate rolled their eyes, smiling. It was no secret that D'Wolf owned Cuban plantations and was personally invested in the trade. The previous year, one of D'Wolf's own ships, the *Collector,* had even been lost to Cuban pirates.[1]

When D'Wolf finished speaking, another New Englander followed him. Massachusetts senator Harrison Gray Otis proposed clarifying the resolution with the words "'for the better protection of the commerce of the United States'" to avoid any confusion from President Monroe about the bill's purpose.[2] Although the bill related to Cuban piracy had been proposed by a senator from Louisiana, now a cohort of Northerners with personal interests in the Cuban slave regime worked to secure its passage. Senator Otis had acted as a legal advisor to the expatriate Cuban plantation owner from Massachusetts, Nathaniel Fellowes, from at least 1808 to 1819.[3]

In the 1820s, elite '15ers used the term "piracy" to shape U.S. foreign policy on behalf of their investments in the slave trade. As elite U.S. investors and the professional class they employed created an informal American economic empire in Cuba, they simultaneously leveraged public law and state power in the United States to deploy the foreign policy apparatus of the nation to protect their investments. Turning from the rise of the U.S.–Cuba trade and the actions of the men who created its economic dimensions to the public machinations of these same U.S. elites in public office, this chapter tracks the strategies these merchant-statesmen employed to co-opt state power in the service of private commerce. In this period, the West India squadron was dispatched to Cuba to punish one brand of piracy for the protection of another—the slave trade. For investors in illicit and illegal trade, piracy was bad for business, and soon the '15er Congress would deploy half of *all* U.S. naval forces to defend U.S. investments in the slave trade and Cuban slave regime.

In fact, at the time of D'Wolf's 1822 speech, the U.S. navy was already there. In 1819, six Boston insurance companies had complained to President Monroe that there had been forty-four attacks on American vessels they insured that year, and the navy had been dispatched to protect American commerce from piracy.[4] Meanwhile, a series of anti–slave trade laws passed, followed by a law calling for the dispatch of a second U.S. squadron to suppress the slave trade.[5] The next year, on May 15, 1820, the foreign slave trade was legally equated with piracy, making it punishable by death.[6] The impact of Caribbean piracy on the slave trade was complex, and these U.S. naval squadrons (one to combat Caribbean piracy, one to suppress the slave trade) had been dispatched with opposing purposes.

As the German merchant Vincent Nolte later reflected, "pirates captured Spanish and other slave ships on the high seas" and resold "the stolen slaves at from 150 to 200 dollars per head, when [Cuban planters] could not have procured as good stock in the city for less than 600 or 700 dollars," directly threatening the profitability of the slave trade.[7] Piracy undercut the slave trade at the same time that the prices of Cuban slaves continued to rise—a fact well known in Washington.[8] In 1821, for example, the U.S. agent at Santiago, Cuba, wrote to Secretary of State John Quincy Adams that he had not complained sooner about two nearby squadrons of pirates precisely because they acted as "a check on the African trade."[9] Investors in the illegal trade also had little recourse if their human cargoes were seized. The U.S. navy had effectively been deployed to punish piracy for the protection of the slave trade.

Moreover, piracy's destabilization of the Cuba trade terrified U.S. investors, who saw the specter of Haiti in any disruption of the regular rhythms of imported provisions and slaves that made agro-industry possible. Americans in the Caribbean routinely described the brutality and lawlessness of "Carthagenian Privateer[s]" that were sometimes crewed—disturbingly, to these North Americans—by "negroes & mulattoes."[10] After the success of the Haitian Revolution and amid persistent hemispheric slave resistance, American investors were concerned that a race war might erupt among the restive enslaved African population of Cuba. Throughout 1818–19, for example, the American commercial agent in Santiago wrote that "scarcely an American vessel enters this port, which is not more or less plundered ... The sea adjacent to this Island," he continued, "is completely infested by Piratical Cruisers, who indiscriminately violate every flag, and commit depredations of the blackest hue."[11] Piracy and lawlessness were predictably characterized as "black in composition" and "black in deed" by Americans. The island was a prison camp, and they knew it.

Amid the anarchical seas of the revolutionary Caribbean, piracy also brought the threat of increased involvement of other geopolitical actors, including—most worrisome for American investors—the anti-slavery British navy. With fresh memories of the War of 1812, every passing British warship stirred rumors of a British plot to reassert hemispheric influence. As the Spanish empire pitched and burned and Spain appeared increasingly unable to quell revolutions throughout the Americas, many Americans feared that Britain might walk away with Cuba. For American investors and national statesmen—now one and the same—a sustained British presence in Cuba represented a worst-case scenario. The British might curtail the slave trade and strangle the U.S.–Cuba trade. British involvement would also represent an immediate and constant threat to the Gulf Coast and Atlantic seaboard of the United States. This, in turn, might threaten U.S. economic development and hemispheric influence, while setting the stage for a new round of Anglo-American conflict. Piratical opportunism was shaped by the smuggling, graft and illicit commerce that characterized the U.S.–Cuba trade, and piracy would soon become the pretext for the exercise of public power on behalf of this same commerce. U.S. investors were not ready to watch their profits disappear behind the British flag.

"Orders to Proceed on the Work of Death"

The price of James D'Wolf's seat in the U.S. Senate was dinner. On November 5, 1820, D'Wolf plied members of the Rhode Island legislature with food and drink, and, as William Russell, one of his opponents, reflected the following day, "Mr James DWolf yesterday gave a dinner to both houses of our assembly & in the even[in]g he had a majority for (in this room of abetters [sic]) seneter [sic] congress for 6 y[ea]rs, from 3d March next."[12] These were often the terms in which the elites leveraged their familiarity with local networks into national power. The operations of the state were often highly personal, and, in fact, James D'Wolf probably would have never made his move into national politics if not for his involvement in the slave trade and the Cuban slave regime. Although he had significant power in the state legislature, in 1820 the nationally appointed anti–slave trade advocate Barnabas Bates replaced D'Wolf's brother-in-law Charles Collins as port collector of Bristol. This had the potential to undermine all of D'Wolf's operations.

The D'Wolfs were quick to respond. Collins destroyed all of the port records, and James D'Wolf ran for the U.S. Senate, where he remained determined to destroy Bates's career. It took years, but D'Wolf won. In April 1824, he wrote to his brother John:

> The Senate has been graciously pleased to *non-concur the President's nomination of Barnabus Bates as Collector of the Port of Bristol* ... Victory to me is great, but I beg you to keep still and show no sort of rejoicing only in secret, tickle inwardly as much as you please, but nothing more... Have the laugh out, shake your sides one or two hours in his house or someplace where nobody will see you."[14]

By the 1820s, it was no secret that James D'Wolf remained deeply involved in the slave trade. In fact, just months before his rise to the

U.S. Senate and at the same moment that participation in the slave trade became a capital offense, two of D'Wolf's slave ships were spotted on the West African coast. Moreover, Secretary of State John Quincy Adams knew about it. As historian James Noonan makes plain, in the complex case of the seized slave ship *Antelope*, Adams had received a copy of a legal opinion that identified "a portion of the Africans" as slaves from "the *Exchange* of Bristol, Rhode Island." This was the tender for the slave ship *Rambler*, owned by D'Wolf. At a time when records of the illegal trade were routinely destroyed, the secretary of state had received direct evidence of D'Wolf's active involvement. Yet, as Noonan puts it, "no one in Washington had had any appetite for linking the Senator from Rhode Island with a federal crime punishable by death."[13]

Although D'Wolf had joined the Senate determined to destroy the career of Barnabas Bates, he was also well placed to shape U.S. foreign policy for the sake of economic development grounded in slavery.[14] He argued that a new sort of man was needed in Congress: "practical men … acquainted with the details of business, and with the relations which subsist between the great Interests of the nation."[15] After serving as a director of the U.S. national bank's Providence branch, D'Wolf would also be appointed as one of "twenty five gentlemen" tasked to "the Committee of Inspection and Investigation of the affairs of the [U.S.] Bank" in September 1822.[16] In his career, the rise of U.S. finance and Cuban slavery were intimately and directly linked.

But even if other members of Congress shared D'Wolf's sensibilities and material interests, the '15ers were not a uniform bloc. Maryland was not Rhode Island was not New York, and regional and local interests often trumped "Atlantic" commercial concerns. James D'Wolf, for example, was involved in 246 votes during his tenure in the Senate. In this time, he voted with the majority 137 times (56 percent). And while the senators who were most consistent in voting with D'Wolf were also New Englanders, men who might have been expected to regularly join with D'Wolf often did not. The New Hampshire–Cuba merchant and senator John Parrott, for example, only voted with D'Wolf 51 percent of the time. While there were certainly patterns of legislative coordination in Congress, individual votes often came down to specific interests and backroom negotiations.[17] When it came to defending the expansion of the U.S.–Cuba trade and the slave trade, however, this was the "era of good feelings" indeed.

After James D'Wolf's 1822 speech in favor of expanding the U.S. navy, the House of Representatives called for $120,000 for the suppression of piracy.[18] In Havana, the U.S. consul John Warner made the geopolitical purpose of an additional naval force explicit in a letter to his longtime ally, Delaware senator Caesar Rodney: "2/3 of the white inhabitants of the Island are decidedly in favor of this Island being attached to the United States as a state, not as a colony," Warner wrote. "The British Government have wished it as a colony … a good naval force and a good negotiator might do much. The piracies already committed and continued, would be a sufficient reason for sending a considerable force here."[19] In Warner's estimation, piracy served as a convenient pretext for the expansion of American naval power to secure American influence and counter British machinations in Cuba. As reports on Cuban piracy accumulated in Washington, U.S. investors worried that the British might take the island before Congress could agree on the character of additional naval appropriations.[20] The South Carolina congressman Joel Poinsett made this explicit in his 1822 writings from Cuba, in which he warned of the "political and commercial" consequences should a "great maritime power" seize Cuba.[21]

By April 1822, the situation had reached a boiling point. That month, James D'Wolf—frustrated with the slow-moving U.S. Congress—demanded action from Secretary of State John Quincy Adams:

> Mr D'Wolf, a Senator from Rhode-Island, came in great alarm, expecting that the British Government will within a month take possession of the Island of Cuba. I thought his apprehensions at least premature, and endeavored to reason and to laugh him out of them—not altogether successfully.[22]

Adams remained an ally of U.S. investors in Cuba, and he readily acknowledged that the island was rapidly becoming essential to the U.S. economy and functioned as a de facto pipeline for specie into the United States.[23] He rightly concluded that the survival of the U.S.–Cuba trade, free from British interference, was essential to U.S. economic development. "The Cuban question," Adams wrote, was of "deeper importance and greater magnitude than [any that] had occurred since the establishment of our Independence."[24]

The economic future of the United States and its hemispheric influence depended on the U.S.–Cuba trade and the continuance of the slave trade, both of which were threatened by the weakness of Spain and the ambitions of Great Britain. And the British were on the move. That month, James D'Wolf was not alone in his concerns about British annexation of Cuba: On April 10, 1822, Congressman Garnett of Virginia argued, "What, sir, is more reasonable … than to suppose that Spain, finding herself about to lose all her American territories, will seek to turn to some account those that remain to her, by selling them to some purchaser who will be able to retain them? … Now, suppose Spain should cede Cuba to England…"[25]

In Cuba, the Creole elite also fretted about exactly this possibility, and in the fall of 1822, they dispatched secret representatives to the United States "to inquire," in the words of John Quincy Adams, "if the government of the United States will concur with them" in a plan to be "admitted as a State into the American Union." In September 1822, James Monroe called a cabinet meeting to decide the matter. The famous slaveholding politician and now Secretary of War John C. Calhoun was eager to take the island but did not see a way to seize it without another war with Great Britain. Adams was less enthusiastic: "I thought it advisable to take a different course; to give [the Creole elite of Cuba] no advice whatever." Adams recorded that he was apprehensive of just how much support the Cuban representatives had from the island's population and that he worried about an open confrontation with both Spain and England. In October 1822, Monroe followed Adams's advice.[26] Later that month, Senator Caesar Rodney forwarded missives from a Spanish merchant in Havana to the administration, warning that the Creole elite were preparing to declare independence. In November 1822, William Crawford, the secretary of the treasury and a longtime ally of Americans invested in Cuba, passed along information he had received from the French that "the British Government had been for two years negotiating with Spain for the Island of Cuba, and had offered them for it Gibraltar and a large sum of money."[27] Then, on November 24, 1822, a new British squadron arrived in Havana.[28]

On his arrival, the British commander immediately went from the harbor docks to the house of the Spanish captain-general, ostensibly to ask for assistance in combating Cuban pirates.[29] Americans in Cuba anxiously watched the Anglo-Spanish negotiations, fearful of anything that might encourage a greater British presence on the island. To make matters worse, on November 29, 1822, reports of new pirate attacks were published in Cuba, and the Consulado—which included some of the richest, most powerful men on the island—considered appealing to the British naval commander for direct assistance in fighting piracy. Earlier that year, Spanish merchants had collected $20,000 to fund the fight against pirates, but it had not been enough.[30] American investors were terrified that if elite Spanish and Creole merchants sided with the Royal Navy out of desperation, the British might never leave.

Although it remained small by comparison, the U.S. navy had been expanded following the War of 1812, and by December 1822, nine U.S. naval vessels were deployed in the West India Squadron around Cuba, with two more immediately on the way. By comparison, just one U.S. ship had been dispatched to the African coast for the suppression of the slave trade. Predictably, since their dispatch two years earlier, the West India Squadron had enjoyed significantly more success than anti–slave trade naval squadrons, capturing more than thirty piratical and privateering vessels around Cuba while anti–slave trade vessels consistently returned empty-handed.[31] Although naval vessels were periodically directed to suppress the slave trade, the larger West India Squadron worked to protect it by campaigning against pirates.

The cynicism of the anti–slave trade naval deployment—a move intended to quiet restive members of Congress, rather than to fight the slave trade—was even apparent in the composition of the ships' commanders. Mathew Calbraith Perry, the commander of the *Shark* in the West India Squadron, had received the appointment in February 1822 to sail "for the protection of our commerce" after returning from an unsuccessful cruise for slave traders along the West African coast and Cuba. His failure to apprehend slavers was hardly surprising, given Perry's personal familiarity with the trade. In 1814, his brother

Raymond had even married James D'Wolf's daughter, Mary Ann—the namesake of a D'Wolf Cuban cafetale.[32] In this case, elite U.S. investors in the slave trade and its products leveraged naval appointments exactly as they used public diplomatic posts, placing allies and family members in key positions whenever possible. But they could not control the British.

In December 1822, as the Spanish Consulado met with British naval commanders in Havana, U.S. policymakers responded.[33] President Monroe used his annual address to Congress to urge an increase in the size of the navy to combat the threat to U.S. commerce by Cuban pirates, and the Committee on Naval Affairs called for an additional $44,000 in appropriations.[34] Days after Monroe's speeches, American newspapers reported the meeting of the British commander and the Spanish captain-general, and by the end of the month, they speculated that the Anglo-Spanish meetings had transferred Cuba into British hands.[35] On December 20, 1822, Congress authorized $160,000— intended to cover the previous $120,000 request and the new $44,000 request—for the "protection to the citizens and commerce of the United States in the Gulf of Mexico, and the seas and territories adjacent."[36] By point of comparison, the public revenue of the United States for 1821 had been approximately $19.5 million, of which the entire balance of naval expenditures for the year was just over $3.3 million.[37]

The merchant-statesmen who had crafted the bill for the protection of their commerce were understandably pleased. The day of the bill's passage, for example, Senator James D'Wolf wrote to his brother that "the Bill for Destroying the Pirates about Cuba has been pass[e]d and Capt[ain] Porter has received his orders to Proceed on the work of Death against those horrible outlaws."[38] But passing laws did not automatically make the British leave, and as the British lingered in Cuba, rumors and misinformation quickly spread.[39] In the early months of 1823, the hysteria in the U.S. press over a potential British seizure of Cuba intensified, fed by the anxious pro-annexationist speculations of British newspapers such as the *London Sun*.[40] In the Senate, Caesar Rodney proposed a resolution in January 1823 offering bounties to naval officers for the capture of pirates, and the U.S. commercial agent in Havana, John Warner—a family friend of Rodney—wrote to Secretary of State

John Quincy Adams that he was sending a box of "Champayn [sic] for Mr. Rodney" and "should he not be with you take charge of it & drink my health."[41]

As Adams, Rodney and Warner toasted to their successes, James D'Wolf continued to fume, convinced that the British were still preparing to seize Cuba. In February 1823, he called on John Quincy Adams for a second meeting. This time, Adams did *not* record the encounter in his diary or correspondence, but D'Wolf was careful to note Adams's commitment to Cuban investors in a letter to his brother:

> It gives me Pleasure to inform our Bristol friends Capt. J[ohn] Smith & G[eorge] DW[olf] in Particular that the Secty of State Mr. Adams has just told me that I may be perfectly easy about the English making any attempt to git [sic] possession of Cuba, that he has an oficial [sic] promise that no such intention exists which to me is quite consoling and have no doubt it will be so to all our friends who have such Deep Interest in that Island.[42]

D'Wolf's relationship with Adams during Adams's tenure as secretary of state was never as close as D'Wolf's relationship with Secretary of the Treasury William Crawford and with Second Auditor of the Treasury William Lee, who served as D'Wolf's personal allies within the Monroe administration. Still, Adams was friendly with the fellow New Englander. A year later, for example, D'Wolf remarked, "I believe I stand tolerably well with Adams."[43] For D'Wolf, this set Adams apart from President Monroe. Just weeks after approaching Adams about Cuba, D'Wolf met the president and described Monroe as "a timid man [with] week [sic] nerves &c &c." The only way to sway "the imbecility of the man," D'Wolf said, was through contacts such as William Lee, who was the "confidential friend of Mr. Munro [sic]." According to D'Wolf, Lee would "do any thing in his power to serve me" to influence the indecisive Monroe: "The man [Monroe] is so feared of doing wrong that he is incapable of acting," D'Wolf said. "When you have an old woman to deal with you cannot calculate what will be done," and "if Mr. Jefferson was President I should have no difficulty" in shaping public policy.[44] Instead, D'Wolf was forced to rely on intermediaries within the administration to secure public offices and ensure presidential support for the Cuba trade. He was similarly disgruntled with Congress:

> We have a great many great talkers in Congress. We are really a great talking government. In times of war our words are louder than our cannon and in peace much louder than our wisdom. The people of these states are paying immense sums of money to support about 300 lawyers to give their most elegant talk, which the people pay for printing... millions a year they pay to support it.[45]

Unsurprisingly, such candid, critical appraisals were not meant to survive, and James D'Wolf regularly told his brother John to destroy all such correspondence: "I hope you do not expose any of my letters," he wrote in March 1824, "but commit them to the fire when you have read them."[46] Yet, despite Adams's assurances to D'Wolf, Monroe's cabinet continued to meet for urgent discussions of Cuba. From the dispatches of Joel Poinsett and the Spanish nobleman Juan José Hernandez, the administration was well aware of the imminent danger of British annexation. On March 14, 1823, Adams recorded the annexationist, anti-British arguments that erupted between John C. Calhoun and Secretary of the Navy Smith Thompson and his own determination to maintain the status quo. "The debate almost warm," Adams noted, "Talk of calling Congress, which I thought absurd. Memorandum: to be cool on this subject."[47] This statement more fully encapsulates Adams's approach to Cuba than his more famous "law of political gravitation," which he would espouse later that year.

These later remarks, which scholars have sometimes interpreted as representing perpetual North American ambitions for Cuban annexation, were more accurately an argument *against* any immediate action on Cuba:

> There are laws of political as well as of physical gravitation; and if an apple, severed by the tempest from its native tree, cannot choose but fall to the ground, Cuba, forcibly disjoined from its own unnatural connexion with Spain, and incapable of self-support, can gravitate

only towards the North American Union, which, by the same law of
nature, cannot cast her off from its bosom.[48]

In fact, Adams was something of a scholar on gravity and had recently
completed a treatise on the possibilities of commercial systems of meas-
urement—a "hurried and imperfect work" that he nevertheless believed
might be his most important literary contribution "to the last ends of
human exertion and public utility."[49] Concepts for the book had taken
root years earlier during Adams's time in St. Petersburg, where he had
reflected on the laws of nature and their relationship to national systems
of trade while defending American sugar and coffee cargoes in the Baltic.
Now, well aware of Cuba's importance and an ally to Americans invested
in the slave regime, Adams was determined "to be cool" for the sake of
the status quo, which depended on the illegal slave trade.

In Washington, the U.S. navy's ongoing complicity in the slave trade
was an open secret that riled antislavery members of Congress. In February
1823, Congressman Charles Mercer of Virginia detailed how the British
had only condemned twenty slaving vessels, "and the court established
at the great slave mart of Cuba, not one!"[50] Throughout the 1820s, as
the West India Squadron wandered the island's coastline, approximately
eight thousand enslaved Africans arrived in Cuba annually.[51] And on
occasion, when U.S. naval officers did attempt to intervene in the slave
trade—including in investigations of American participation—they
found that Spanish jurisdiction trumped U.S. law. In October 1823, for
example, Matanzas merchants Zachariah Atkins and Thomas Wuturn
petitioned the Spanish captain-general via their Spanish associate Felix
de Acosta about "the American sloop, *Two Brothers*," which had just
been seized in Matanzas harbor by the U.S. warship *Wild Cat*. The *Two
Brothers* had sailed from Newport, Rhode Island, for the New England
merchant Johannes Fosberg and others, before arriving in Cuba with
"four persons of color without papers, or any documents to prove they
were not slaves." The U.S. commander Lieutenant Wolbert refused to
give up the vessel, arguing that it had been captured "in the act of violating the Spanish laws as also the American governments." Whether
or not the four suspected men onboard were actually slaves picked
up by the vessel en route to Cuba—as was common in the Caribbean

circuit—the ship's destination became clear when Atkins surrendered the *Two Brothers*'s bill of lading: It was "bound to the Coast of Africa" with a cargo of goods— "Tobacco," "aguardiente," "powder," "sugar" and "glass beads"—that were likely intended to purchase enslaved Africans.[52]

Despite the notarized evidence of a "cargo for Africa," the Spanish captain-general lobbied the commander of the West India Squadron, Commodore David Porter, to free the ship on Atkins's behalf. "I can not help stating that she [*Two Brothers*] was so in a Spanish port," Captain General Vives wrote Porter. "I hope your Lordship convinced of the justice of this claim, will disapprove the conduct of said commander."[53] Soon, Porter himself would become embroiled in Congressional controversies surrounding the public-private activities of the U.S. navy. In the fall of 1823, however, Congress was on recess, and the Monroe administration—particularly John Quincy Adams—came under British pressure to confront the Cuban situation and the slave trade.[54] In December 1823, Adams's response on behalf of elite American investors would create the foreign policy initiative that would come to be known as the Monroe Doctrine, signaling his commitment to the promise he had made D'Wolf just months earlier: the informal American empire in Cuba would never become British.

EIGHT

Presidents

Bells were ringing in the cracked stone towers of the Cathedral of Saint Christopher. It had been damaged in an earthquake seven years before, but now, as John Mountain entered the cobblestone square in 1823, he saw the Spanish celebrating. A parade of soldiers fired pistols and rifles into the air, and people threw flowers. What was happening? Mountain asked, and someone told him in halting English that the empire was restored, the king had returned to power. As the Spanish drank and laughed, Mountain returned to the U.S. consulate. It was unnaturally cool for mid-December, and back in the U.S. offices, an American captain explained that a French frigate had just arrived with the same news: The Spanish monarchy was restored.

What does it mean for us? Mountain wondered. What should we do? That night, he wrote to Secretary of State John Quincy Adams, describing the celebrations and the unease he felt. Any change in the status quo might be catastrophic for Americans like Mountain, who were outsiders in this regime. Unlike most of the consular officials, Mountain had not worked as a merchant prior to arriving in Cuba. And although he had been drawn into several moneymaking schemes—including the purchase and resale of a portion of Key West with his superior, U.S. consul John Warner—John Mountain believed in the larger mission. All was well for the Americans, Mountain told Adams, but "how long we shall remain so is very uncertain." The following month, as the new year began, business was booming, and "the great extent of our commerce" that Mountain recorded in the U.S. consular offices operated in perfect safety. Despite the many ships that filled Havana's harbor, Mountain told Adams there had not been a single "recent act of piracy." The slave trade continued unabated.[1]

It often took weeks or months for news to travel from North America to Cuba, and so Mountain was unaware that, at that very moment, Adams and his allies in Congress were simultaneously using the threat of piracy to reshape U.S. foreign policy to protect American investments in the outlawed slave trade and related slave regimes. In fact, this was the main reason the president had warned European powers against any attempt to play a larger role in the hemisphere in his December 1823 address to Congress, with verbiage that would later become known as the "Monroe Doctrine." The doctrine was crafted to protect the illegal slave trade and was entirely consistent with the existing anti-British, pro-slavery foreign policy of the administration. It was, moreover, the next logical step in the incorporation of the apparatus of U.S. foreign policy into the private trade networks of elite Americans invested in Cuba. Just as diplomatic appointments had long been essential to merchants' trade networks, so too the navy had been deployed—and would soon be strengthened even further—to protect U.S. trade and the slave trade on which it depended. The "No Transfer Principle of 1811" had now become a hemispheric, "status quo," non-annexationist policy writ large.[2]

"The Confidence of Our Merchants"

The Monroe Doctrine has had a profound impact on U.S. foreign policy. When considering any influential diplomatic prerogative, it is worth taking a step back to consider how past generations have interpreted it. For starters, it should come as no surprise that Cuba was interpreted as central to the doctrine by some of its earliest professional scholars. In 1936, for example, historian Edward Tatum rightly drew attention to the island's importance in the discussions of Monroe's cabinet—and particularly in John Quincy Adams's own mind. More recently, however, many scholars have emphasized Cuba's importance in the formulation of U.S. foreign policy in terms of the doctrine's *future* implications, rather than in its creation.[3] That is, the tangled history of late nineteenth- and twentieth-century U.S. involvement in Cuba has obscured the actual circumstances in the early 1820s that gave rise to the doctrine itself. The legacy and implications of the Monroe Doctrine have often taken precedence over questions of purpose.[4] In part, this is the result of work by a number of twentieth-century historians whose research established the basic motivations (liberalized trade in the Americas) and authorship (John Quincy Adams) of this diplomatic innovation.[5] What more is there to know? the story goes. As it turns out, there is a great deal more to be said—particularly with respect to the impact of commerce and slavery on politics.

Scholars such as Edward Tatum, Dexter Perkins and Ernest May stressed political over economic factors in early-nineteenth-century U.S. foreign policy—to the point of excluding a serious discussion of commercial concerns from chronicles of the back-and-forth of cabinet and diplomatic negotiations in 1822–3.[6] To be sure, politics and diplomacy matter, but so do sources—and many historians revere the scrupulous records of John Quincy Adams. Just as he did during his tenure as U.S. consul in Russia, Adams continued to keep exacting notes during his time as secretary of state, chronicling many cabinet meetings and private conversations for which no other record exists. And while Adams may not have lied, per se, this does not mean that he always told the truth. In Russia, he explained that the sugar arriving in U.S. vessels had originated in the United States before delivering an extended lecture on Cuban sugar. In Washington, he omitted an 1823 meeting with James D'Wolf from his daily diary. Trained as an attorney, John Quincy Adams often recorded his own words—"I assured him that, with the exception perhaps of coffee, all the articles of colonial trade were produced within the United States"—with little or no commentary on the accuracy of these words. The son of a president, John Quincy Adams was extremely cognizant of the importance of his own legacy. What Adams said and what he actually believed were sometimes very different things. Simply put, it is not enough to take Adams at his word.

But Adams, unlike many historians, certainly recognized the vital importance of Cuba to the future of the United States. In treatments of the United States and Cuba within larger hemispheric histories, the

Spanish-American War and the later twentieth century are highlighted as decisive moments of U.S. involvement on the island,[7] and more generally, the field of early U.S. and antebellum foreign relations has been described as "the Great American Desert" for lack of recent scholarly attention.[8] While there have been important exceptions to these deterministic trends in U.S. scholarship—including the excellent work of J. C. A. Stagg, James Lewis, Jr., Rafe Blaufarb and Peter J. Kastor[9]—typically, in the forward-looking march to American empire, these decades of the early nineteenth century have been treated as a precursor to Manifest Destiny, rather than as decisive moments in themselves.[10] That said, not all scholars have neglected the importance of Cuba in the Monroe Doctrine's formulation. Cuban scholar Herminio Portell-Vilá's work in the first volume of *La Historia de Cuba* provides a more comprehensive accounting of the importance of Cuba, but also leaves a serious accounting of commercial investments by the wayside.[11] Counterposed to these works is Russian scholar Nikolai Bolkhovitinov's careful emphasis on U.S. trade interests in the promulgation of foreign policy.[12] Today, the pendulum has begun to swing decisively in this direction, and many scholars, political scientists and policymakers now take the impact of commercial concerns on foreign policy for granted. The single most important aspect of the 1823 ban on future European intervention in the hemisphere was U.S. investment in Cuba and in the slave trade; this meant that the doctrine was avowedly anti-British.

Other European powers were of only marginal importance. While Russia has long been included in analyses of the 1823 policy shift, Russian influence has typically been framed in terms of Russian interest in the Pacific. Recent scholarship has suggested, however, as historian Andrei Grinev writes, that "no weighty or direct evidence of the presence in the [Russian] government of a grandiose plan of expansion is found." It is certainly true that the unilateralism of Russian foreign policy in the North Pacific outraged the American and British press in 1821, but by 1822, tsarist policy forced the Russians to pull back.[13] Recent scholarship suggests that private Russian commercial interests alone promoted the expansion.[14] That Adams had the future support (for the 1824 election) of U.S. merchants invested in the Pacific Northwest in mind is certainly true. These same elites, however, were invested in Cuba and had much more to lose in a British seizure of the Spanish colony than in Russian competition in the Pacific. Nor were the two trades easily separable: The fur trade was directly tied to U.S. investment in the Asia trade, which depended on Spanish specie from Havana.

Moreover, although members of James Monroe's cabinet certainly fretted over the possibilities of an intervention in the Americas by the Holy Alliance (composed of Russia, Austria, Prussia and German states), John Quincy Adams consistently stressed the unlikelihood of such an invasion. The French were also secondary for American policymakers. Certainly the French royalist regime represented a threat and had proven its determination to seize opportunities that might win it respect and legitimacy. The French had also amassed naval forces in Europe and the Caribbean, which could potentially target Cuba.[15] However, countering genuine French moves in the hemisphere would have required the strength of British, not American, naval forces, and for many American statesmen, including members of Monroe's cabinet, the British threat was far more deadly—not simply because of the strength of the Royal Navy, but because the Royal Navy was actively anti–slave trade. Although Brian Loveman has rightly acknowledged that "the panoply of intermestic issues confronting the Monroe administration, from tariff debates and suppression of piracy and the slave trade to the 'peace of the world,' provided a very complex background for the December 2, 1823, message," every one of these issues can be tied to the centrality of Cuba in the U.S. economy and the slave trade on which it depended.[16] The expansion of North American slavery and the cotton South, too, depended on and encouraged the expansion of Cuban agro-industry. Despite the complex geopolitical circumstances of 1823, the Monroe Doctrine's purpose was as straightforward as its target: It was shaped to protect the outlawed transatlantic slave trade. This meant that Cuba needed to remain Spanish.

Although ex-president and frequent advisor to the Monroe administration Thomas Jefferson may have famously mused in October 1823 that "I have ever looked on Cuba as the most interesting addition which could ever be made to our system of states," the protection of American-owned Cuban estates, *not* Cuban statehood, was the doctrine's purpose.[17] James Monroe did agree with Jefferson in theory, however. In

June 1823, for example, Monroe had acknowledged that "I have always concurr'd with you in sentiment, that too much importance could not be attached to that Island, and that we ought if possible to incorporate it into our union." Just as they had for at least a decade, the Spanish and Creole elite in Cuba, Monroe wrote, viewed "an incorporation with the UStates" as "the most desirable event that can occur," but "we"—at the urging of John Quincy Adams—"have advised them to cling to Spain for the present."[18]

The "status quo" was all-important. Adams, for example, in reflecting later on the repressive and calculating regime of Spanish captain-general Vives, suggested that Vives "was precisely the man to tranquilize and conciliate the submission" of Cuba, and that Vives was so effective post-1824 "that the government of the United States heard nothing further of intended insurrection [by the Creole elite] in Cuba during the remainder of Mr. Monroe's administration, and the whole of mine."[19] Like his commercial allies, John Quincy Adams rightly recognized that a revolt against Spanish rule would destabilize the Cuban slave regime and encourage foreign intervention in the slave trade. Monroe shared this sensibility. Most importantly, James Monroe wrote in June 1823, the Spanish elite in Cuba must resist "any attempt to get possession of the Island by England." U.S. relations with Cuba continued to be framed almost wholly in terms of the danger of potential British annexation.[20] The French might seize the island—an uncertain prospect for U.S. investors—but the British would ruin it by strangling the slave trade on which the slave regime depended. This is precisely why, in the fall of 1823, John Quincy Adams and President Monroe broke with a proposed bilateral statement that had been suggested by the British earlier that year.[21]

The Monroe Doctrine was not only conceived, as John Johnson has suggested, around a defense of free, legal commerce in the Americas, but it was also focused on the maintenance of the slave trade.[22] In crafting U.S. foreign policy, John Quincy Adams now carried his protection of U.S. investment in the slave trade from the Baltic to Washington. Liberalized trade in the Americas depended on the expansion of the illegal slave trade. As Francisco de Arango had suggested decades earlier, a surge in enslaved labor in Cuba encouraged free trade—and vice versa.

Some scholars have misinterpreted this U.S. policy as inconsistent. As Ernest Obadele-Starks writes, for example, "the Monroe Doctrine was shaped to encourage free seas and open trade ... [yet] despite evidence of a foreign slave trade, Monroe expended few resources to alter the practice along the African coast and scarcely effected any change to it in the Western Hemisphere."[23] In 1822–3, for example, the highly publicized case of a seized slave ship, the *Antelope*, in which Adams's commercial allies—including James D'Wolf—had a stake, was indefinitely "continued."[24] These historians have missed the point. James Monroe and John Quincy Adams certainly *did* expend resources on behalf of the slave trade: In the early 1820s, they worked doggedly to protect the status quo, rather than to quell it.

In his December 1823 address, President Monroe also claimed that because U.S. naval vessels had not seized a single U.S. ship involved in the slave trade, "there is good reason to believe that our flag is now seldom, if at all, disgraced by that traffic."[25] The likely audience for this falsehood was the British Royal Navy. Although the U.S. navy was ill equipped to respond to the reports of continued American involvement in the slave trade, U.S. vessels were not the only ships on the water. In ongoing negotiations with the British throughout 1823, Adams had refused to cede the right to search U.S. vessels to the Royal Navy and wrote to the Cuban investor and senator Samuel Smith that he had refused "to *concede* more to the British."[26] For years, the British had attempted to gain the right to search U.S. vessels for slaves; now President Monroe had ducked the issue altogether by publicly disavowing the private reports of U.S. slave trading he had received from the West India Squadron. If Americans were supposedly no longer involved in the slave trade, the British had less reason to lurk around Cuba.

The anti-British sentiment infusing Monroe's famous declaration that "the American continents ... are henceforth not to be considered as subjects for future colonization by any European powers" did not represent an interventionist break in U.S. foreign policy so much as a fight for the status quo on behalf of elite American investors. U.S. elites expected to wield the foreign policy apparatus of the state—including the U.S. navy—on behalf of the informal American empire in Cuba. By now, however, this was increasingly problematic. In 1823, there seemed to be fewer official justifications for such expenditures, when James Monroe announced the successful suppression of pirates around "the Island of Cuba" and the restoration of "the confidence of our merchants."[27] This was the same news that vice consul in Havana John Mountain would repeat to John Quincy Adams in the coming months. Now, James Monroe had not only denied American involvement in the slave trade, but, in another wedge against British designs on Cuba and the slave trade, he had also declared the extinction of Caribbean pirates. If there were no more pirates, the Royal Navy would no longer be needed in the hemisphere. Here, however, Monroe miscalculated. After all, if there were no longer any piratical cause for British naval forces to linger around Cuba, then there might also be less justification for the U.S. naval buildup around the Spanish island.

By declaring the successful completion of the West India Squadron's mission in his address, President Monroe had publicly acknowledged his own ignorance of the U.S. navy's actual activities. Combating piracy had been one function of the 1820–3 naval deployments, rather than their primary purpose. Elite American investors intended to incorporate the navy as another element in the service of trade and the slave trade *as needed*. Once the pirate threat was contained, the U.S. navy— like merchant-diplomats in foreign ports—could be tasked with other commercial objectives, such as shipping cargoes on freight and the transportation of specie. This is precisely why, just one month after the president announced the extinction of Cuban pirates—at the same moment that John Mountain noted the tranquility of U.S. commerce in Havana—American investors pushed for more.

In January 1824, Senator John Parrott of New Hampshire proposed a bill to build "an additional number of sloops of war" to secure the Cuban trade. The move was highly personal. Not only was Senator Parrott a merchant captain with a decades-long history of investments in Cuba, but in 1823 his cousin, Bonaparte Toscan, had been captured by Cuban pirates onboard the *Gossypium*, a ship that Parrot may have even employed in the Cuba–Baltic trade in 1812.[28] After the legislative maneuvering surrounding previous naval bills, Parrot's commercial allies had praised "the promptness with which you have acted, in the affair of the pirates."[29] Although $160,000 had been allocated for the protection of Cuban commerce in December 1822, in early 1824 it became clear that Parrott and his allies had larger ambitions. They now wanted $850,000 in additional funding at a time when 48 percent of *all* commissioned U.S. naval forces were already deployed in the Caribbean, primarily on behalf of the U.S.–Cuba trade.[30]

Opponents of the new naval bill highlighted its audacity to arrive at a time when piracy was supposed to have been suppressed by the disproportionate deployment of U.S. naval forces to the Caribbean. Senator Macon of Maryland, for example, worried that increasing the size of the navy might encourage Americans to want "to whip Spain and take Cuba from her," and Senator Lowrie of Pennsylvania complained that although "it is said that the vessels are wanted for the suppression of piracy," Lowrie had "been told, from the proper Department, that the enterprise was successful, and that piracy was suppressed."[31] Even allies of elite investors, such as Mathew Calbraith Perry—commander of the *Shark* in the West India Squadron—fretted, "The western members are in full force against the representatives from the Atlantic States, and I fear might succeed in their plans of destroying commerce and consequently the Navy."[32] Here, Perry made explicit what often went unsaid: Atlantic commerce and naval deployments were viewed as inseparable by American investors.

Amid the 1824 naval controversy, the contentious presidential election and the threat of British, French and revolutionary invasions of Cuba, John Quincy Adams abruptly broke from his past pro-slavery positions and pushed for a diplomatic arrangement with Great Britain to curtail the slave trade. This was calculated, in part, to appease England and prevent the worst-case scenario of a Spanish transfer of Cuba into British hands; in part, it was also a matter of domestic politics. Adams's proposal—if the British equated the slave trade with piracy, the U.S. would allow naval searches—was, in the estimation of historian John Noonan, "inconsistent ... with past and present Administration action," which had provided tacit support for the illegal slave trade.[33] Predictably, the U.S. senators most invested in the slave trade immediately opposed Adams's treaty. James D'Wolf and John Chandler of Maine even broke with the rest of the Senate and attempted to kill discussion altogether. The treaty passed, but ultimately this didn't matter: The Senate was forced to cut various search provisions to win support from the many senators invested in the trade, and in the aftermath, the British refused to ratify the much-weakened version.[34]

Meanwhile, John Parrott's naval bill had stalled. Senator James Lloyd of Massachusetts, who had been active in the U.S.–Cuba–Baltic trade a decade earlier, made the reason plain when he "repelled the idea, which had frequently been expressed, that the Navy was peculiarly an Eastern or sectional interest."[35] This was an open lie, and when Congress reconvened in December 1824 after the summer recess, investors from key ports in the U.S.–Cuba trade—including New York, Boston, Philadelphia, Bristol-Warren, Rhode Island, and Portland, Maine—lobbied Congress in an attempt to save the bill. On December 2, 1824, a cohort of New York merchants led by William Bayard gathered at the Tontine Coffee House in downtown Manhattan to draft a petition on "the evils which threaten not only our direct trade to Cuba, but also our commerce to every part of the Gulf of Mexico." "The squadron to the Cuba station," they wrote, "should be re-inforced [sic]."[36] A week later, merchants in Portland, Maine, followed suit, writing that "for many years, the trade to Cuba ... has occupied the principal part of the tonnage of this collection district."[37] The Philadelphia chamber of commerce also joined in, defending the "important and lucrative branch of commerce" between "the United States with the Island of Cuba" and asking that the navy be expanded to protect it.[38] Unsurprisingly, the Rhode Islanders of Bristol-Warren were also eager to protect "our Commerce in the vicinity of Cuba."[39] The petition submitted by Boston merchants—which today has unfortunately gone missing in the U.S. National Archives in Washington, D.C.—was no doubt similarly phrased.[40] Elite U.S. investors in the Cuba trade did not intend to allow the naval bill to die quietly.

As the bill began to gain momentum in early 1825, no one doubted the value of the U.S.-Cuba trade: The real question was whether or not the new naval expansion was necessary. As Senators Van Buren and Samuel Smith of Maryland joined the call to arms—urging a blockade of the island and the potential arming of merchant ships—Senator Macon responded that "there was something in this business which he could not understand. Insurance from New York to New Orleans, the

Senate was informed, was but one to one and a half per cent." In the naval wars of the 1790s–1800s, Macon said, "insurance was not so low as five per cent."[41] Macon wasn't wrong: In 1797, insurance to Jamaica had risen to 15–20 percent for a "single passage,"[42] whereas in 1825 the New York–West Indies rates had fallen to 1.25–2 percent and only 1.25–1.5 percent to Cuba.[43] In short, the piratical threat was negligible as far as insurers were concerned; one quarter to one half percent seasonal spikes correlated to hurricane season, not piracy.[44] But if the U.S. navy was not engaged in combating piracy, just what *was* it doing? And why was there now such a determined push to expand its presence on the island? Amid continuing geopolitical uncertainty in the Caribbean, and the fallout from the contested 1824 presidential election that had confirmed the continuation of a pro–slave trade U.S. foreign policy by elevating John Quincy Adams to the presidency, apprehensive members of Congress would get their answer in the court-martial of the West India Squadron's commander, David Porter.

"A Thirst For Making Money"

When David Porter assumed command of the West India Squadron, he stepped into the contradictory position of issuing orders for public naval vessels that had been deployed to protect private U.S. investment in Cuba (including in the slave trade) in the face of British naval power. Although members of Congress were likely unaware of Porter's ties to Cuba, this deployment was not his first encounter with the Spanish colonial authorities there—or with Cuban pirates. In 1810, David Porter had captured three French pirate ships that had harassed the Cuba–New Orleans trade, before applying to the Spanish Consulado in Havana for a reward of ten thousand pesos that had been advertised in *Avisos de la Habana*. When the Consulado refused to pay, arguing that because Porter had been operating as a captain in the U.S. navy, rather than as a private citizen, he was ineligible to receive the prize money, Porter began an extended petition in 1810, employing Vincent Gray as his intermediary. Now that he was back in the Caribbean, Porter used his appointment as commodore of the West India Squadron to lobby the Consulado, beginning on March 29, 1821, and continuing into 1825, for more than $60,000 in compensation. Perhaps most telling, as the case dragged on and the likelihood of a cash settlement diminished, David Porter asked the Spanish for a land grant in the eastern part of the island in lieu of payment.[45] The Consulado refused.

By 1825, however, Spanish merchants were not the only ones irritated with David Porter. In attempting to address the contradictions of his assignment by appeasing both sides, he had angered virtually every party in the U.S.–Cuba trade, including U.S. investors, expatriate American agents, and the Spanish authorities.[46] From the start, the secretary of the navy had made the squadron's commercial purpose explicit to Porter when he had commanded Porter to transport gold and silver specie on behalf of private merchants.[47] In theory, Porter was aware of the contours of his assignment, but in practice, he found it difficult to serve as a private courier and public naval commander. As early as April 1823, he exclaimed that there were "certain American merchants who wished the whole squadron to be at their disposal."[48] Still, in the course of his assignment, the West India Squadron transported specie worth over $1 million—and possibly much more—at between 1.25 and 2 percent freight, with two-thirds of the freight fee paid to the ships' commanders and one-third to David Porter himself.[49] Among the many beneficiaries of this practice was a U.S. merchant-consul at Tampico, Nathaniel Ingraham—son of William Shaler's New York commercial ally—who organized and profited from the specie shipments from the Mexican port.[50] Yet, U.S. investors were far from monolithic, and when U.S. warships were preoccupied with the transport of private specie, they invariably neglected the hunt for Caribbean pirates, who continued to intermittently harass the slave trade.

American agents for U.S. investors in the slave trade became outraged when the navy neglected its stated mission (combating piracy for the protection of the U.S.–Cuba trade) to transport specie on private account. On October 1, 1824, "vice consul" John Randall wrote from Havana of the common practice of "the carrying of specie for our merchants in vessels of war the whole effect of which, is to give a trifling premium of insurance to one class of the community, which would otherwise be paid to another class." Similarly, on October 30, 1824, John Mountain forwarded an extract of a letter from "Mr. Lattin[g], of Matanzas," in which John Latting fumed that the navy was consumed by "a thirst for making money," rather than a desire to fight pirates.[51] Randall and Latting likely had more than sugar and coffee on their minds: Insurers might cover commodities, but they wouldn't pay for seized illegal slaves.

By 1825, Spanish complaints about Porter's conduct—likely driven in part by Porter's insistent demands for compensation from the Consulado and by his frustration with the Spanish refusal to stem the slave trade—led the Spanish to demand action from U.S. authorities. The Spanish claimed that Porter had violated Spanish sovereignty in pursuing pirates on land in Puerto Rico. Porter's enemies were happy to oblige them. Highly politicized, Porter's court-martial represented the Adams administration's first major geopolitical test: In an attempt to appease the Spanish and U.S. investors, the court was stacked against Porter, giving him little chance of acquittal. However, due to Porter's prominence and to general anti-Spanish sentiment in the United States, the court could not hit him too hard: Porter was suspended for six months. The verdict quieted Spanish officials without isolating Porter's allies. One man who did not go quietly, however, was David Porter himself. Insulted by U.S. and Spanish authorities, David Porter soon followed a predictably transnational impulse and defected to the side of the very revolutionaries who plotted to take Cuba: He assumed command of the Mexican navy.[52]

By 1824–5, all appeared to be going according to plan. Elite members of the generation of 1815 had successfully leveraged state power to protect their investments in the slave trade and informal American empire in Cuba as they advanced their own careers. In these early decades, the secretary of state's office was the natural stepping-stone to the White House. James Monroe had served as secretary of state under James Madison, just as Madison had under Thomas Jefferson. By 1824, John Quincy Adams was ready to make his move. But in a country divided by sectional interests, this was not an easy fight for the patrician from Massachusetts, and when the dust settled, the war hero Andrew Jackson had won the most electoral votes. For the first and only time in U.S. history, none of the four candidates in the presidential election had secured a majority. Other candidates, including the Kentucky congressman Henry Clay and Secretary of the Treasury William Crawford, helped to split the vote. The U.S. House of Representatives was then compelled to decide the outcome, and here the master negotiator Henry Clay engineered Adams's victory in what came to be known as "the corrupt bargain." The press reported that Clay had arranged for Adams to win on the condition that Clay be made secretary of state. One secretary of state succeeded the next to the presidency, and Henry Clay intended to be next in line.

In February 1825, after the chaos of the disputed 1824 presidential election, John Quincy Adams, the consummate ally of U.S. investors in Cuban slavery, finally assumed the presidency. James D'Wolf greeted the event by writing to his brother: "Can go out now. The clouds disperse and fair weather. I hope for 4 years at least."[53] Adams's new secretary of state, Henry Clay, was also no stranger to Americans invested in Cuba, including James D'Wolf. In 1814, D'Wolf had invested in land and a distillery in Clay's home state of Kentucky and had even employed Clay as his attorney, explicitly referencing his Cuban investments in numerous letters to Clay.[54] In March 1825, John Parrott's contentious naval appropriation was split and passed: Up to ten warships would be built in the first year, at a cost of $500,000 "for the suppression of piracy."[55] And although the threat of foreign invasion from circling British, French and revolutionary forces continued to loom, the island of Cuba remained in Spanish hands.

The illegal slave trade—which accelerated as greater legal barriers were placed in its path—remained the driver of Cuban agro-industry, and the Monroe Doctrine now worked in tandem with the West India Squadron to protect it. As Cuba rapidly grew into the second-largest trading partner with the United States, elite members of the '15ers flexed the muscles of the Early Republic state to protect the growth of informal empire. Yet, this process of U.S. capitalization and investment in Cuban slavery still depended on two highly unpredictable components: the rise of international capital markets and the behavior of enslaved human beings. In 1825, American investors faced a turning point. How they responded to a series of controversies and crises in that year would determine the direction of American investment on the island for decades to come.

NINE

Speculators

Edward Spalding felt old. He had spent the seven years since his 1816 wager with his friend Benjamin Bosworth—the famed "Kiah Butterworth"—chasing women and profits from one end of the Atlantic Ocean to the other. Now, the Cuban port of Matanzas looked like a polished jewel, with columned buildings and flowery latticework facing the main square. The port seemed to grow larger and wealthier every day, and Edward Spalding had seen it happen. As he sat in the offices of the slave-trading house of Latting, Adams and Stewart, he opened a letter from his cousin in Bristol, Rhode Island, Joseph Torrey. He still kept the letters Torrey had sent him earlier in the year during a trip to secure sugar, coffee and slaves on the island.

Torrey had joked that "the Bachelor's Pew," which Spalding and his friends owned at St. Michael's Church, "was ornamented with five beautiful ladies, all of whom thought more of one of its absent proprietors than of all [other] subjects." "I congratulate myself," Torrey wrote, "as you are particularly fond of ladies."[1] Now, Torrey told Spalding that although he had not "attend[ed] the service of 'Christmas Eve,'" he had "heard, with great sorrow, that the Bachelor's Pew was thickly studded with ladies."[2] Edward Spalding put the letter down. He remembered Benjamin Bosworth on the prowl for women and wealth. The world was much less certain than it had been when they had started. Now, his cousin wanted money, and Bosworth was dead.[3]

"I find you to be a sober merchant," Torrey told Spalding, "stating briefly the circumstances of important revolutions, the exports &

business of a colony."[4] The demands of this new capitalism had sapped
the enjoyment from Spalding's correspondence, transforming him from
an irreverent opportunist into a "sober merchant." Early in the following
year, Torrey wrote to "Ned Spaldinque" (Edward Spalding) that, "Poor
Mrs Bosworth seems to derive great additional hope from" the "unex-
pected news" that a New Englander who was believed to have perished
at sea was discovered "after an unheard of absence of nearly two years ...
in the Castle at Havana." "But I fear," Torrey wrote, "the prison of her
husband, is more obdurate than the dark cells of the Moro."[5] Benjamin
Bosworth had been lost at sea, and he wasn't coming back.

As this commercial system of sugar, slaves and gold took a toll on the
men who created it, it also transformed the United States. The towns
and villages in New England where Edward Spalding had grown up were
transforming almost beyond recognition, as a boom in cotton production on the North American frontier stoked the fires of Northern and
Atlantic industry. Spalding's home state of Rhode Island had been the
first U.S. site of standardization and mass production of textiles, based
on British designs. And the rise of hundreds of mills along the river
valleys of New England dramatically refigured the landscape. Within
a few short years, Spalding had seen familiar New England cities, such
as Boston and Providence, double in size.[6] Nothing seemed certain.
Benjamin Bosworth was gone, and soon much of the network he had
helped to create from Bristol to Matanzas would follow him down.

   The integration of U.S. economic development with Caribbean and
European commodity markets brought sea changes in the fortunes
of U.S. investors. And although the U.S.–Cuba trade fueled North
American development, the operations of this economic integration were most apparent when things went wrong. In 1825, capitalist
hedging and catastrophic weather on both sides of the Atlantic demonstrated the deep economic entanglement of the U.S. economy with
the slave regime of Cuba, when the maneuvers of a cutthroat commercial agent in New York and Matanzas combined with a flood in St.
Petersburg and Cuban crop failures to decimate the economy of Bristol,
Rhode Island. In the mid-1820s, professional agents such as Edward
Spalding, who had worked for years to profit from the rise of Cuban

slavery and the slave trade, watched the links they had created stretch and snap.

The dramatic and simultaneous rise in the slave frontiers of North America, Cuba and Brazil bred speculation, leading planters to borrow against their future crops from foreign investors, particularly in the United States and Europe. When business was good, investors and planters alike reaped the rewards, leveraging wealth into greater investments in the slave regime. But when things went wrong, it became apparent just how deeply entangled this network had become. In 1824–5, the success and rapid failure of Edward Spalding's friends and allies at the Matanzas commercial house of Latting, Adams and Stewart demonstrated the extent of this early transnational market integration in striking detail. Not coincidentally, there was also a simultaneous financial panic in North American cotton markets. As Edward Baptist suggests, "in the winter of 1824–25, cotton buyers were convinced that the 1824 crop had been small" only to discover that it had been large, destabilizing commodity prices and credit markets on both sides of the Atlantic and forcing the Second Bank of the United States to intervene. The bank's response was to force "smaller, state-chartered banks to redeem their own credit in highly convertible currency, like gold dollars, British pounds, or banknotes of the BUS itself."[7] All three of these "highly convertible currencies" relied on the U.S.–Cuba trade, either directly via specie funneled into the U.S. (and British) economy, or indirectly via the sugar and coffee dispatched to European commodity markets.

Even more to the point: the same "animal spirits" that excited the ambitions of U.S. cotton speculators also led American investors in Cuba (including many of the same men) to attempt to manipulate Cuban commodity markets. That the U.S. senator from Rhode Island James D'Wolf invested in Cuban slave plantations and North American agricultural land while serving as the director of U.S. banks and insurance companies and investing in European and Asian commerce was not a contradiction. Instead, due to his successes, D'Wolf represented one of the most explicit examples of network consolidation by an elite within the system. Although I concentrate on the unstudied Cuban wing of this exchange, U.S., Cuban and European markets would shake simultaneously, precisely because Cuban slavery and the slave trade that drove its development were integral to North American and trans-atlantic economic systems of exchange. In the 1820s, as Edward Spalding reflected on the death of Benjamin Bosworth in Matanzas, he was also sitting at ground zero of an impending financial collapse—at the successful commercial house of Latting, Adams and Stewart.

"There Is No Longer Any Safety in Business"

By the 1820s, John Latting—the New York merchant and slave trader who had become the U.S. vice consul in Matanzas in 1810—had part-nered with a wealthy Virginia merchant named Francis Adams.[8] Adams brought a wealth of connections that included his state representa-tive brother-in-law Thomas Newton, Jr., as well as the elite Howland family of Connecticut and New York.[9] Adams had used his influence with powerful New York commercial houses to obtain an appoint-ment as U.S. agent to Trieste in 1819, and in 1823, Adams arrived in Matanzas with a similar appointment as a "commercial agent." He promptly purchased a portion of the nearby Mount Vernon planta-tion.[10] John Latting's other business partner, Robert Stewart, primarily worked as the commercial house's representative on the southern coast of the island at Trinidad, where his relative James Stewart was serving as an unrecognized consul.[11] The strategy of placing relatives and personal allies in public posts to leverage the diplomatic apparatus of the state to improve the prospects of private commerce remained the typical course for American merchants invested in the Cuba trade. Controlling every public and private aspect of the trade at Matanzas could reduce the risks of the U.S.–Cuba trade, but it could not insulate American investors entirely—particularly when they overreached.

In August 1824, while on a trip to New York, Francis Adams wrote to Edward Spalding that he had received news from St. Petersburg of the low prices listed for sugar in Russia. "I think we have reason to be pleased," Adams wrote, "that prospects are *now* discouraging." Adams planned to use the published account currents of commodity prices in St. Petersburg to buy from Cuban planters at a reduced rate, then time these shipments to match another peak in European demand. "It will keep down the ideas of sugar planters," he confided to Spalding, "& the price may open low enough to induce orders and enable us to execute them on terms which will be safe to all parties." Because the Europeans would be unable to calculate demand on sugars purchased in February 1825 (arriving in Europe in May) "before October or November" of 1824, Adams planned "to draw in our advances on planters [and] discontinue shipments on our own acct."[12] Adams intended to force planters to sell at the lower price by calling in the money owed from indebted planters, then hold stockpiles until prices in Europe peaked again. But Adams's plans quickly imploded.

In late 1824, crops failed in Cuba, and in the Baltic, St. Petersburg was hit by a major storm. Writing to New England from the scene of devastation in Russia in November 1824, the Brothers Cramer detailed the "awfull & dreadfull inundation" in which "thousands of lives & thousands of dwellings [were] swept away." The damage was as extensive as it was potentially lucrative for the lucky few to have protected stocks of sugar on hand:

> The cellars, lower warehouses filled with water, most all the property on the customhouse wharfs damaged, & in short a destruction of which there never was before … the first article [of interest] is sugars. We have fared better than most of our neighbours in consequence of our sugars being deposited under the shed on three rows of bricks… [but there would now be an] advance in prices…[that might] produce more money than the whole would have produced had the misfortune not occurred, this is the prevailing opinion here."[13]

As news of the catastrophe slowly travelled across the Atlantic, there were agricultural failures in Cuba. Many planters who had heavily borrowed to invest had now been manipulated into selling at a loss to Adams. This left the planters desperate to recover sums they were owed from one another. Francis Adams, meanwhile, had over-leveraged money he did not have, counting on the arrival of crops in early 1825 and a rise in European prices. This was exactly the moment when news of the Russian catastrophe reached the United States. In Russia, sugar prices spiked 35–40 percent, and every sensible U.S. merchant invested in Cuba eyed St. Petersburg. Writing from New England to Matanzas, Edward Spalding's elite backers urged him to use his "experience in Cuba" to send new shipments of Cuban sugar and coffee to "the Baltic as soon as possible" to beat their competitors. The "grand object," John D'Wolf wrote from Boston, "now appears to be dispatch."[14] The urgency of high prices drove merchants to borrow even more.

And then the rains came. In January and February 1825, as indebted planters and commercial agents frantically struggled to get their crops to market, torrential rains demolished many of the roads and upset the normal routines of the harvest. "We have had a dreadful season for Planters," Edward Spalding warned, "the rains [have] been equal to those of the rainy season, and all the sugar Planters have been prevented from grinding for the last 8 or 10 days."[15] In Matanzas, Francis Adams could not deliver his many promised consignments, and his failure triggered a panic, causing more investors to call in their debts at the very moment commercial houses and planters could least afford to pay. William Savage, for example—whose relative Thomas was still in Havana—wrote from Boston that he was owed "Thirty thousand dollars" in an "account with Messrs Latting Adams & Stewar[t]" in his regular trade with Matanzas.[16] And the Rhode Islander George D'Wolf, who had significant investments leveraged with numerous merchants in Cuba, soon found himself embroiled in lawsuits related to the commercial house's insolvency. In early 1825, he tallied $18,496.31 he was owed by nineteen different merchants, not counting other sums invested with Vincent Gray and Zachariah Atkins.[17] One claim sparked another and another, in a ripple that soon shocked the entire network.

As Adams struggled to clear his name in Matanzas, American merchant John Morland grew suspicious of cargoes consigned to the failing house. "They had better make these good sales," Morland wrote, otherwise "I shall get a letter for the Intendant" to allow inspections of the ships.[18] Meanwhile, Adams attempted to exploit lags in communication to balance what he owed against various creditors, causing Morland to fume that "Mr. Adams is even worse than I believed man to be." Because the entire apparatus of agro-industry had been built on credit that depended on reputation and careful timing of crops, any major seasonal disruption could bring the entire operation to a halt. This is precisely what happened. As the Matanzas commercial house's finances deteriorated, another Boston merchant exclaimed, "Never was the firm nor myself concerned in so rascally and in so unfortunate a business. If a bill of Lading ceases to be a security there is no longer any safety in business."[19]

In Cuba, Americans scrambled to save what they could through the Spanish administration, including—in the case of Joseph "José" Wilson—"nine boxes" of "tile or brick" being held "in the store of Latting, Adams & Stewart."[20] Meanwhile, Adams's partner John Latting tried to remain above the fray.[21] In this tumult, George D'Wolf's finances collapsed, and his deep investment in the banks and insurance companies of Bristol soon derailed the port's entire economy, costing more than $1 million in this Rhode Island town alone. In the entire D'Wolf network only James D'Wolf seems to have emerged unscathed. For his part, George D'Wolf fled from his American creditors to live out his days on the Arc de Noe plantation in Cuba.[22] Francis Adams would not survive. Although it is unclear if he committed suicide, was killed or died by natural causes, in 1825 Francis Adams was dead and would be buried on his own plantation near Matanzas. He would not be the only U.S. citizen to die in Cuba that year.

The impact of the failure of Latting, Adams and Stewart demonstrates just how significantly the U.S. economy depended on American investment in Cuba. Cuban crop failures and rains in Matanzas coupled with financial manipulation and a Russian storm had cost millions of dollars within the United States. In the wheel of Atlantic trade networks, Cuba was a central spoke, with significant implications for U.S. global trade and the rise of U.S. finance. By the time of the 1824–5 financial catastrophe, virtually every U.S. ship involved in transatlantic trade made a point of stopping in Havana. The 1822 voyage of the Appleton ship *Minerva* was typical: The ship traveled from Boston to England (where it acquired bills of exchange in London), and later to Batavia, Canton and Cuba (for specie doubloons). From Cuba, the *Minerva* traveled to Boston, Lisbon, then back to Cuba.[23] Moreover, the island's role as a vital depot in global trade routes linking the United States with Europe and Asia was well known. In 1824, Daniel Webster—the personal friend and attorney of many elite New England investors in the Cuban trade, including George D'Wolf—made this explicit in a speech to the U.S. Congress:

> If a vessel take our own products to the Havana, or elsewhere, exchange them for dollars, proceed to China, exchange them for silks and teas, bring these last to the ports of the Mediterranean, sell them there for dollars, and return to the United States—this would be a voyage resulting in the importation of the precious metals. But if she had returned from Cuba, and the dollars obtained there had been shipped direct from the United States to China, the China goods sold in Holland, the proceeds brought home in the hemp and iron of Russia, this would be a voyage in which they were exported.[24]

For Webster, Cuba was the central driver in the expansion of U.S. foreign trade—not only due to the steady supply of sugar and coffee leaving the island, but also to Americans' access to Spanish gold and silver specie, which continued to be directly linked to the slave trade. Specie was essential to the expansion of Asian trade and the financial infrastructure of the United States, which depended on a stockpile of specie for the issuing of banknotes and credit. And Cuba was a key supply point for Spanish doubloons at a time when the Spanish dollar remained the de facto global currency.[25] Although the U.S. Mint had been established in 1792, an 1816 law allowed foreign coins—including "the gold coins of Great Britain, Portugal, France, Spain, and the dominions of Spain, and the five-franc pieces of France" to be "declared to be a tender" in the United States. The reality of specie exchange was even simpler. In 1819, a report by the Finance Committee of the U.S. Congress concluded what many Americans already knew: "The silver which is most frequently brought into the United States in the common course of commercial business is the Spanish dollar; but individuals have no inducement of interest to send this coin to the Mint." Investors had good reason to keep their bullion in the form of Spanish dollars: "In Canton," the Finance Committee explained, "and many parts of the East Indies, the Spanish dollar is valued much higher than that of the United States, or than any other coin, in proportion to the quantity of pure silver which it contains."[26]

Scholars such as James Fichter have acknowledged that "capital, often in the form of specie (silver coin), was fundamental to American and British trade in Asia and to east-west interaction generally" contributing to the more complex leveraging of credit and wealth via corporate and insurance investment schemes. But the source of this specie has often been taken as a *fait accompli*.[27] In fact, global trade and domestic economic development ran not simply on specie, but on *Spanish* specie of the type flowing from Spanish mines in the Americas and through Cuba. In effect, the Spanish terms of exchange in the U.S.–Cuba trade established the foundation on which the expansion of economic development and global commerce depended. And in Spanish Cuba, the terms of specie export were explicitly linked to the slave trade.

That many elite Americans who invested in Asian trade and who would grow wealthy from their Eastern trade contacts—from John M. Forbes to Nathaniel Silsbee, Thomas Perkins, John Cushing and William Gray—were also heavily invested in Cuba was not coincidental. Havana was essential to American investment in Canton precisely because of the Spanish-made specie that moved through Spanish warehouses on the island.[28] The New England–Cuba trade surged at the very moment of increased New England investment in Asia precisely because of, while simultaneously enabling, this global expansion. By the 1820s, Cuba—not Jamaica or rival "West Indies" islands—had become the linchpin to this trade. In September 1825, Daniel Webster argued that the British islands were rapidly becoming irrelevant. "Whether in present enjoyment; or in future prospect," he said, "Our whole trade to the British West Indies ... is trifling, compared with that to Cuba and Hispaniola."[29] British trade restrictions, the slave trade, and the Spanish island's geography made Cuba decisive for U.S. merchants. Cuba was the commercial key to the hemisphere precisely because it was *not* British.

Still, the threat of foreign invasion loomed. In October 1825, an article in *The National Gazette* of Philadelphia titled "The Invasion of Cuba," which purported to be a fragment of a revolutionary missive, claimed that a powerful naval squadron with ten to twelve thousand soldiers was preparing to invade the island from Colombia.[30] News circulated of European forces being readied for Cuba: In Spain, a large expedition was being outfitted, and, as British warships continued to circle, American merchants in Haiti worried that a French force near Port au Prince was also "in reality bound for Cuba."[31] The Mexican Congress too was under pressure from expatriate Spanish-Cubans to launch a secret invasion of their own.[32] In this tense atmosphere, even the slightest mistake might cost Spain the island of Cuba. American investors who eyed the movement of British, French and Spanish fleets around the island worried that, even if neither side wanted war, the possibilities of inadvertent hostilities in this tense atmosphere were very real.[33] Spain might be provoked into another war and lose the Pearl of the Antilles.

In October 1825, Henry Clay wrote to John Quincy Adams that his informants in Cuba had notified him "that matters are fast hastening to a crisis there, and that there must be shortly an explosion." The Creole elite "dread[ed] the black troops of Columbia," Clay said, "and prefer a connexion with Mexico, but look anxiously and ultimately to the U. States." If a Mexican army landed in Cuba, Clay said, the Creole elite would revolt against Spain, and as tensions mounted and Mexico prepared an invasion force, Clay became increasingly suspicious of France's Caribbean fleet, which was disproportionate "to any of the ordinary purposes of a peaceful commerce."[34] If Cuba did indeed "explode," the United States, France and England were all prepared to step in. In fact, for American planters living on the island, Cuba had already exploded. In the summer of 1825, a transnational U.S.–Cuban slave insurrection erupted among American, Spanish and French slave plantations in Guamacaro, near Matanzas. The course of this insurrection—which has gone unnoticed in the historiography of U.S. slave revolts—and its aftermath would help to shape and confirm the nature of American investment in the slave regime.

TEN

Executioners

On Nathaniel Fellowes's plantation outside Havana, the Reverend Abiel Abbot packed mementos of his time in Cuba—a jar of scorpions, a box of oranges and his spare black hat—and prepared to return to Havana and then to New England. It was four in the morning, and Fellowes was dressed "in his night gown" when he said goodbye and wished Abbot well. After spending the winter of 1828 on the Spanish island for his health, Abiel Abbot was ready to return to Massachusetts. He never got there: Shortly after leaving Havana, Abbot died at sea. Typically, scholars have presented Abbot's posthumous collection of correspondence as representative of the origin of nineteenth-century North American involvement in Cuba. Yet on visits to numerous American-owned Cuban plantations, Abbot documented the extensive investment of American citizens from the U.S. North in the Spanish slave regime. Almost immediately after his arrival at Matanzas, Abbot was escorted to "the battle ground of 1825." Here, he wrote, "a few gentlemen by uncommon daring, killed a few, and put to flight six or seven hundred insurgent negroes." "Four gentlemen, if I mistake not," he said, "put the whole multitude to rout."[1]

The reality of this "little known rebellion" near Guamacaro, Cuba, in 1825 was far different, and the American response would help to shape the course of the informal U.S. empire in Cuba and solidify the role of the slave trade in the North American economy for a generation. Each year, the churn of this commercial network brought tens of thousands of enslaved people to replace the dead at the slave plantations of Cuba and Brazil. And Americans from the U.S. North rushed to a deeper south, eager to cash in. As slave-ship captains and commercial operatives like Benjamin Bosworth and the Virginian merchant Francis Adams passed away, other U.S. investors arrived to take their place. The intense debate over Missouri statehood had demonstrated that slavery's place in the future of the United States was far from settled. In North America, the '15ers shelved the issue rather than face it. Farther south, they were less conflicted.

As the new U.S. republic was created on the backs of enslaved North American laborers, many American investors feared a future day of reckoning. Still terrified of the specter of Haiti, American writers imagined race war and lobbied to expel African Americans from the country altogether. Slave conspiracies and revolts in the United States prompted national debates about emancipation or aspirations for amelioration. Northerners, including many later abolitionists, raised funds to send blacks to the newly created West African colony of Liberia, with its capital of "Monrovia" named for the same U.S. president who determinedly protected the slave trade. Northerners were no strangers to the slaveholding South, and while some may have readily assimilated, scholars such as Dennis Rousey have suggested that Northerners in the U.S. South were "likelier to harbor antislavery feelings." In Cuba, this was simply not the case.

The presence of Cuban slaveholders from the U.S. North alters the geography of American slavery. Northern participation in the "agro-industrial graveyard" of the Cuban slave regime both reinforces and complicates scholars' recognition of slavery as a national, rather than sectional, bedrock of U.S. state formation. When convenient or profitable, the character of U.S. slavery was also transnational. In Cuba, a Rhode Islander traded a factory account book for a plantation invoice that listed 103 enslaved men, women and children; a New Yorker forced enslaved Africans to build stone walls around their own homes to prevent escape; and a Connecticut merchant, convinced that leniency would trigger revolt, turned his manor into a fortress, surrounded by armed guards and dogs. Harboring no illusions about the human cost of their coffee and sugar crops, Americans from the U.S. North made their homes in the center of Cuban slave labor camps. And they did so remarkably easily.[2]

"The Eye of the Traveler Is Constantly Delighted"

At approximately one in the morning on June 15, 1825, enslaved Africans on a small French plantation near the village of Guamacaro, Cuba, east of the port of Matanzas, attacked and killed their owner. They quickly moved to a larger neighboring estate, where more enslaved Africans slipped out of their quarters to join them. Drawing on a deep knowledge of warfare, the Africans rushed the mansion and executed the owner, an Englishman named Armitage, along with his wife and two oldest sons. The owner's third child, a three-year-old boy, was spared when an enslaved "mulatto" woman begged for his life. The woman carried the boy, along with her own child, into the yard. The Africans moved through Armitage's house, looting clothing along with knives and forks—anything that might be used as a weapon. They left the silver.[3]

In the chaos, the "mulatto" woman slipped away with another enslaved worker and carried the children two miles to a neighboring plantation, the Mount Hope, where she woke the American manager, Stephen Fales. One of Fales's daughters was away at another American plantation, the San Juan in Camarioca, but Fales was terrified for the safety of his wife, his other daughter and his son, who were still asleep. Fales quickly hustled them out of the house, past the slave *bohíos* (huts) to the edge of the field, where they ducked past rows of coffee trees into Caribbean jungle and began a long walk. It was thirty-six miles to the Wilson's San Juan estate.

In the early morning hours, the Africans likely sang, beating drums as they moved from Armitage's plantation to attack three nearby Spanish estates, burning the buildings with the same New England–manufactured spermaceti candles used to light the sugar ingenios at night. At a roadside tavern, the Africans—now numbering well over a hundred—executed two more Spaniards before arriving at another American coffee plantation, the Santa Ana. This cafetal was owned by the Connecticut native Ebenezer William Sage, who was away in Boston and had left his cousin, S. A. Rainey, in charge. Hearing gunfire from the tavern, Rainey rode his horse out to the fields of sugarcane and coffee trees, where enslaved Africans had already begun the day's work with hoes and machetes. The Africans had heard the shots too. Rainey urged his workers to drop their tools and return to their homes so he could lock them in. But they didn't move. Behind Rainey, the Africans reached the house, and while some Africans searched for weapons and liquor, others fired on Rainey. He fled on horseback. All but three of the enslaved men at the Santa Ana joined the African army.

On the road nearby, the Africans ambushed and executed another New Englander, Samuel Bartlett, then divided into two companies. The first company attacked another Spanish ingenio, but they soon began to quarrel and their advance slowed. Meanwhile, the second, larger company neared a cafetal that was owned by a former ship captain from Baltimore named Mr. Taylor. Taylor heard them coming. Armed with heavy firearms, pistols and swords, Taylor barricaded himself inside his mansion with the enslaved people on his plantation. Outside, two hundred Africans surrounded his house with torches and machetes, shouting for his slaves to join them.

By now, however, word had traveled from Guamacaro to Matanzas, and, as American merchants in the port looked on, Spanish dragoons readied their horses, dogs and guns. Meanwhile, the white planters near Guamacaro also assembled. Fleeing the Santa Ana, S. A. Rainey took a jungle road to La Carolina, a cafetal owned by the Bostonian George Bartlett, whose brother Samuel had just been killed. At La Carolina Rainey joined a small army of planters, guards and overseers. Around eight in the morning they rode out to launch a counterattack against the Africans who had surrounded Taylor's cafetal. A battle ensued.

By ten or eleven in the morning, every owner of a nearby estate had been notified to ready arms and sever any potential communication between enslaved laborers and the "insurgents." Around noon, the Matanzas dragoons arrived on horseback to join the fight, creating an army of at least four hundred men. With three types of Cuban dogs that were infamous throughout the Atlantic for their ability to hunt and kill human beings, the Spanish tracked the Africans throughout the day, killing or capturing as many as they could. The next day, a second company of dragoons arrived from Havana and "continued the work of extirpation." This "work" was not quick. An African with military experience, Lorenzo Lucumí, led the African army in combat for ten days until he was assassinated. Most of the remaining Africans were soon overpowered by the Spaniards' superior numbers and weaponry. Yet, even as Africans were hanged on the docks of Matanzas or returned to their owners, other participants in the revolt escaped capture altogether, including the insurrection's organizer, Pablo Gangá.[4]

In 1825, Cuba remained a Spanish colony, and, as Manuel Barcia Paz has demonstrated, the Guamacaro Revolt was the first nineteenth-century rebellion in Cuba to be "totally organized and commanded by African-born slaves." As Barcia makes plain, the revolt was African in motivation and execution and can be traced, like other revolts in Cuba and Brazil, to the Fulani jihad that had enslaved Oyo warriors, beginning in 1804 and peaking in the 1820s and 1830s. Although the majority of the twenty-three plantations attacked in the 1825 insurrection were not U.S. plantations, the revolt also impacted Americans: Bartlett, Fales, Rainey, Sage, Taylor and Wilson were all U.S. citizens. Even the Englishman Armitage had lived in the western United States before bringing his family to Cuba. In the revolt's aftermath, Spanish authorities would blame the insurrection, in part, on the levity of foreign planters. Although the Rhode Island D'Wolfs—who invested in numerous U.S. slave plantations in Cuba—were notorious for their role as Atlantic slave traders, there is no evidence that most of the Northerners had slaveholding experience prior to arriving in Cuba. Stephen Fales may have been an exception.

During his work as a ship captain in the D'Wolf commercial empire, for example, Stephen Fales's mother had written his sister in June 1806 that "your brother Stephen in Charlestown … [is] very happy in his humorous way." Indeed, "how could it be otherways for he says to one go and he goeth and to another come and he cometh." Years before arriving as an administrator in Cuba, Fales was entirely satisfied at his exercise of total control over the people with whom he had come into contact. How could it be otherwise? One month later, Fales "sent his profile" portrait back to Rhode Island, along with "one of the blacks with a kiss to each of his Sisters." Slavery and good wishes were inseparable within the context of New England trade networks that had long since disproportionately linked the U.S. North with Cuba.[5]

Nowhere was this more apparent than on the Cuban plantations owned by members of the D'Wolf family of Rhode Island. By now,

the D'Wolfs and their allies would invest in at least six Cuban plantations as part of a commercial empire that included shipping, finance,
land speculation and industrial development. In 1818, eschewing
typical distinctions between New England factories and Caribbean
coffee plantations, future U.S. senator James D'Wolf had appointed the
same man—George Munro—who had recently supervised D'Wolf's
Arkwright Mills in Coventry, Rhode Island, to administer his Mary Ann
cafetal in Cuba. Scholars have increasingly noted the use of technologies
and innovation on plantations—particularly in the Caribbean—and
D'Wolf apparently saw no contradiction in shifting Munro from
weaving to whipping.[6]

On Munro's arrival at the Mary Ann in mid-December 1818, ninety-
six of the enslaved workers were native Africans; another seven children
had been born on the estate. D'Wolf instructed Munro to "treat the
Negroes … with all the humanity in your power" to compel them
to work as "other Coffee Estates [do] from a similar gang." The following month, Munro's friend Byron Diman wrote to him from the
D'Wolf counting house in Bristol, eager to learn "how you get along the
Negroes." Without apparent irony, he enclosed a dozen chains.[7]

In February 1820, James D'Wolf wrote to Munro about the arrival
of white laborers, who had been dispatched from the United States to
build shelters on the plantation for the enslaved Africans. "Never suffer
any of the white people to have any thing to do or say to any of the
negroes," D'Wolf wrote, "not even to speak to one of them, for if there
is the least intercourse you will have great difficulty in governing the
negroes or the whites." Notorious for his legacy as a slave trader, James
D'Wolf was attempting to impose a North American construction of
binary racial slavery on an island where terms of bondage and race were
sometimes more fluid. Unfortunately, Munro himself remains silent:
The only surviving record of his presence on the plantation is his signature on the plantation inventory.[8]

Stephen Fales's correspondence provides a more comprehensive
picture. As the periodic administrator of the D'Wolf Mount Hope
cafetal—the same man who would wake in 1825 to cries from the
neighboring Armitage estate—Fales had arrived from New England in
1817. Once his family joined him, Stephen freely permitted his young

son Thomas to play "with the little Negroes" and to learn Spanish until, three years later, Thomas had "quite forgotten his mother tongue." Northerners like the Fales often attempted to transplant their interests to Cuba, bringing the concerns of the New England parlor to the Cuban countryside. Americans traded, socialized and even married in Cuba. In 1819, for example, Stephen Fales may have attended the Cuban wedding of the Bostonian George Bartlett to his wife, a native of Philadelphia, at Bartlett's nearby *La Carolina* cafetal. "We have," Fales later reflected, "the best neighbours in the world." This also included the Englishman Armitage, who moved with his family to a nearby cafetal in 1822 and who was, in Fales's estimation, "a brother to me & mine." And, just as Fales's son Thomas became fluent in Spanish, Stephen Fales also embraced elements of Spanish culture in Cuba. In an attempt to create an Anglo-American and Spanish cultural blend, Stephen Fales—like other American expatriates—even adopted a Spanish name. "We make out to pass our time much more agreeably than you could suppose," Stephen "Esteban" Fales wrote in April 1824, and "our long residence has assimilated our manner of living to the Spaniards."[9]

Yet, no matter how "agreeably" he and his family lived, the reality of the Caribbean slave plantations continually intruded. Many of Fales's concerns, from education and improvement for his children to family squabbles and business investments, were typical of middle-class New England. Others were not. Immediately after Fales arrived, for example, he was "obliged to report more deaths of our Negroes" and track down runaways who had been stolen by another American, William Bowen. "That gentlem[a]n," D'Wolf wrote, "fell so obviously in love with my property that he makes it his own when ever he can." D'Wolf was also certain that Bowen had information on "several more of our de[a]d & missing Negros." Discipline and submission among his "property" were important, D'Wolf wrote in October 1817, but "never suf[f]er any capritious [sic] or wanton cruelty practiced upon them as has be[e]n the case." Based on a legal dispute one year earlier related to Bowen's neglect of the estate, it is likely that D'Wolf had Bowen in mind. Whether or not Fales continued to torture the enslaved Africans, he was compelled—by the demands of the coffee crop and the plantation's U.S. investors—to work them to death.[10]

With the start of the rainy season in June 1822, for example, he wrote, "the poor negroes have but little time for rest [and] consequently my presence is wanted in the field as I have no white men on the place." No distant administrator, Fales supervised the Africans as an overseer, almost certainly with whip in hand. And although Stephen Fales took numerous business leaves from the Mount Hope, the brutality took a toll. After five years at the cafetal, Fales admitted that the violence had changed him, numbing whatever humanitarian sensibilities he had once had. "Since my living in this country," he confided to his sister in August 1822, "I have seen so many sudden deaths that they do not affect [me] so awfully as formerly."[11]

Closer to Havana, at the D'Wolf's Buena Esperanza and Arc de Noe estates, the New Yorker Joseph Goodwin tersely catalogued a similar regime in his plantation diary from 1821 to 1827. Here, Goodwin counted over 240 enslaved laborers, although their number was never constant. Slave names regularly overlapped from one estate to the next, suggesting that workers were routinely shifted between the plantations. An undated register of the eighty-two "Negros belonging to the Ingenio Nuevo Esperanza," for example, listed the names of ten men who had been brought "with their families from the Mount Hope Coffee Estate"; ten women were also tallied as "From the Mt. Hope." In addition to two names that had been crossed out and removed from the total ("Justo" and "Carolina"), an addendum at the bottom noted that people marked with a small x (such as "Basindo," "Clotilda" and "Juliana") "have died" and people listed with a cross ("Felix" and "Carlos") had "run."[12]

In mid-April 1821, two weeks after his arrival as administrator, Goodwin noted, "The first Negro I struck was this evening for laughing at Prayers." Line by line, his writings provide a glimpse of the toil and death, runaways and suicides that characterized the lives of enslaved Africans on cafetales and ingenios in Cuba. That summer, for example, Goodwin discovered two runaway Africans hanging by ropes in the jungle, their bodies decayed after at least three days' exposure. Rather than reflect on "the unfortunate circumstance," Goodwin coldly remarked, "suffice it to say they are no more." This was a shame, he said, since "they were the two best Bosals on the Plantation." It is impossible to know if they were the same "Felix" and "Carlos" listed as missing in the ingenio inventory, precisely because marronage was so constant. The "best Bosals" suggests that these Africans may have been worked hard, pushed by Goodwin's Spanish overseer and his armed guards until death seemed preferable to the lash. During harvest season, enslaved workers on Cuban ingenios routinely labored for up to twenty hours each day.[13]

Like Rhode Islander Stephen Fales, the New Yorker Joseph Goodwin could not claim ignorance of the brutal reality of these Cuban plantations. When two more Africans—"Pablo" and "Padro Marea"—who had run away "came back" the following day, for example, Goodwin catalogued how he planned to torture them: "Their punishment will be as follows, four days in the Sapo heavy ironed, four days in succession after prayers, twenty four lashes on the naked bottom each, after which lanced and well rubbed down with rum and salt."[14]

But the runaways continued, and so Goodwin assigned his enslaved laborers not only tasks traditionally associated with the Caribbean coffee frontier—such as clearing jungle and "trimming," "weeding" and "cleaning" coffee leaves—but also forced them to "collect stone" to build walls. Amid the tens of thousands of coffee trees at the Arc de Noe and Buena Esperanza, Goodwin oversaw the construction of walls, which not only encircled the plantations to discourage runaways, but also likely separated the bohíos, where enslaved Africans lived, from the grounds. Indeed, Theresa Singleton has demonstrated that "enclosing slave quarters within a prison-like wall" on Cuban coffee and sugar estates was a "known practice." Goodwin knew this practice well and sometimes acted—like Stephen Fales—as overseer himself. In fact, Goodwin may have demanded *more* labor from his enslaved workers than some Spanish planters: The Africans on these American plantations regularly worked on the Sabbath, and feast days were often ignored. Only Christmas seems to have been sacrosanct.[15]

Although Goodwin may not have followed the Spanish labor traditions, he, like Fales, readily embraced the Spanish "manner of living," and the Spanish were happy to include him. In July 1821, for example, Joseph Goodwin dined with a company of Spanish planters at a "Superb Palace," where he played "Billiards," before enjoying a lavish dinner, dessert and cigars. In Cuban ports, American merchants routinely socialized with the Spanish, and on the coffee and sugar frontier, American planters and administrators were welcomed into the circles of the Spanish and Creole elite. In fact, the estates' owner, George D'Wolf—nephew of James—was not only a friend to U.S. president James Monroe, but also to the Spanish captain-general of Cuba.[16]

In April 1825, just months before the Guamacaro Revolt, George D'Wolf arrived in Cuba with a small group of fellow New Englanders and "a disposition to make trouble and difficulty on the Estates with the Negroes." Goodwin was concerned that D'Wolf would "spoil" the Africans and offered him "one negro to do with him as he pleased ... but to no effect." "I shall go on patiently," Goodwin fumed, "a few days longer." Goodwin's notes suggest that the New Englanders, enjoying the novelty of the slave plantation, had arrived with domination and rape on their minds. On a visit to Bristol, Rhode Island, four years earlier, Goodwin had described George D'Wolf as "the Prince of the Place." "I should be ungrateful," he wrote, "if I forgot Genl George DWolf and Family after receiving the kind treatment while in this place." Now, years later and perhaps fearing both a breakdown in discipline and resistance from the Africans, Goodwin "prevail[ed] upon G.B.D.Wolf to return home" for days. Based on the stockpile of arms in his personal quarters, which included "two Blunderbusses[,] two pair[s] of Pistols, two Broad Swords, Plenty of Chain and round shot, together with 4 Canisters of Powder and fixed am[m]unition," Goodwin was well aware of the danger. But there was no revolt, and when George D'Wolf did eventually leave, he took "a Black girl by the name of Jane" with him to Havana, "bound to the United States." "I shall go on," Goodwin wrote after D'Wolf and his entourage departed, "friend or no friend." When D'Wolf left, Goodwin's attention returned to coffee, sugar and walls. And it paid off: By August 1825, Joseph Goodwin—a native of Hudson, New York—was purchasing newly arrived enslaved Africans for himself.[17]

Back in the Matanzas region—just before the uprising—Joseph "José" O. Wilson of the San Juan estate was invited to attend the marriage of Stephen Fales's daughter Mary to a man named James William Brown. Amid the wedding celebrations, another supervisor of the Mount Hope, Asa Anthony, worried about the prolonged absence of an enslaved woman named Ines, who had been sent on an errand over one month earlier. In a move suggestive of the uncomfortable mobility American planters were forced to allow enslaved people in Cuba, Anthony wondered if he should "send to the Havana to inquire for her?" Although it is impossible to know if Ines knew of the Africans conspiring to revolt, Spanish authorities certainly feared African information networks, which crisscrossed plantation walls. Because of their growing influence in the Cuban slave regime, U.S. citizens found themselves at the center of these Atlantic circuits.[18]

In the aftermath of the 1825 Guamacaro Revolt, as Joseph Wilson's wife Sarah later reported, free blacks from the surrounding neighborhoods would also be summarily "shot as being principals in this affair." It is difficult to know if Sarah expected such violence before arriving at the San Juan plantation in July 1818. On reaching the cafetal, she was reasonably satisfied that her family would "be comfortable & look at least as well as our neighbours." But she also acknowledged the extreme mortality surrounding her new home: "We have buried three children," she wrote, "but they had long been weakly." Her inability to speak Spanish and lack of "female society" drove Sarah to supervise the construction of a plantation hospital, which she came to resent. "Negroes," she wrote, "are such miserable beings, wild and—everything thats bad." Even more frustrating for her, those few Africans who she deemed "*valuable good,*" died just as frequently as the others. As Sarah tended to the hospital and sewed clothing for her children, she found time to write for the comforts of home, asking for hair combs, "an Iron Griddle for baking," "neck kerchiefs" and "nice riding whips," as "it is always necessary to keep our horses harness in order in this country." Horses, like dogs, were an essential component of control in the Cuban slave plantation, and Americans always rode armed. In the 1820s, as enslaved Africans died around her, Sarah Wilson wrote to her friend John D'Wolf—the brother of James—for more goods from New England: "I am sorry," she said, "to give you so much trouble for shoes."[19]

From food to furniture to clothing, Northerners in Cuba tried to stock their plantation manors with all the comforts of home. Along with items typical of the New England–Caribbean circuit—such as "flour," "beef" and "new hhds"—the *Cashier,* for example, sailed from

Rhode Island to Cuba in 1819 with accounting books, "Pens" and two types of chairs, "Fancy" and "Windsor." In addition to typical cargoes, American ships routinely entered Havana in the early 1820s with tables, cotton, clothing and paper, some of which had no doubt been personally requested by Americans already living on the island. In fact, after the Guamacaro Revolt, Sarah Wilson noted that Stephen Fales's wife recognized an African man as a "slave of Armitage" when "a handkerchief was found with him marked with Mr. A's name," condemning the African with an article of clothing his dead owner may have requested from the United States.[20]

In the immediate aftermath of the insurrection, Americans in Cuba welcomed the hardening of disciplinary lines on the plantations. Four days after the Guamacaro Revolt, on June 19, 1825, Joseph Wilson wrote from San Juan that although some were suspicious of the Africans on his estate, he had overheard his slaves "say those negros were fools and would all be killed by the Spaniards." Still, Wilson was worried. "I am in want of six blunderbusses for the use of the plantation" from Matanzas or Havana, at any price. A week later, Wilson repeated the request, specifying that he did not want pistols: The larger, more deadly blunderbusses were necessary to prepare for an attack "of the kind they have had lately in the other neighborhood." Wilson hoped that the recent executions by the Spanish of enslaved and free blacks would "be a strong lesson"—not to the enslaved, but "to all of us to be on our guard," adding that "such things take place in all slave holding countries." In this telling reflection, Wilson did not reconsider the violence of the Cuban regime or his participation in it; instead, he suggested armed preemptive measures. Wilson, like other New Englanders, had no illusions. His home was at the center of a slave labor camp—manageable only through the use of extreme violence—and he knew it.[21]

Similarly, at the Mount Hope, Stephen Fales was happy to report on June 21, 1825, that his "Negroes [were] perfectly contented and submissive." On the day of the insurrection, the enslaved Africans under his supervision had been "unconscious of what was going on" thanks to the plantation's location, which was "retired from the main road." If the "insurgents" had reached the estate, Fales had "no doubt our names would have been added to the 'Killed.'" Now, the Spanish issued orders that any Africans discovered in "the woods" should be killed on sight, and when the militia publicly executed, mutilated and burned suspected African "insurgents," even Stephen Fales was disturbed at the "shocking scene to see the dead beside the road" that had "been burnt" and left "in such a state that it was impossible to bury them." The Spanish blamed the revolt, in part, on the permissiveness of foreign planters, and they intended to set an example for the enslaved.[22]

At the Santa Ana plantation, however, this conflicted with the interests of American investors, who sought to protect their slaves just as they would any other highly capitalized investment. After the insurrection, six Africans from the estate had been killed in the fighting, and another six were imprisoned at Matanzas, awaiting sentencing. The Northern plantation administrator, S. A. Rainey—who had narrowly escaped on June 15—now struggled to convince the Spanish that "twelve [dead] would be a sufficient example" and to "have as few arrests as pos[s]ible." Even as rumors of new slave plots circulated, Rainey "secreted and protected" many of the Santa Ana's workers "who were engaged" in the Guamacaro insurrection. "Be assured," he wrote to both his cousin Ebenezer William Sage in Boston and to the estate's New York investor, N. Talcott, "everything that can be done for your Interest shall not be neglected." Sage's brother-in-law, the fellow Connecticut native and manager of the nearby Ontario estate Ephron Webster, was shocked that planters would protect their guilty slaves for pecuniary interests, rather than see them hanged. And after five of the six captured Santa Ana Africans—Felix, Isidro, Gregorio, Caitano and Ramon—were executed, Webster wrote simply that they "are now on the Estate in front." In Boston, Sage knew what Webster meant; Rainey had already told him. "According to the sentence," Rainey wrote Sage, "the Head and hands were cut off and nailed on posts or trees on the places of their former abode. The Head of Felix I had put … near the Negro Hog Pens." Even as Rainey continued to lobby the Spanish to save the valuable lives of African laborers for their owners in the U.S. North, he dutifully nailed the rotting heads and hands of these five African men to trees and poles on the Santa Ana grounds.[23]

Such graphic displays were only the beginning. After the Guamacaro Revolt, Matanzas province became even more heavily militarized. As

at the Buena Esperanza and Arc de Noe, walls were common in many
Cuban slave plantations, but after the 1825 insurrection, the governor
of Matanzas province issued new security regulations to enforce the
practice, requiring owners of estates with enslaved laborers to "build
fencing or a palisade around the [slave] houses" between 3.4 and 4.25
meters high. By January 1826, Americans such as Stephen Fales could
happily report that "most of the Negroes concerned [in the insurrection]
are either executed or under sentence," and the planters were "in complete readiness" to prevent another uprising. The Spanish also required
planters to send half of their enslaved laborers two days each month
to construct roads, and in April 1826 a road was completed, linking
Matanzas with Camarioca, to allow for an even more rapid response
from Spanish dragoons. That same month, Sarah Wilson remarked that
"ten ['little negroes'] have died [of disease] within the last month and
eight of them within the last week." "I assure you," she wrote, "it is very
painful to see the little things that have been raised under my own eyes
suffer as they have done." A middle-class woman from New England,
Sarah might have thought to question her place in the Cuban slave plantation, but she did not. By November 1826, she wrote of happiness, not
death, and, throughout the 1820s and early 1830s—when a cholera
epidemic would kill Africans faster than they could be buried—Sarah
continued to urge her husband to protect his Cuban investments.[24]

By February 1828, when the Massachusetts reverend Abiel Abbot
arrived in Cuba, New Englanders were comfortably armed. On a tour
that began and ended with Boston expatriates—from George Bartlett's
La Carolina plantation near Matanzas to Nathaniel Fellowes's Reserva,
Fundador and Pequena Cabana plantations outside Havana—Abiel
Abbot witnessed a sustained Northern presence in the Cuban slave
regime.[25] He documented Northern-owned slave plantations, describing a "fine square of negro huts or boheas" surrounded by walls that
rose "ten feet high." He noted that the enslaved were engaged in "a great
extent of wall building" to create a "beautiful and permanent fence."
He alluded to constant security measures to prevent slave "thieving and
conspiracy" and the use of "dogs, the lash, and sometimes the punishment of death." After a recent visit to South Carolina, Abbot praised
the brutality of the gang system on American plantations in Cuba as far

superior and suggested that the enslaved Africans in Cuba "accomplish one third more labor than the tasked slaves of Carolina." From "daybreak," he wrote, "they labor till the light is gone, and renew it on some plantations, by the light of the moon or stars, or a blazing fire." Driven by the whip, Africans worked silently, "and it is confidently said," Abbot wrote, "that on estates there is a loss of from 10 to 15 per cent of their laborers each year."[26] He dutifully reported on the escalating punishment system employed at the American Lemonal plantation, noting that discipline was meted out by the whip in increments of three lashes, twenty-five lashes, and two hundred lashes. As he left the grounds, Abbot "heard the snap of the lash, but no other noise." A half mile down the road, he "heard ten lashes more."[27]

In Abbot's estimation, such violence paid off. Near the Buena Esperanza, where Joseph Goodwin may have still been employed, Abbot wrote, "Plantations of coffee, beautifully laid out and neatly cultivated are almost continuous, and the eye of the traveller is constantly delighted with the finest specimens of agriculture." This was the direct result of Goodwin's brutality, and in 1828 a New England reverend reveled in the wealth it created.[28]

On the Spanish island, U.S. planters had taken the Guamacaro Revolt to heart. They well knew that the Africans on their plantations were ready to resist, whether through marronage, suicide, insurrection or more covert methods. Despite increased security, for example, there were hundreds of reported acts of violence by the enslaved after 1825 in Matanzas province alone. It is hardly surprising then that by the time of Mary Gardner Lowell's visit to American-owned Cuban plantations in 1831–2, the 1825 Guamacaro Revolt had become a cautionary tale on the island. A woman from the same elite Northern families typically associated with shipping, industry and finance in the early United States, Mary Gardner Lowell saw another side of their commercial empires and became well acquainted with the reality of Cuban slave labor. "It is a rare thing," she noted, "to see an old negro."[29]

Lowell learned the history of the 1825 Guamacaro Revolt from the wife of Connecticut native Ebenezer William Sage, who suggested that the revolt "began on the estate of Mr. Armitage" precisely because the Armitage family "were extremely indulgent to their blacks & had not the least suspicion of danger." Guamacaro did not lead Sage to reconsider the brutality of his Santa Ana and Ontario plantations, but to follow Spanish planters in embracing increased militarization and violence. As Joseph Wilson and the Spanish authorities had suggested, the revolt was interpreted as the natural result of *leniency*, not oppression. Ebenezer William Sage responded not with thoughts of humanity, but with dogs and guns. By 1832, Sage's paranoia about his enslaved laborers led him to ban household slaves from his home at night, and he regularly beat enslaved children if they were found too near the stone, single-story house. Like Goodwin, Sage slept with "two or three pairs of pistols, guns & swords." Even his house "itself [was] a sort of castle," situated on a hill overlooking the fields and surrounded by "noisy dogs" that were "very savage." Here too, the Africans were forced to build stone walls as armed guards looked on. By the time of Mary's visit, however, the mounted skulls and hands seem to have been taken down.[30]

In Cuba, Americans from the U.S. North and their Spanish auxiliaries peered down open avenues with dogs and guns as enslaved Africans labored, surrounded by tall hedges or walls. Although nineteenth-century, American-owned Cuban plantations have tended to elude scholars, contemporaries were well aware of them. In his famous 1841 *Amistad* defense, for example, John Quincy Adams acknowledged the interests of "American citizens who own plantations in the island of Cuba, which they cultivate by the labor of slaves." That many of these U.S. planters were also Northerners went unsaid, and with good reason, as these plantations would persist throughout the century. The behavior of Cuban planters and administrators from the U.S. North complicates both national and sectional formulations of American slavery. It suggests that the capitalism of the U.S. North and Caribbean slavery were interdependent, not merely in the push-and-pull of "trade" but in the ease with which Northerners changed their names and raised the Cuban whip. The brutality of the Northern response in Cuba demonstrates how readily the logic of the Caribbean slave regime impacted transnational cultural sensibilities. The moral geographies of the U.S.–Cuban Atlantic World were as malleable as the trade routes they followed. Trading factories and counting houses for ingenios and cafetales, Northerners became untroubled planters and administrators in the heart of the Caribbean.

"One child died this morning," New Yorker Joseph Goodwin wrote tersely in 1822, "all han[d]s trimming coffee and carrying stone, pleasant day, cold night." And, as Africans were worked to death around her a year later, Sarah Wilson urged a friend in Rhode Island to visit: A trip to Cuba "would do you good," she wrote without irony, "why it would take fifteen years off." She, like many Americans from the U.S. North, was at home among the dead.[31]

CONCLUSION

Illegal Slave Trade, American Empire

At the age of nine, Herman Melville spent the summer of 1828 with his aunt Mary in Bristol, Rhode Island. Her husband, John D'Wolf II, was away at the time, but Uncle D'Wolf visited Melville in New York over Christmas and New Year's Eve. The encounter made a strong impression on the young boy, and, as Melville later put it, D'Wolf was "the first sea captain I had ever seen."[1] In his visit over the holidays, Uncle D'Wolf likely regaled the boy with stories of his voyages to Russia and may even have recounted the time that his ship slammed into the side of a giant whale that "was like striking a rock."[2]

By the time Melville published *Moby-Dick* in 1851, the post-revolutionary '15ers had passed on. Growing up in New England, Herman Melville's generation had listened to the stories of these "white haired" old men all their lives and imagined the daring, adventurous world they must have inhabited when the country was young, before it prepared to tear itself apart over North American slavery. That this imagined seafaring past bore little resemblance to the desperation and brutality of the saltwater carrying trade was beside the point. In the years after the '15ers passed on, their lives became mythologized. This was particularly true for the elites. In the U.S. North, many of the wealthiest families of the nineteenth century could trace the origins of their fortunes to seafaring in the first decades of the 1800s. Exactly how ancestral ship captains had made their money was often vague or obscured, as the moral distinctions of the 1820s and 1830s helped to clarify the winners and losers of the "market revolution." The North

American slave frontier expanded and eastern cities grew rapidly, dislocating thousands of workers and casting immense uncertainty on an industrializing economy. As workhouses replaced charities, members of a new middle class and capitalist elite claimed public space, remaking respectability and the private sphere for the sake of stability. By the 1830s, many of the white-haired ship captains from the post-revolutionary generation lay dead or dying, and in this new marketplace the persistence of money and power was simply equated with greatness.

The true origins of many of these fortunes were grounded in the illegal slave trade, gold, sugar and coffee found further south. The stories Herman Melville heard came from this world. Captain John D'Wolf II had been the first American to travel overland from Siberia to St. Petersburg, Russia, in an attempt to link the Pacific fur trade with the eastern Russia trade. He had traveled there on behalf of his uncle, James D'Wolf, in 1808—the same year that the United States had outlawed the slave trade and one year before John Quincy Adams would arrive to protect the commodities it continued to generate. This is how many old seafaring fortunes were made and protected: with ruthless ingenuity.

By the late 1820s, elite Americans had successfully leveraged the apparatus of the U.S. state, including the navy and the formulation of the Monroe Doctrine, to protect their investments from foreign, primarily British, interference. The new informal American empire was based not on political or military domination, but on secondary resource extraction and economic influence within the Spanish empire. In Cuba, the Spanish administration not only funded the intensive militarization necessary to secure the island's slave plantations, but also encouraged the illegal slave trade that made the agro-industrial graveyard possible.

Many of the men who had been instrumental in the expansion of U.S.–Cuba trade in the first decades of the nineteenth century, from Alexander Everett to John Forbes and William Shaler, never forgot the island. When he became president in 1825, John Quincy Adams also remembered his friends. In 1809, Alexander Everett had witnessed the flow of Cuban sugar and coffee into the Baltic, and in April 1825 Adams sent his former legation secretary to the imperial center as U.S. consul to Spain. Unsurprisingly, the three "principal objects" that Secretary of State Henry Clay outlined for Everett's mission—piracy, commercial claims, and "Commerce in the Ports of Spain"—all centered on Cuba and the slave trade.[3] Years later, Everett would eventually travel to Cuba, where he met many of the same Americans—including Golden Dearth and John Morland—on whose behalf he had worked in Russia in his youth. By the time of Everett's arrival in Cuba in 1840, Morland was "an old gentleman between 60–70" years old and was "the acting Consul" in Havana.[4] Similarly, after John M. Forbes, who had worked in Copenhagen for U.S.–Cuban merchants during the Napoleonic Wars, secured a consular appointment to Buenos Aires, his brother James G. Forbes lobbied (unsuccessfully) to become the U.S. commercial agent at Havana.[5] Even William Shaler, who had been exiled from Cuba in 1811–12, returned to the Havana consulate later in life, where he was employed until his death in 1833.[6]

Meanwhile, Americans—many from the North—continued to immigrate to Cuba, often becoming naturalized Spanish citizens. By the late 1820s, many North Americans were well aware of the growing U.S. presence in Cuba and of the Spanish administration's continuing encouragement of "white" immigration. As the South pushed west, the North also pushed farther south—into Cuba. U.S. citizens and merchants such as thirty-six-year-old Nathaniel Johnson of Philadelphia, New Englander Nathaniel Clarke and Connecticut native and Matanzas trader Moses Gyron applied for Spanish naturalization papers (on October 11, 1824; November 12, 1824; and August 29, 1825, respectively). Some Americans—such as "José Harvis" of Hartford, Connecticut—had lived in Cuba for years: Harvis's application on January 12, 1829, certified that the twenty-eight-year-old had lived in Matanzas for sixteen years, where he had even been baptized.[7] Others, like Rhode Islander Joseph Corlis, viewed 1820s Cuba as a potentially lucrative alternative to traditional routes of North American expansion. "Finding nothing to do at Tallahassee," he wrote his brother John in January 1825, "I intend to try my fortune at Cuba" with the help of "letters of introduction ... to some of the first people in Cuba." "At Matanzas," Corlis planned to check in with "W[illia]m Bowen" and then "go immediately to W[illiam] Jencks['s] plantation & get into employment as soon as possible."[8]

Many American expatriates in Cuba were identified as merchants, but in the 1820s, growing numbers—including twenty-nine-year-old

"Herrique Hopeful" in February 15, 1820, and twenty-six-year-old "Carlos Pedro de Butien" on December 10, 1825—were also termed "agriculturalists" and "farmers."[9] The Spanish encouragement of "white" immigration to Cuba had never been *only* about encouraging foreign investment. From the time of Francisco de Arango's 1790s ruminations on Cuba's future, North American and European immigration had always been framed in racial terms as a contrast to Haiti: Eventually, "white" immigrants were intended to balance out the overwhelmingly large numbers of enslaved African laborers and to prevent potentially revolutionary incidents like the 1812 Aponte Rebellion and the 1825 Guamacaro Revolt. This is precisely why less affluent "agriculturalists" and "farmers" were permitted into the country as the decades wore on.

Nor was "white" immigration from North America to Cuba confined to U.S. citizens. Although numerous French migrants from Haiti had been driven out of Cuba in 1808–9, after 1817 a number of French investors began to return. Many of their stories were typically Atlantic: The Frenchman Jules de Mun, for example, had been born in Saint Domingue and educated in France, and had fled Europe during the revolutionary purges of the 1790s. By then, however, Saint Domingue was in turmoil, and de Mun moved to Cuba, where he owned a cafetal from 1803–8 until he was exiled to the North American continent. Post-1808, de Mun followed the Mississippi River north of New Orleans and settled in St. Louis, where he invested in the fur trade until 1820, when he returned to Cuba.[10] As a U.S. agent at Santiago noted in July 1824, "The Agricultural importance of this district is gradually extending itself, and as that increases, its consequence is advanced to a corresponding extent in a commercial point of view. Emigrations from the state of Louisiana are of frequent occurrence." By 1824, this included not only planters like Jules de Mun but also "indigent individuals."[11] Rarely did this Atlantic population stay fixed. By 1830, de Mun had left Cuba and was on his way back to St. Louis.

"A Very Serious Plan to Combine and Enlarge the United States"

In the late 1820s, immigration to Cuba also took on an experimental, transnational corporate framework that has gone entirely unnoticed by historians. In March 1826, a group of American investors in New York proposed something novel: the creation of a corporate town called Moa near the port of Barracoa in northeast Cuba. The plan, "Report of the Committee of the Moa Land Company to the Board of Directors," which was published on April 17, 1826, was explicitly designed to encourage "white" American immigration to Cuba through land grants to U.S. farmers and merchants. In a unique legal move, the New York investors—led by President John Stearns—sought to create a town owned and operated by American citizens within a Spanish colony and governed by corporate rules, rather than U.S. or Spanish law.

Moa would be run by "Agents" of the company, who would not only "select the best location for a Town" in a space of 640 acres, with the center reserved "for a Market, Court-House, Church, and other public buildings," but who would also "set a price on the town lots and planta- tions" and "receive for their service fifteen per cent" on the sales. The organizers were ambitious and planned to erect sawmills, along with tra- ditional coffee, sugar and cotton plantations that would trade via regular convoys by way of nearby Barracoa. The company's laws, as written by "M. Myers," "D.P. Campbell" and "J.J. Boyd," would dictate the organi- zation and discipline of the township. "All differences arising between the settlers," the corporate proposal noted, "shall be settled by referees" and the company agents. "Should any settler behave disorderly," the board of directors of the company—not the Spanish or U.S. authorities—would be allowed to dispossess and remove the troublemaker.[12] Unfortunately for the U.S. investors, things would not go precisely as planned.

The Moa Company dispatched three agents to survey potential settle- ment sites, and by November 25, 1826, the Spanish governor of Barracoa had agreed to allow—in conjunction with the Spanish consul in New York—the dispatch of a group of "white" settlers for the island. That month, forty-six people, including men, women and children, boarded the U.S. ship *Revenge* for Cuba. Many of the new settlers were not U.S. citizens but newly arrived, predominantly Irish, immigrants.[13] Scholars of race and "whiteness" have long stressed the degree to which antebellum Irish immigrants to the United States were associated with other "racial types," particularly blacks, in major cities. From the late 1820s through the 1830s, for example, David Roediger suggests that Irish immigrants and

African Americans "lived side by side in the teeming slums of American cities," performed similar labor, and were typically "poor and often vilifed."[14] The socially constructed racial status of pre-famine Scotch-Irish immigrants to the United States was by no means fixed and was typically more "black" than "white." Ironically, the Moa Company of New York attracted a group of immigrants to settle Cuba—under a Spanish policy intended to encourage "white" immigration to the island—whose own racial status in the United States was much more ambiguous. For the Spanish, however, these immigrants were white enough.

Settlement did not proceed as smoothly as many had hoped it would, however, and in February 1827, the settlers petitioned the Spanish captain-general for assistance, swearing fidelity to the Spanish king and begging for military, medical and provisional assistance.[15] Meanwhile, in the United States, the Moa Company ran a campaign in the press to encourage further immigration to their colony. In April 1827, U.S. newspapers, including *The New-York Gazette* and Cincinnati's *Saturday Evening Chronicle*, advertised that "the *Company of Moa*" would be "patronized by the authorities of Cuba, and in conformity with a decree of the king of Spain, 'on the subject of increasing the *white* population of the Island of Cuba' [italics original]." Moreover, the settlement's explicit purpose was "to demonstrate by actual experiment that the land can be cultivated *without* the labor of *blacks*; and to set an example [italics original]" that might eventually replace the slave trade. "A number of settlers had arrived there," the papers announced and been "favorably received by the authorities at Barracoa."[16]

Although the Spanish captain-general had welcomed the settlers to Moa, other Spanish administrators were less enthusiastic. In July 1827, military officials in Barracoa eyed the "suspicious operations on the part of foreigners" in Moa and warned that the neighboring mountains had always been a haven for runaway Africans who had formed a sizeable maroon community. In August 1827, the military commander of Cuba submitted a report to the captain-general outlining what he perceived as an American plot in the colony:

> how delicate is the grand enterprise in the establishment of foreigners
> at Moa—is it not an element in an ambitious project of the American

government and a very serious plan to combine and enlarge the United States with the precious jewel of the Island of Cuba.[17]

Openly concerned about a U.S. annexationist plot in Moa—which, military officials pointed out, lacked Spanish settlers and a firm Catholic grounding—Spanish authorities in Barracoa worried that they would be unprepared if Americans used Moa as the staging point for a larger invasion of the island. By October 1827, the captain-general had issued guidelines to assimilate the new, non-Spanish colony, encouraging Spanish immigration and requiring the colonists to build a church—including a house for a parish priest—barracks, a military hospital and government quarters. A Virginian doctor living in Barracoa, "Santiago [James] Anderson," was tasked with medical issues. The colonists were also required to focus on sugarcane as their primary crop, suggesting that they had not enthusiastically embraced the rigors of Caribbean sugar cultivation common on Cuban plantations. But as the finances of the colony deteriorated in 1827–9, investors in the colony lobbied to become Spanish citizens and allow further North American immigration. As he had for three decades, Vincent Gray was instrumental in advocating in Havana for these Americans.[18]

By the end of the decade, more Americans were enticed to join the transnational corporate homestead experiment. On June 19, 1829, James Anderson lobbied the Spanish authorities for permission to settle in Moa as a naturalized Spanish citizen. Anderson had lived in Cuba since 1821, but he had only been in continual residence in Barracoa since 1825. He was two months short of the five years of residence required to become a naturalized Spanish citizen. Still, the Spanish authorities seem to have made an exception for the doctor. The following year, on April 23, 1830, the New Yorker "Andres Sheffield" applied to join him and increase the population of the small expatriate town.[19] From 1829 to 1831, while receiving regular provisions of meat, rice and flour, the colony struggled to conform to Spanish expectations. By the fall of 1831, a Spanish administrator, José Rodriguez Rubio, had been appointed to lead the colony, and in February 1832, fifty-four new Spanish colonists arrived from Teneriffe in the Spanish ship *Micaela*.

Soon after the colonists arrived, however, Moa came under attack.

As the military authorities had warned, maroons from the nearby jungle surrounded the village, and the governor of Barracoa dispatched a small company of ten soldiers with twenty rifles to help the settlers defend themselves. It was no use. The colonists abandoned the village, but Spanish authorities were not willing to give up so quickly, and in August 1832, a new, more defensible location was selected to give the American company another chance.[20] The investors' hopes do not seem to have been realized, however, and the transnational start-up village of Moa quickly faded in importance behind the booming illegal slave trade. The same year Moa collapsed, for example, more than fifteen thousand enslaved Africans arrived on the island.[21] U.S. plantations in Cuba would endure throughout the century; the Moa experiment would not.[22]

By the 1830s, many members of the generation of 1815 lay dead or dying, but for observers, the future of the world—and certainly of the U.S. economy—appeared to be naturally linked to the expansion of slavery across the Western Hemisphere. It was profitable and productive. In North America, technological improvements and innovations in violence produced record cotton crops. As scholars such as Edward Baptist and Mark Smith have demonstrated, there was nothing premodern or antiquated about the labor regimes of the U.S. South, and enslaved workers were compelled by the systematized crack of the lash and the regimented discipline of the clock to "slave" for the sake of U.S. and European markets.[23] In Cuba, the productivity of enslaved laborers continued to rise post-1830, outpacing both competing Caribbean sugar plantations and American and British manufacturers.[24] Meanwhile, the growth of the enslaved and free Afro-Creole population in Cuba actually stagnated in the 1830s and 1840s during a period of intense slave imports, as slaves were "productively" worked to death in the "agro-industrial graveyard."[25]

By 1830, Cuba had become the world's largest sugar producer, with 104,971 metric tons; by 1840, Cuban sugar production reached 161,248 metric tons; in 1850, it hit 294,952 metric tons. Significant American investment continued to promote coffee alongside sugar, until twin hurricanes devastated the island in 1846 and 1848.[26] Americans were now not only deeply embedded in Cuba, but they had also begun to reach farther south to the massive slave regime of Brazil. As Louis Pérez has demonstrated, these natural disasters were key to the decisive shift to sugar in Cuba, solidifying a specialization in world markets between Cuba (sugar) and Brazil (coffee).[27] As Dale Tomich argues, "by 1860, Matanzas had forty-four of the island's sixty-four fully mechanized [sugar] mills" and dominated "the island's sugar crop," going "from 25 percent in 1827 to 55 percent by mid-century."[28] In 1850, the United States accounted for 39 percent of Cuban trade and Spain accounted for 27 percent; by 1859, the U.S. share had risen to 48 percent; and by 1865, "the island exported 65 percent of its sugar to the United States and 3 percent to Spain."[29]

In these decades, the significance of U.S. investment increased rather than diminished in importance. In 1827, American merchants in Havana estimated that 87 percent of the 1,053 ships to arrive in port were American-owned,[30] and the U.S. trade with Cuba occupied a position rivaled only by U.S.–English trade. In the 1830s, Liverpool, London and Havre were the only three foreign cities to trade more heavily with New York City than Havana or Matanzas. And whereas Cuba represented just 7 percent of total New York foreign-trade tonnage, in other U.S. ports its share was much more significant. For both Boston and Philadelphia, just one foreign port—Liverpool (in the case of Boston, Liverpool was virtually identical to Havana)—occupied more shipping tonnage than Havana, Matanzas or Trinidad, Cuba. The percentage of the tonnage of foreign trade represented by Cuban trade in Boston and Philadelphia was 19.23 percent and 16.93 percent, respectively.[31]

Many elite Americans in Cuba, meanwhile, expanded the scope of their investments and became easier to track. Roland Ely's studies of U.S.–Cuban commerce and mercantile investment, for example, offer a much more detailed and comprehensive account of individual U.S. merchants' interests post-1828—and especially post-1840—than pre-1828.[32] Moreover, post-1828, in an era of North American expansion and dreams of continental empire, Americans increasingly began to treat Cuba as a part of their economic and cultural orbit. Travel narratives, histories and diaries—many published—became (relatively) commonplace.[33] Many of the elite American authors of these works came from families that invested in Cuba, not simply contemporaneously, but with legacies entangled in smuggling, the slave trade and U.S. foreign policy that extended back to the early years of the nineteenth century. Both Julia Ward Howe, who published *A Trip to Cuba* in 1860, and Samuel Hazard, who wrote *Cuba with Pen and Pencil* in 1873, were direct descendants of New Englanders who had owned and operated Cuban plantations since at least 1808.[34] The Samuel Hazard who visited Cuba in the 1870s was the namesake of the Samuel Hazard who had served as the U.S. consul to Archangel in 1811 to protect shipments of Cuban sugar and coffee into the Baltic during the Napoleonic Wars. The longevity of such familial ties was not "inevitable" but was instead the direct result of their ancestors' Cuban investments and use of the American state decades earlier to protect the intensification of these investments.

By 1833, for example, the New York Howland family invested not only in sugar and coffee plantations, but also in iron and copper mines, which would eventually combine to become the basis of the American Mining Company. Similarly, Hezekiah Bradford—whose New England family had invested with the D'Wolfs in slave plantations decades earlier—partnered with Thomas Smith to run the Compania de Minera near Cienfuegos.[35] The Atkins family—whose forebearer Zakariah Atkins had operated a slave trading house in Matanzas in 1808—would become the largest individual sugar planters in Cuba and major players in the American Sugar Refining Company, which, in 1900, handled 67 percent of the total sugar consumed in the United States.[36]

As Americans attempted to siphon and leverage the wealth flowing from slave ships, plantations and mines, the island's wealth rose dramatically. In the estimates of Roland Ely, the real incomes for planters and merchants in Cuba may have increased by as much as fifty times from 1790 to 1839.[37] American interests continued to create, as Louis Pérez suggests, "alternative financial structures like the Moa Company, new insurance systems, and additional shipping agencies" in Cuba, and "more and more, too, U.S. capital goods became vital factors in the expansion of industrial and transportation infrastructure of the island," including steamships, railroads and telegraph lines. By the 1840s, streetlamps in Havana and Matanzas glowed from American-made gasworks.[38] As some Americans longed to annex the island, telegraph lines crisscrossed the Cuban countryside in 1851, and by 1867—as the slave trade finally waned and Chinese contract laborers arrived—a submarine cable linked Cuba with Florida.[39] The first railroad in Latin America, built by the American Richard Cruger in 1834–8, connected Havana with Guines.[40] Although it would be another decade before railroad tracks were laid in Spain,[41] local, small-scale railroad lines were quickly incorporated into Cuban plantations, linking distant sugar fields with centralized mills and allowing the agro-industry to reach new levels of consolidation and production. Highly sophisticated estates now involved thousands of enslaved workers on grounds that covered thousands of acres.[42]

The illegal slave trade had become a fundamental, interlocking component in a global system of investment, credit and commerce. The rise of this trade was not inevitable. Instead, it was the result of the incorporation of the foreign policy apparatus of the Early Republic state—including diplomatic appointments and the dispatch and aggrandizement of the U.S. navy—into the service of the private trade networks of elite '15ers. Much of the Cuban plantation regime operated as a nineteenth-century Caribbean gulag: a heavily militarized system of slave camps that depended on a constant influx of enslaved Africans. That a pro-slavery, anti-British U.S. foreign policy could defend "free trade" in the Americas while encouraging the expansion of the Cuban slave regime and the illegal slave trade was not a contradiction. Instead, it represented a guarantor of circuits of global commodity and specie trade, linking the United States with Europe, Africa, the Americas and Asia. Although true annexationist ambitions would arise in the United States years later, in the earliest decades of the nineteenth century, the growth of informal American empire in Cuba depended on "status quo" Spanish rule. The Monroe Doctrine represented one of the most decisive enunciations of this foreign policy.

As the generation of 1815 passed away, the world they had created—a network of economic development built on Cuban slavery and the slave trade—endured. Although some of the elite '15ers had miscalculated or withdrawn their investments in Cuban slavery, many had not. The success of elite members of this generation in translating their financial investments into state influence and naturalizing their fortunes is evident in the celebratory accounts of their eventual worldly demise. As

Robert Dalzell has suggested, law, culture and financial power helped to justify and sustain the existence of the vast fortunes accumulated in these first turbulent decades of the nineteenth century.[43] When John Quincy Adams's old benefactor and ally William Gray died in 1825, he left an extensive estate worth approximately $900,000, not including more than $1 million he was owed in unpaid European claims. His antiquarian biographer and descendant Edward Gray eulogized Gray in a celebratory manner: "All through his life Mr. Gray worshipped truth, and made it a point that his word should be as good as his bond ... He had strong convictions and the courage to live up to them."[44] More recently, Frank Cassell described Samuel Smith's 1838 funeral procession as being composed of "thousands of plain citizens [who] spontaneously joined the procession. Unlike the others these people had no official reason to be present; only genuine sorrow and respect could explain their actions."[45] Indeed, the lives of the elites who had worked to protect the expansion of the U.S.–Cuba trade and the slave trade with the apparatus of the U.S. state have spawned an entire reverential historical genre.

George Howe's antiquarian account of James D'Wolf's 1837 death is more revealing. Although Howe was himself a descendant of D'Wolf, he could not easily ignore his predecessor's obvious and persistent links with the slave trade. James D'Wolf had been among the first American investors to arrive in Cuba, and he remained one of the most aggressive and unapologetic supporters of the slave regime as he rose from slave ship captain to U.S. senator. When D'Wolf died, he left an estate—which included Cuban plantations; lands and distilleries in Rhode Island, Maryland, Kentucky and Ohio; cotton mills; financial investments; and numerous ships—that was valued at more than $5 million, reportedly making him the second-richest person in the United States. In a memorable fable of "Captain Jim's" death in Bristol, Rhode Island, George Howe describes D'Wolf's last days as witnessed by one of his servants: Late in D'Wolf's life, a black coach rolled up to his mansion, and a well-dressed gentleman "in black, with silver shoe-buckles just like his own" asked for D'Wolf, but he was turned away. The gentleman returned a second time, pushed inside, and brought out "Captain Jim." James D'Wolf said goodbye to his servants, climbed into the stranger's black coach, "and no one ever saw Captain Jim deWolf again, never."[46]

Acknowledgements

I owe a debt of gratitude to a great many people who made this project possible. First, thanks are due to all of those whose comments, suggestions, and advice helped to make this book stronger along the way, including Seth Rockman, Manuel Barcia, Robin Blackburn, Caitlin Annette Fitz, Jim Green, and Mike Vorenberg. Thanks also to my editor at Verso, Andy Hsiao, and to my agent, Peter Rubie.

A heartfelt thank you also to Douglas Cope, Jorge Flores, Elliot Gorn, Karl Jacoby, Tara Nummedal, Ethan Pollock, Amy Remensnyder, Joan Richards, and Vazira Zamindar. My colleagues have been a great source of support and inspiration. In particular, I'd like to thank Ryan Hayes Dowd, Jon Gentry, Michele Mericle, and Richard Wiebe. Thanks are also due to Will Brucher, Sara Fingal, Sonja Glaab, Danny Loss, and Theresa Williams.

Thanks also to the numerous participants at the 2011 Slavery's Capitalism conference, where I presented a draft selection from this project. And I would be remiss if I did not thank the knowledgeable staff and archivists at numerous institutions. In particular, I would like to begin by thanking the Rhode Island Historical Society, the Bristol Historical Society, the John Hay Library and the Rockefeller Library at Brown University, and the John Carter Brown Library. Farther north, I'd like to thank the staff of the Massachusetts Historical Society, the Baker Library at Harvard Business School, the National Archives and Records Administration in Waltham, the Phillips Library, Peabody-Essex Museum in Salem, and the New Hampshire Historical Society.

Down the coast, I owe thanks to institutions from New Haven to Miami: the Beinecke Library at Yale University, the New York Public Library, the U.S. National Archives and Library of Congress in Washington, D.C., and the Cuban Heritage Collection (with their amazing reading room) at the University of Miami. Thanks also to the staff at the Filson Historical Society in Louisville, Kentucky.

For the Cuba leg of this project, I owe deep gratitude to Adrián López-Denis and Evelyn Pérez, without whom this simply would not have been possible. Special thanks also to the staff at the Archivo Nacional de Cuba and at the Rare Books Collection at the University of Havana Library. This project has benefited from the generous support of Brown University, the John Carter Brown Library, the Filson Historical Society, and the Cuban Heritage Collection at the University of Miami. Overdue thanks are due to my family, for all of their constant support, including my parents, younger brother, Daniel, and brother-in-law, Jesse Freeman. Most of all, thank you to my children, Ellie and William, and to my patient wife, Ceceley: this is dedicated to you.

Notes

Abbreviations

AAS	American Antiquarian Society, Worcester, MA.
AGI	Archivo General de Indias, Seville, Spain.
ANC	Archivo Nacional de Cuba, Havana, Cuba.
ASP-C&N	American State Papers, Commerce and Navigation.
ASP-Fi	American State Papers, Finance.
ASP-FR	American State Papers, Foreign Relations.
ASP-NA	American State Papers, Naval Affairs.
BHS	Bristol Historical Society, Bristol, RI.
CHC	Cuban Heritage Collection, University of Miami, Miami, FL.
DNA	National Archives, Washington, D.C.
FHS	Filson Historical Society, Louisville, KY.
HAY	John Hay Library, Brown University, Providence, RI.
HBS	Baker Library, Harvard Business School, Boston, MA.
HFA	Harvard University Fine Arts Library, Cambridge, MA.
JCB	John Carter Brown Library, Providence, RI.
LOC	Library of Congress, Washington, D.C.
LSU	Special Collections, Louisiana State University, Baton Rouge, LA.
MHS	Massachusetts Historical Society, Boston, MA.
NARA-MA	National Archives and Records Administration, Waltham, MA.
NHHS	New Hampshire Historical Society, Concord, NH.
NYHS	New York Historical Society, New York, NY.
NYPL	Special Collections, New York Public Library, New York, NY.
PEM	Phillips Library, Peabody-Essex Museum, Salem, MA.
RIHS	Rhode Island Historical Society, Providence, RI.
UHL	University of Havana, Rare Books Library, Havana, Cuba.
YALE	Beinecke Library, Yale University, New Haven, CT.

Introduction

1 John Quincy Adams, April 7, 1822, in *Memoirs of John Quincy Adams*, Vol. V (Philadelphia: J. B. Lippincott & Co., 1875), 486.

2 "It gives me Pleasure to inform our Bristol friends Capt. J[ohn] Smith & G[eorge] DW[olf] in Particular that the Secty of State Mr. Adams has just told me that I may be perfectly easy about the English making any attempt to git [sic] possession of Cuba, that he has an oficial [sic] promise that no such intention exists which to me is quite consoling and have no doubt it will be so to all our friends who have such Deep Interest in that Island." James D'Wolf (Washington) to John D'Wolf (Bristol), February 6, 1823, Box 9, Folder 2, D'Wolf Papers, BHS.

3 "Letter from John Adams to Abigail Adams, 3 July 1776, 'Had a Declaration ...,'" Adams Family Papers, MHS.

4 James D'Wolf (Washington) to John D'Wolf (Bristol), February 9, 1825, Box 9, Folder 9, D'Wolf Papers, BHS.

5 James D'Wolf (Washington) to John D'Wolf (Bristol), February 25, 1822, Box 8, Folder 28, D'Wolf Papers, BHS. Similarly, D'Wolf wrote in March 1824 in reaction to Barnabas Bates's potential renomination as port collector in Bristol, that "Bates name will be sent into the Senate & I have not much hope of stoping him from being reappointed, if we had half a man for Presdt he would not be sent in but when you have an old woman to deal with you can not calculate what will be done." James D'Wolf (Washington) to John D'Wolf (Bristol), March 14, 1824, Box 9, Folder 7, D'Wolf Papers, BHS.

6 Marcus Rediker, *The Slave Ship* (Viking: New York, 2007).

7 *Hampden Federalist & Public Journal* (Springfield, MA), November 29, 1820.

8 *Village Record, or Chester and Delaware Federalist* (West Chester, PA), November 22, 1820.

9 "After [James D'Wolf's] election, but before he took his seat in the Senate, William Smith of South Carolina charged that of the fifty-nine Rhode Island vessels carrying slaves to Charleston between 1800 and 1804 ten had belonged to DeWolf." Elizabeth Donnan, *Documents Illustrative of the Slave Trade in America*, Vol. III (Washington, D.C.: Carnegie Institution of Washington, 1930–35), 380.

10 David Eltis and David Richardson, *Atlas of the Transatlantic Slave Trade* (New York: Yale University Press, 2010).

11 Christopher Kingston, "Marine Insurance in Britain and America, 1720–1844: A Comparative Institutional Analysis," March 24, 2005, 21. Marine insurance provides an example of a trade that creatively leveraged these investments. Marine insurance funds often acted as a de facto loan, because many policies did not have to be paid, as Glenn Crothers suggests, until "six months *after* the policy had been written, enabling merchants to use the money they earned from the voyage to pay for insurance." Glenn Crothers, "Commercial Risk and Capital Formation in Early America: Virginia Merchants and the Rise of American Marine Insurance, 1750–1815," *Business History Review* 78 (Winter 2004): 629–30.

12 See Herman Kross and Martin Blyn, *A History of Financial Intermediaries* (New York, 1971); Holger Engberg, "Capital Formation and Economic Development: The Role

of Financial Institutions and Markets," in Bernard Wasow and Raymond Hill, eds., *The Insurance Industry in Economic Development* (New York: New York University Press, 1986); Howard Bodenhorn, *A History of Banking in Antebellum America: Financial Markets and Economic Development in an Era of Nation-Building* (New York: Cambridge University Press, 2000); Robert E. Wright, *Origins of Commercial Banking in America, 1750–1800* (Landham, MD: Rowman & Littlefield, 2001).

13   James Fichter, *So Great A Profit: How the East Indies Trade Transformed Anglo-American Capitalism* (Cambridge, MA: Harvard University Press, 2010), 112–13. "Banks lent to the same clubby group of family members, business associates, and old partners whom they trusted and with whom they had long done business as merchants. These men were, as the Massachusetts Bank reported in 1792, 'opulent Merchants of extensive business and credit, but a small part of whose property is in the funds of the Bank.' 'Insider lending' provided a means for merchants to monitor each other ... The only loans that passed were those in which the applicant was a friend or family member of a director, or a bank director himself, in which case it was wise for the other directors to vote yes lest their own loans be shot down." James Fichter, *So Great A Profit*, 263.

14   Robert Dalzell, *Enterprising Elite: The Boston Associates and the World They Made* (Cambridge, MA: Harvard University Press, 1987), 4.

15   One of the most cited works on sugar's role in capitalist systems of exchange and social production is Sidney W. Mintz, *Sweetness and Power: The Place of Sugar in Modern History* (New York: Viking, 1985); see also Stuart Schwartz, *Sugar Plantations in the Formation of the Brazilian Society: Bahia, 1550–1835* (Cambridge, New York: Cambridge University Press, 1985); Dale Tomich, *Slavery in the Circuit of Sugar: Martinique and the World Economy, 1830–1848* (Baltimore: Johns Hopkins University Press, 1990); John F. Richards, "Landscapes of Sugar in the Antilles," in *The Unending Frontier: An Environmental History of the Early Modern World* (Berkeley, CA: University of California Press, 2003), 412–60.

16   Rediker, *The Slave Ship*.

17   James D'Wolf (Washington) to John D'Wolf (Bristol), March 19, 1824, Box 9, Folder 7, D'Wolf Papers, BHS.

18   See, for example, Frances Gregory, *Nathan Appleton: Merchant and Entrepreneur, 1779—1861* (Charlottesville: University of Virginia, 1975), 115. The business records of the D'Wolf financial empire, which constitute a major source for this study and which are housed at archives from New England to Washington, D.C., and Havana, are highly idiosyncratic, rather than systematic.

1   Smugglers

1   Ledyard Seymour to Thomas Jefferson, received January 8, 1802, *The Papers of Thomas Jefferson Digital Edition*, ed. Barbara B. Oberg and J. Jefferson Looney (Charlottesville: University of Virginia Press, Rotunda, 2008) [hereafter TJPD]. Interestingly, although I do not uniformly subscribe to a racial reading of the term *assassin* in its use in the

Cuban context, Jeremy Popkin has argued that the term was part of a rigid trope in writings on the Haitian revolution, in which black attackers were termed "assassins." The use of language in the revolutionary Caribbean to denote the perceived appropriateness of acts of violence in relation to racial categories demands further study. Jeremy Popkin, *Facing Revolution: Eyewitness Accounts of Haitian Insurrection* (Chicago: University of Chicago Press, 2007), 6–9.

2   "Between 1790 and 1867 over 780,000 African slaves were imported to Cuba, making the island the greatest slave-importing colony in the history of the Spanish empire and the center of the nineteenth-century slave trade to the Caribbean": Laird Bergad, *The Cuban Slave Market, 1790–1880* (New York: Cambridge University Press, 1995), 38–39, 51. See also Antonio Santamaría García and Alejandro García Alvarez, *Economia y colonia: la economía cubana y la relación con España, 1765–1902* (Madrid: CSIC, Instituto de Historia, Departamento de Historia de América, 2004), 79.

3   Louis Pérez, ed., *Impressions of Cuba in the Nineteenth Century* (Lanham, MD: Rowman & Littlefield Publishers, 1998), xii.

4   Laird Bergad, *Cuban Rural Society in the Nineteenth Century: The Social and Economic History of Monoculture in Matanzas* (Princeton, NJ: Princeton University Press, 1990), 27, 322, footnote 28.

5   Hugh Thomas, *Cuba: The Pursuit of Freedom* (New York: Harper and Row, 1971), 140–1. See also Louis Pérez, "Cuba and the United States: Origins and Antecedents of Relations, 1760s–1860s," in Louis Pérez, ed., *Cuban Studies 21* (Pittsburgh, PA: University of Pittsburgh Press, 1989), 77.

6   Louis Pérez, "Cuba and the United States," 71.

7   Robert Greenhalgh Albion, *Rise of New York Port, 1815–1860* (New York: C. Scribner's Sons, 1939), 182–3.

8   Moreno Fraginals, *The Sugarmill: The Socioeconomic Complex of Sugar in Cuba, 1760–1860* (New York: Monthly Review Press, 1976), 30. By comparison, total annual U.S. government expenditures in 1800 were approximately $11 million. Although exchange rates are notoriously difficult to assess in this period, the Spanish silver or gold peso served as the de facto currency of choice—both in the United States and globally—into the nineteenth century.

9   For example, the Spanish colonial state maintained historically low taxes on Cuban exports relative to other colonies: citing the work of John Coatsworth, Roger Betancourt suggests "that in 1800 Cuba had 8.325 dollars of export revenues for every tax dollar paid compared to Mexico's one dollar! Cuba's rate was the lowest of the six colonies" of Argentina, Brazil, Chile, Mexico, and Peru. Roger Betancourt, "Why Cuba Remained a Colony While Latin America Became Independent," University of Maryland and Development Research Center, 2011, econweb.umd.edu. See also John Coatsworth, "Economic and Institutional Trajectories in Nineteenth-Century Latin America," in John Coatsworth and Alan Taylor, eds., *Latin America and the World Economy since 1800* (Boston: Harvard University Press and David Rockefeller Center for Latin American Studies, 1998), 19–54.

10 See Herman Kross and Martin Blyn, *A History of Financial Intermediaries* (New York, 1971); Holger Engberg, "Capital Formation and Economic Development:

The Role of Financial Institutions and Markets," in Bernard Wasow and Raymond Hill, eds., *The Insurance Industry in Economic Development* (New York, 1986); Howard Bodenhorn, *A History of Banking in Antebellum America: Financial Markets and Economic Development in an Era of Nation-Building* (New York, 2000); Robert E. Wright, *Origins of Commercial Banking in America, 1750–1800* (Lanham, MD: Rowman & Littlefield Publishers, 2001).

11   James Fichter, *So Great A Profit: How the East Indies Trade Transformed Anglo-American Capitalism* (Cambridge, MA: Harvard University Press, 2010), 112–13.

12   Dale Tomich, *Through the Prism of Slavery* (Lanham, MD: Rowman & Littlefield Publishers, 2004), 63–4.

13   Barbara H. Stein and Stanley J. Stein, *Edge of Crisis: War and Trade in the Spanish Atlantic, 1789–1808* (Baltimore, MD: Johns Hopkins Press, 2009), 222.

14   See Linda Salvucci, "Development and Decline: The Port of Philadelphia and Spanish Imperial Markets, 1783–1823" (Ph.D. dissertation, Princeton University, 1985), 94–95.

15   Javier Cuenca Esteban, "Trends and Cycles in U.S. Trade with Spain and the Spanish Empire, 1790–1819," *Journal of Economic History* XLIV (June 1984): 540–1. See also Linda Salvucci, "Atlantic Intersections: Early American Commerce and the Rise of the Spanish West Indies (Cuba)," *Business History Review* 79 (Winter 2005): 806. In 1790, the "young United States" was notoriously indebted: Alexander Hamilton calculated that "the federal government owed $54 million, almost $12 million to foreigners; on top of that, he estimated individual states had debts that added up to $25 million. To put this in perspective, from 1784 to 1789, the Continental Congress was able to bring in only $4.6 million—and half of that was borrowed money." Simon Johnson, and James Kwak, *White House Burning* (New York: Random House, 2013), 15.

16   Citing Cuenca's extensive research, Linda Salvucci suggests that "gross government revenue on imports from the Spanish colonies often approached a fifth of total American customs receipts from merchandise" in the early decades of the nineteenth century ("Development and Decline," 43). In this same period, customs duties were the young United States's only reliable source of revenue. Stephen Budiansky, *Perilous Fight: America's Intrepid War with Britain on the High Seas, 1812–1815* (2011), 35. Republican political economy depended on this vibrant re-export trade and the formulation of a robust pro-slavery U.S. foreign policy to protect it. See Drew McCoy, *The Elusive Republic: Political Economy in Jeffersonian America* (Chapel Hill, NC: University of North Carolina Press, 1980); Paul A. Varg, *New England and Foreign Relations, 1789–1850* (Lebanon, NH: University Press of New England, 1983), and Henry Adams, History of the United States during the Administrations of Jefferson and Madison, Vol. III (New York, 1891).

17   I refer to this study as U.S. history in a transnational context because of the scope and premise of my argument. Like David Armitage's conception of a cis-Atlantic perspective, in which local elements are examined in relation to one another and to the Atlantic as a whole, I analyze the actions of historical actors from a perspective that takes both the national and transnational seriously as mutually informative, legitimate paradigms. See David Armitage, "Three Concepts of Atlantic History," in David

Armitage and Michael J. Braddick, eds., *The British Atlantic World, 1500–1800* (New York: Palgrave Macmillan, 2002), 11–27.

18 See also H.C. Prinsen Geerligs, *Cane Sugar and Its Manufacture* (London: N. Rodger, 1909); José A. Benitez, *Las Antillas: Colonización, Azúcar e Imperialismo* (Havana: Casa de las Americas, 1977), 47, 56.

19 José A. Benitez, Las Antillas, 47, 56); H.P. Davis, *The History of Haiti* (New York, 1929); Roland Ely, La Economia Cubana (Havana, 1961). See also Geerligs, *Cane Sugar and Its Manufacture.*

20 The total land devoted to sugar is taken from the estimated size of caballerías (33.16 acres) and the number 5,000 used by Moreno Fraginals, *The Sugarmill: The Socioeconomic Complex of Sugar in Cuba, 1760–1860* (New York: Monthly Review Press, 1976), 20–1. The total arable land in Cuba is approximately 13,910 square miles.

21 Louis Pérez, "Cuba and the United States," 65–6. The number of French planters from Haiti who arrived in Cuba after 1791 is unclear, and frequent estimates of 30,000 likely understate the migration. The exact composition and contours of French planter migration throughout the Atlantic world are difficult to track, as some French planters, after arriving in Cuba, continued on to Louisiana and other points in North America. Adding to the confusion, thousands of French migrants also arrived in Cuba from Louisiana after 1803 before being expelled again in 1808–9 following the Napoleonic invasion of Spain. The "white" population of Cuba increased dramatically in the 1790s and early 1800s, rising from approximately 133,559 in 1791 to 234,000 in 1804. Hugh Thomas, *Cuba*, 77; William R. Lux, "French Colonization in Cuba, 1791–1809," *The Americas* 29 (1972): 57–61.

22 U.S. imports of sugar from the French West Indies dropped by two-thirds from 9.3 million pounds (1790) to 3.1 million pounds (1799). *American State Papers, 1789–1809: Commerce and Navigation* (Washington, D.C.: GPO, 1832), 1: 37, 441.

23 Francisco de Arango, *Discurso sobre la agricultura de La Habana y medios de fomentarla* (1792); Free trade in slaves was allowed throughout the Spanish empire in 1789. Dale Tomich, "The Wealth of Empire: Francisco Arango y Parreno, Political Economy, and the Second Slavery in Cuba," *Comparative Studies in Society and History* 45 (January 2003): 4–28.

24 See Robert Paquette, *Sugar Is Made with Blood* (Middletown, CT: Wesleyan University Press, 1988).

25 Eric Williams, *From Columbus to Castro: The History of the Caribbean, 1492–1969* (New York: Harper & Row, 1970), 150–1; Seymour Drescher, *Econocide: British Slavery in the Era of Abolition* (Pittsburgh: University of Pittsburgh Press, 1977), 78–83.

26 Dale Tomich, *Through the Prism of Slavery*, 81–4; Leví Marrero, *Cuba: Economía y Sociedad, Azúcar, Ilustración y Conciencia, 1793–1868* (Madrid: Editorial Playor, 1983–1992), 149–51.

27 Douglas A. Irwin, "New Estimates of the Average Tariff of the United States, 1790–1820," *Journal of Economic History* 63 (June 2003): 506–13; "By 1800, over 40 percent of total U.S. imports were re-exported to other destinations." Douglas A. Irwin, "New Estimates of the Average Tariff of the United States, 1790–1820," 510. In 1797, the Committee of Ways and Means submitted a report to the U.S. House,

suggesting that high duties on goods such as brown sugar discouraged importation for domestic consumption and encouraged re-exportation, precisely because of the drawbacks (refunded port duties) merchants could claim in re-shipping abroad, rather than importing. American State Papers, Finance, Vol. 1, 493–4.

28 Charles Fenwick, *The Neutrality Laws of the United States* (Washington: Carnegie Endowment for International Peace, 1913), chapter 2; Richard Peters, ed., *Public Statutes at Large of the United States of America* (Boston: Charles C. Little and James Brown, 1845–6), 381–4, 520; David Head, "Sailing for Spanish America: The Atlantic Geopolitics of Foreign Privateering from the United States in the Early Republic" (Ph.D., University of Buffalo, 2009), 6.

29 Linda Salvucci, "Development and Decline," 87.

30 Louis Pérez, "Cuba and the United States," 63.

31 James Fichter, *So Great A Profit*, 112–13.

32 Drew McCoy, *The Elusive Republic: Political Economy in Jeffersonian America* (Chapel Hill: University of North Carolina Press, 1980), 166, Douglass North, *The Economic Growth of the United States* (Englewood Cliffs, N.J.: Prentice-Hall, 1961), 36–8, 221, 249.

33 Roger R. Betancourt, "Why Cuba Remained a Colony While Latin America Became Independent: Implications for the Current 'Transition,'" University of Maryland and Development Research Center, December 2011.

34 The *Hope* had recently sailed from New York to New Orleans before being seized by the French and sent to Cuba for trial. Hawley had then used his "personal interference." George C. Morton, November 18, 1795, Roll 1, Dispatches from U.S. Consul at Havana, DNA.

35 Daniel Hawley (New York) to Timothy Pickering (Philadelphia), April 18, 1799, Roll 1, Dispatches from U.S. Consul at Havana, DNA; George Cushing (Havana) to "Hond Uncle," August 20, 1800, George A. Cushing Letterbook, 1799–1802, Mss. 766, HBS.

36 George Cushing (Havana) to "Hond Uncle," August 20, 1800; George Cushing (Havana) to Samuel Parkman, October 30, 1800, George A. Cushing Letterbook, 1799–1802, Mss. 766, HBS.

37 George Cushing (Havana) to Samuel Parkman, October 30, 1800.

38 *Columbian Centinel* (Boston), June 27, 1801; January 26, 1811.

39 Henry Hill (Havana), November 1/10, 1805, Roll 1, Dispatches from U.S. Consul at Havana, DNA.

40 "Notes on John Morton," TJPD.

41 George Cushing (Havana) to "Hond Uncle," August 24, 1800; George Cushing (Havana) to Samuel Parkman, October 30, 1800.

42 John Morton (George Town, D.C.) to James Madison, June 4, 1801, Roll 1, Dispatches from U.S. Consul at Havana, DNA. Christopher Perry was the father of both Oliver H. Perry and Raymond Perry, who would marry James D'Wolf's daughter, Mary Ann, in 1814. Samuel Morrison, *"Old Bruin": Commodore Matthew C. Perry, 1794–1858* (London: Oxford University Press, 1968), 14–16, 54; John H. Schroeder, *Matthew Calbraith Perry: Antebellum Sailor and Diplomat* (Annapolis, MD: Naval Institute Press, 2001), 9–10.

43   By December, John Morton was back in Havana. Although Morton would resign
      from the consular office the following year, the brothers would remain active in
      Havana for years. See also John Morton to James Madison, June 4, 1801; John
      Morton (Ship Calliope, off Port-Penn, Delaware) to James Madison, October 30,
      1801; John Morton (Havana) to James Madison, December 11, 1801, Roll 1,
      Dispatches from U.S. Consul at Havana, DNA; Roy F. Nichols, "Trade Relations and
      the Establishment of the United States Consulates in Spanish America, 1779–1809,"
      Hispanic American Historical Review 13 (1933): 300–1; Palmer, *Stoddert's War: Naval
      Operations during the Quasi-War with France, 1798–1801* (Columbia, S.C.: University
      of South Carolina Press, 1987), 228–9. By early 1802, John Morton had had enough
      and resigned. He was replaced by the young Washington merchant Robert Young.
      James Madison (Department of State) to John Morton, April 7, 1802, J.C.A. Stagg,
      ed., *The Papers of James Madison Digital Edition* (Charlottesville: University of Virginia
      Press, Rotunda, 2010) [hereafter JMPD].
44   Drew McCoy, *The Elusive Republic*, 214–16.
45   James Madison (Washington) to Charles Pinckney; James Madison (Washington) to
      Marquis de Someruelos, January 19, 1804, JMPD. In 1789–93, John Hollins had
      owned the fourth largest shipping fleet by tonnage in Baltimore. Geoffrey Gilbert,
      "Maritime Enterprise in the New Republic: Investment in Baltimore Shipping, 1789–
      1793," *Business History Review* 58 (Spring 1984): 20.
46   Carlos Martinez de Yrujo (Washington) to James Madison, February 2, 1804, JMPD.
47   "Sobre futura provisión de harinas de los Estados Unidos consultada a doce com-
      erciantes de esta plaza," 1805, Junta de Fomento de la Isla de Cuba, Negociado de
      Comercio Legajo 79, Expediente 2819, ANC.
48   George A. Cushing to "Querido Amigo Pancho," August 10, 1802; George A. Cushing
      (Boston) to "Nat.," August 16, 1802, George A. Cushing Letterbook, 1799–1802,
      Mss. 766, HBS.
49   Linda Salvucci, "Development and Decline," 17.
50   H.L. Howard (Havana) to Elizabeth (Matthew) Wainwright, December 23, 1809,
      Box 4, Elizabeth (Matthew) Wainwright, 1803–11 (incoming correspondence),
      Wainwright Papers, NYPL. As late as 1812, the Spanish captain-general declared
      that American merchants only resided in Havana "by permission, and under cover
      of Spanish Houses, but they can be ordered away at any moment." Stephen Kingston
      (Havana) to James Monroe (Washington), July 10, 1812, Roll 2, Dispatches from
      U.S. Consul at Havana, DNA.
51   Josiah Blakeley (St. Jago) to James Madison (Washington), November 1, 1801, Roll
      1, Dispatches from U.S. Consul at Santiago, DNA.
52   Josiah Blakeley (St. Jago) to James Madison (Washington), December 26, 1801, Roll
      1, Dispatches from U.S. Consul at Santiago, DNA. See also American State Papers
      02, Foreign Relations, Vol. 2, 7th Congress, 1st Session Publication, No. 173.
53   Josiah Blakely (St. Jago) to James Madison (Washington), July 1, 1805, Roll 1,
      Dispatches from U.S. Consul at Santiago, DNA.

2   Lawyers

1   The following account is taken from numerous sources, including the *New York Commercial Advertiser* (New York), April 19, 1805; John Morton (Havana) to James Madison, April 26, 1805, Roll 1, Dispatches from U.S. Consul at Havana, DNA; and *New York Gazette and General Advertiser* (New York), May 17, 1805. Other American merchants who openly backed Gray were prominent men from Pennsylvania, Massachusetts and Rhode Island, including John Murdock, James Gorham, Edward Landers, Amos Green and J.B. Russel. James Gorham was a member of a prominent Massachusetts family with a presence in the U.S. Congress and links to D'Wolf. Amos Green was a Boston merchant, and Edward Landers was likely from Newport, Rhode Island. And while the Boston-Cuba merchant and planter Nathaniel Fellowes has already been discussed, the other men's identities are less certain. John Murdock may have been from Pennsylvania: a Margaret Murdock, listed as having attended a Moravian Seminary in Bethlehem, Pennsylvania, was the daughter of a John Murdock from Havana, Cuba. John Murdock would also be involved, along with Vincent Gray, in slave ship cases in the late 1810s and into the 1820s in the cases of the *Louisa*, *Merino*, and *Constitution*. On Amos Green see *Herald of the United States* (Warren, RI), March 7, 1807. On Edward Landers see *United States Chronicle* (Providence, RI), October 28, 1802; *The Newport Mercury* (Newport, RI), October 27, 1810; *The Newport Mercury* (Newport, RI), May 29, 1813; and *Rhode-Island American, and General Advertiser* (Providence, RI), October 12, 1819. On John Murdock, see William Cornelius Reichel and Joseph Mortimer Levering, *A History of the Moravian Seminary for Young Ladies: at Bethlehem, PA* (Bethlehem, PA: The Seminary, 1901), 385.

2   John Morton (Havana) to Vincent Gray, July 15, 1802, Roll 1, Dispatches from U.S. Consul at Havana, DNA.

3   Vincent Gray (Havana) to James Madison, March 2, 1803, Roll 1, Dispatches from U.S. Consul at Havana, DNA.

4   Vincent Gray (Havana) to Alexander Hamilton (New York), April 26, 1803, AHP.

5   Vincent Gray (Havana) to James Madison, January 14, 1805; Vincent Gray (Havana) to James Madison, January 14, 1805, Roll 1, Dispatches from U.S. Consul at Havana, DNA.

6   Vincent Gray (Havana) to James Madison, April 28, 1804 and May 8, 1804, Roll 1, Dispatches from U.S. Consul at Havana, DNA. Just months after sharing the home of an American slave trader in Havana, Humboldt would exclaim that the "abominable law that permits the importation of Negroes in South Carolina is a disgrace." Humboldt to William Thornton, June 20, 1804, in Moheit, 299–300.

7   "Citizens of one party to the treaty within the jurisdiction of the other would be made according to the order and authority of the law and … allowed to employ advocates." James Madison (Washington) to Vincent Gray, April 6, 1803, JMPD.

8   Vincent Gray (Havana) to James Madison, January 2, 1805, Roll 1, Dispatches from U.S. Consul at Havana, DNA.

9   Vincent Gray (Havana) to James Madison, January 14, 1805, Roll 1, Dispatches from U.S. Consul at Havana, DNA.

10   Josiah Blakely (St. Jago), September 30, 1805, in Andrew Hadley (St. Jago) to Henry Hill, October 15, 1805, Roll 1, Dispatches from U.S. Consul at Santiago, DNA.

11   Henry Hill (Havana), July 8, 1805, Roll 1, Dispatches from U.S. Consul at Havana, DNA.

12   Henry Hill (Havana) to James Madison, July 22, 1805, Roll 1, Dispatches from U.S. Consul at Havana, DNA.

13   Henry Hill (Washington) to James Madison, January 12, 1805, JMPD.

14   Josiah Blakely (St. Jago), September 30, 1805, in Andrew Hadley (St. Jago) to Henry Hill, October 15, 1805, Roll 1, Dispatches from U.S. Consul at Santiago, DNA; Henry Hill (Halifax, Nova Scotia) to James Madison, May 10, 1806, Roll 1, Dispatches from U.S. Consul at Havana, DNA.

15   Andrew Hadley (St. Jago), December 15, 1805; Andrew Hadley (St. Jago) to Henry Hill, October 15, 1805, Roll 1, Dispatches from U.S. Consul at Santiago, DNA.

16   J. Ramage (Havana) to Henry Hill, January 26, 1807, Roll 1, Dispatches from U.S. Consul at Havana, DNA.

17   Henry Hill (New York) to James Madison, February 27, 1807, Roll 1, Dispatches from U.S. Consul at Havana, DNA.

18   H.L. Howard (Havana) to Elizabeth (Matthew) Wainwright, December 23, 1809, Box 4, Elizabeth (Matthew) Wainwright, 1803–1811 (incoming correspondence), Wainwright Papers, NYPL.

19   James Anderson (Havana) to James Madison (Washington), January 11, 1808, Roll 2, Dispatches from United States Consul at Havana, DNA.

20   George A. Cushing (Havana) to Nathl Jones, April 10, 1800, George A. Cushing Letterbook, 1799–1802, Mss. 766, HBS.

21   The New England–Cuba merchant, Thomas Amory Coffin, for example, routinely charged a 5 percent commission fee, which he suggested was "the lowest that any undoubted Respectable House will transact Business for," and while "Spanish & Portuguese Houses make other advantages which would destroy the reputations of a Merchant here," Coffin claimed not to add miscellaneous charges to increase his pay. Thomas Amory Coffin to Andrew Thompson & Co., October 15, 1797, Letterbook 1, 1797–1798, Thomas Amory Coffin Papers, Mss 766, A524, HBS.

22   James Anderson (Havana) to James Madison (Washington), January 11, 1808, Roll 2, Dispatches from United States Consuls at Havana, DNA.

23   "Exp sobre la construccion de un muelle … de D. Juan Latin y D. Antonio Gleau," 1810, Real Consulado y Junta de Fomento, legajo 3285, ANC; Laird Bergad, *Cuban Rural Society in the Nineteenth Century: The Social and Economic History of Monoculture in Matanzas* (Princeton, N.J.: Princeton University Press, 1990), 27.

24   "Sobre animar la introducción del hielo de los Estados Unidos para bebidas frescas," 1801, Real Consulado y Junta de Fomento de la Isla de Cuba, Negociado de Comercio, Legajo 72, Expediente 357, 2793, ANC.

25   See Theodore Chase and Celeste Walker, "The Journal of James Savage and the Beginning of Frederic Tudor's Career in the Ice Trade," *Proceedings of the Massachusetts Historical Society*, Third Series, Vol. 97 (1985): 103–34.

26   "Sobre animar la introducción del hielo de los Estados Unidos," 1801.

27   See for example *Diario de la Habana* (Havana), November 1, 1820, April 7, 1821, February 28, 1822, and June 17, 1823, UHL.

28   Vincent Gray (Havana) to James Madison (Washington), December 15, 1808; William Shaler (Havana) to Robert Smith, February 3, 1811, Roll 2, Dispatches from U.S. Consul at Havana, DNA.

29   *Alexandria Daily Advertiser* (Alexandria, VA), March 13, 1807.

30   James Anderson (Havana) to James Madison, May 13, 1807, Roll 1, Dispatches from U.S. Consul at Havana, DNA.

31   Years earlier, in 1789–93, William Patterson already commanded the second-largest shipping fleet—by tonnage—in Baltimore. Geoffrey Gilbert, "Maritime Enterprise in the New Republic: Investment in Baltimore Shipping, 1789–1793," *Business History Review* 58 (Spring 1984): 20; Roy Nichols, "Trade Relations and the Establishment of the U.S. Consulates in Spanish America, 1779–1809," *Hispanic American Historical Review* 13 (August 1933): 310; George A. Cushing to "Querido Amigo Pancho," August 10, 1802; George A. Cushing (Boston) to Saml. Cabot (London), October 5, 1802, George A. Cushing Letterbook, 1799–1802, Mss. 766, HBS; George W. Erving (London) to James Madison, October 25, 1804, JMPD.

32   James Anderson (Havana) to James Madison, March 27, 1807, Roll 1, Dispatches from U.S. Consul at Havana, DNA.

33   In fact, by law (on March 22, 1794, and May 10, 1800), no ship could legally be built or outfitted in a U.S. port for the slave trade, and U.S. citizens were banned from serving as crewmembers or owning property on similar ships. Elizabeth Donnan, ed., *Documents Illustrative of the Slave Trade to America* (4 vols.; Washington, 1932), 3: 257–59, 337, 379.

34   Although Cushing considered sending the slave ship to Cuba—wondering "what are the Guinea prospects in the Havana?" and "will slaves be high during the peace?"—he ultimately chose the slave markets of Buenos Aires instead. Cushing's slave ship, the *Louisiana*, was eventually seized by the British in 1804. George A. Cushing (Boston) to Nathaniel Fellowes, June 3, 1802. See also George A. Cushing (Boston) to Willard Briggs, March 31, 1802, George A. Cushing Letterbook, 1799–1802, Mss. 766, HBS.

35   Leonard Marques, "Slave Trading in a New World: The Strategies of North American Slave Traders in the Age of Abolition," *Journal of the Early Republic* 32 (2012): 254.

36   Linda Salvucci, "Development and Decline," 96–8, 124.

37   James Fichter, *So Great A Profit: How the East Indies Trade Transformed Anglo-American Capitalism* (Cambridge, MA: Harvard University Press, 2010), 133–5.

38   James Anderson (Havana) to James Madison, March 27, 1807, Roll 2, Dispatches from U.S. Consul at Havana, DNA.

39   Thomas Amory Coffin to James Hunter & Co., September 27, 1797; Thomas Amory Coffin to James Deering, May 28, 1797, Letterbook 1, 1797–1798, Thomas Amory Coffin Papers, Mss 766, A524, HBS.

40   See Thomas Amory Coffin to Thomas Amory, June 29, 1798, July 8, 1798, Letterbook 1, 1797–1798, Thomas Amory Coffin Papers, Mss 766, A524, HBS.

41   Elbridge Gerry (Cambridge) to James Madison, November 9, 1801, JMPD. Like many elite merchants, Fellowes regularly coordinated his investments in the Cuba

trade with European trade. His ship *Genet*, for example, was seized by "British cruisers" en route from Amsterdam to Boston in 1800 with a cargo of "gin and iron." American State Papers 02, Foreign Relations Vol. 2, 6th Congress, 2nd Session, Publication No. 164.

42 "Expediente seguido por Nataniel Fellowes," 1807, Legajo 379, Expediente 16, ANC. See also *Proceedings of the Massachusetts Historical Society* (Boston: The Society, February 1906), 54.

43 William Shaler (Fundador Estate) to James Monroe (Washington), October 21, 1811; William Shaler (Havana) to James Monroe (Washington), November 13, 1811, Roll 2, Dispatches from U.S. Consul at Havana, DNA; *The Republican Spy* (Northampton, MA), May 20, 1806. This was the second death the younger Fellowes had faced in three years: in October 1803, his "consort," Julia Fellowes, had died en route from Charleston to Havana aboard the *Warren*. *New-England Repertory* (Newburyport, MA), October 19, 1803.

44 Nathaniel Fellowes (Havana) to Harrison Gray Otis, December 1, 1818, Roll 4, Harrison Gray Otis Papers, MHS; "Expediente seguido por Nataniel Fellowes," 1807, Legajo 379, Expediente 16, ANC. Fellowes also owned an additional $50,000 in property and investments in Massachusetts and Havana. *Proceedings of the Massachusetts Historical Society* (February 1906), 54.

45 *The Independent Chronicle* (Boston), July 31, 1806.

46 *New-York Spectator* (New York), January 17, 1810.

47 "Expediente seguido por Nataniel Fellowes," 1807, Legajo 379, Expediente 16, ANC.

48 Nathaniel Fellowes (Havana) to Harrison Gray Otis, September 8, 1808, Roll 4, Harrison Gray Otis Papers, MHS.

49 Karen Robert, *New Year in Cuba: Mary Gardner Lowell's Travel Diary, 1831–1832* (Boston: Massachusetts Historical Society: Northeastern University Press, 2003), 178–9.

50 Account Sheet, Betsy, Box 1, Folder 17, D'Wolf Papers, BHS.

51 Sabens may even have gone to sea on his first voyage as a cabin boy to James D'Wolf's brother, John. Sabens—Coffee Plantation Cuba—Agreement with J. Cataloguer [Joseph Catalogne], 1806, Box 12, Folder 10, D'Wolf Papers, BHS.

52 Sabens's estate was valued at $19,225.25. Estate Settlement, Box 12, Folder 29, D'Wolf Papers, BHS.

53 From 1814–18, for example, he would manage the Mary Ann cafetal, which was named after James D'Wolf's daughter; James D'Wolf (Bristol) to George Munro, November 2, 1818, Reel 9, Part 2, Papers of the American Slave Trade, RIHS.

54 "Dn. James D'Wolf contra Dn. Guillermo B. Bowen por pesos," 1816, Legajo 575, Expediente 6631, ANC.

3   Consuls

1 John Quincy Adams, *The Russian Memoirs of John Quincy Adams, His Diary from 1809 to 1814* (New York: Arno Press & The New York Times, 1970), 83; John

Quincy Adams (St. Petersburg) to Robert Smith (Washington), January 7, 1810, *The Writings of John Quincy Adams*, Vol. III, ed. Worthington Chauncy Ford (New York: Macmillan, 1914), 375–6.

2   So little sugar was produced domestically in the United States that Timothy Pitkin's *Statistical View of the Commerce of the United States* included sugar only as a foreign product of trade; sugar was imported into the United States (and re-exported), not exported from domestic production, as Adams had suggested. See also Alexander Everett (St. Petersburg) to Oliver Everett (Boston), December 13, 1809, Alexander Hill Everett Diaries, 1809–1841, Everett-Noble Papers, Massachusetts Historical Society, Boston.

3   See John Quincy Adams, *Russian Memoirs*, 175, 181–2, 263.

4   In an incisive study of tariffs and revenue, Douglas Irwin has demonstrated "that when re-exports are large, the tariff calculated with gross customs revenue can significantly overstate the actual tariff (adjusted for drawbacks)." Based on Irwin's calculations of the gap between gross customs revenue and net customs revenue, the period from 1797–1811 (notwithstanding a period from 1804–6) were consumed with the re-export trade, much of which increasingly centered on Cuban sugar and coffee. Douglas A. Irwin, "New Estimates of the Average Tariff of the United States, 1790–1820," *Journal of Economic History* 63 (June 2003): 507, 510.

5   The Napoleonic Wars were a positive boon for U.S. merchants invested in Cuba in the decade before Jefferson's embargo: by 1807, U.S. re-exports of sugar and coffee had risen from 1.1 million and 2.1 million in 1792 to 143 million and 42 million respectively. Alfred Crosby, Jr., *America, Russia, Hemp, and Napoleon: American Trade with Russia and the Baltic, 1783–1812* (Columbus, OH: Ohio State University Press, 1965), 74.

6   Two of the best studies of this moment on U.S.–Russia trade and foreign policy (both of which comparatively neglect the Cuba trade) are Alfred W. Crosby, Jr., *America, Russia, Hemp, and Napoleon* and David W. McFadden, "John Quincy Adams and Russia," *New England Quarterly* 66 (December 1993): 613–29.

7   Samuel Flagg Bemis, *John Quincy Adams and the Foundations of American Foreign Policy* (New York: Alfred A. Knopf, 1949); William Earl Weeks, *John Quincy Adams and the Creation of American Global Empire* (Lexington, KY: University Press of Kentucky, 1992); Bradford Perkins, *The Creation of a Republican Empire, 1776–1865* (New York: Cambridge University Press, 1993); William Earl Weeks, *Building the Continental Empire: American Expansion from the Revolution to the Civil War* (Chicago: Ivan V. Dee, 1996); Frank Lawrence Owsley, Jr., and Gene A. Smith, *Filibusters and Expansionists: Jeffersonian Manifest Destiny, 1800–1821* (Tuscaloosa: University of Alabama Press, 1997).

8   See Brian Loveman, *No Higher Law: American Foreign Policy and the Western Hemisphere since 1776* (Chapel Hill: University of North Carolina Press, 2010), 27.

9   See Levett Harris, "Exported from St. Petersburg in American Vessels Ao. 1805," Roll 1, Dispatches from U.S. Consul at St. Petersburg, DNA; Levett Harris, "Particulars of the Goods passed the Sound for the Baltic Markets in American Vessels from the 1st January to the 1st December 1811"; Levett Harris, "Statements as to the Baltick trade & Sound dues in the year 1811," Roll 2, Dispatches from U.S. Consul at St.

Petersburg, DNA; "List of American Vessels at Archangel, 1810," Joseph V. Bacon Memorandum Book, Ship. Mss 42, PEM.

10 This material is taken from a complete survey of 4,428 ship entrances and 3,771 ship clearances published in 210 issues of the *Boston Gazette* (Boston) from January 1, 1810, to January 2, 1812.

11 This material is taken from the Portsmouth, New Hampshire, Impost Books, 1810–1811; Salem, Massachusetts, Impost Books, 1810–1811; Newport, Rhode Island, Impost Books, 1810–1811; and Bristol-Warren, Rhode Island, Impost Books, 1810–1811, NARA-MA.

12 *New York Commercial Advertiser* (New York), February 6, 1810; John Quincy Adams (St. Petersburg) to Thomas Boyston Adams, October 11, 1810, *Writings of John Quincy Adams*, Vol. III, 521.

13 Peter T. Dalleo, "McKean Rodney: U.S. Consul in Cuba: The Havana Years, 1825–1829," *Delaware History* 22, No. 3 (1987), 204–5. See also William Barnes and John Morgan, *The Foreign Service of the United States* (Washington, D.C.: Historical Office, Bureau of Public Affairs, Dept. of State, 1961), and Thomas Bailey, *A Diplomatic History of the American People* (New York: Appleton–Century–Crofts, 1964).

14 *New York Commercial Advertiser* (New York), February 6, 1810; John Quincy Adams (St. Petersburg) to Thomas Boyston Adams, October 11, 1810.

15 Edward Gray, *William Gray of Salem* (Boston-New York: Houghton Mifflin Company, 1914), 26.

16 The stages in the complex national trade restrictions from 1807 to 1812 were succinctly summarized by Thomas Bailey as follows: 1) December 1807–March 1809: Embargo (against all nations); 2) March 1809–May 1810: Nonintercourse (England and France); 3) May 1810–March 1811: Macon's Bill Suspension; 4) March 1811–June 1812: Nonimportation (England only). Thomas Andrew Bailey, *A Diplomatic History of the American People*, 7th ed. (New York: Meredith Publishing Co, 1964), 134. See also Herbert Heaton, "Non-Importation, 1806–1812," *Journal of Economic History* 1 (1941): 178–98, and Donald R. Hickey, "American Trade Restrictions during the War of 1812," *Journal of American History* 68 (1981): 517–38.

17 See *Columbian Centinel* (Boston), April 3, 1813. For a comparison with other leading New England merchants who routinely employed hundreds of sailors, see Edward Gray, *William Gray of Salem*, 75–6.

18 Frank A. Cassell, *Merchant Congressman in the Young Republic: Samuel Smith of Maryland, 1752–1839* (Madison: University of Wisconsin Press, 1971), 138; Samuel Flagg Bemis, *John Quincy Adams and the Foundations of American Foreign Policy* (New York: Alfred A. Knopf, 1949), 154. In a compilation of the wealthiest Baltimore shipowners from 1789 to 1793, Geoffrey Gilbert suggests that Samuel Smith commanded the seventh largest shipping fleet in Baltimore, with fourteen vessels and 1,133 tons. Geoffrey Gilbert, "Maritime Enterprise in the New Republic: Investment in Baltimore Shipping, 1789–1793," *Business History Review* 58 (Spring 1984): 20.

19 Gray's support of the embargo was simultaneously a public affront to Massachusetts Federalists and a geopolitical gambit: Gray believed that English competition, not French privateers and trade restrictions, represented the greatest threat to his

commercial fortunes. For a survey of the dilemma of foreign relations in this period see Louis Martin Sears, *Jefferson and the Embargo* (Durham, NC: Duke University Press, 1927); Burton Spivak, *Jefferson's English Crisis: Commerce, Embargo, and the Republican Revolution* (Charlottesville: University Press of Virginia, 1979); Donald R. Hickey, *War of 1812: A Forgotten Conflict* (Urbana: University of Illinois Press, 1989).

20 William Bentley, September 10, 1797, and September 8, 1799, *The Diary of William Bentley, 1793–1802* (The Essex Institute, 1907), 282, 317; Edward Gray, *William Gray*, 24.

21 This estimate did not include Gray's extensive investments in banking, insurance, land and unrecorded overseas cargoes (which were alleged to be numerous). *Washington Federalist* (Georgetown, D.C.), September 10, 1808.

22 Treasury Reports, American State Papers, Finance.

23 *North Star* (Danville, VT), September 3, 1808; *Salem Gazette* (Salem, MA), August 12, 1808.

24 *Massachusetts Spy, or Worcester Gazette* (Worcester, MA), November 22, 1809. Many of these Federalist attacks, although often motivated by local commercial and political concerns, were likely accurate in their general tenor. For a reappraisal of the much-maligned and sometimes celebrated Federalist party, see Doron Ben-Atar and Barbara B. Oberg, eds., *Federalists Reconsidered* (Charlottesville: University of Virginia Press, 1998).

25 *Salem Gazette* (Salem, MA), March 10, 1809.

26 Quoted in Edward Gray, *William Gray*, 42–4.

27 *Trenton Federalist* (Trenton, NJ), June 4, 1810.

28 *Massachusetts Spy, or Worcester Gazette* (Worcester, MA), November 22, 1809.

29 *Palladium* (Boston), January 13, 1809, quoted in Edward Gray, *William Gray*, 44.

30 Boston Gazette (Boston), August 22, 1811. Yet, for all of his influence and political pivot into Thomas Jefferson's Republican camp, when William Gray applied for an individual exemption from the embargo, he was denied. Henry Stephens Randall, *The Life of Thomas Jefferson*, Vol. 3 (Philadelphia: J.B. Lippincott & Co, 1871), 262.

31 Wendell Blancke, *The Foreign Service of the United States* (New York: Frederick Praeger, 1969), 10–11.

32 Edward Gray, *William Gray*, 34–8. For an overview of smuggling in the face of these trade laws see Herbert Heaton, "Non-Importation, 1806–1812," *Journal of Economic History* 1 (1941): 178–98; Anna Clauder, *American Commerce as Affected by the Wars of the French Revolution and Napoleon, 1793–1812* (Clifton, NJ: Augustus M. Kelley Publishers, 1972); Donald Hickey, "American Trade Restrictions During the War of 1812," *Journal of American History* 68 (1981): 517–38; Joshua Smith, *Borderlands Smuggling, Patriots, Loyalists, and Illicit Trade in the Northeast, 1783–1820* (Gainesville: University Press of Florida, 2006).

33 Francis Gregory, *Nathan Appleton: Merchant and Entrepreneur, 1779–1861* (Charlottesville: University of Virginia, 1975), 36–7.

34 Vincent Gray (Havana) to Madison (D.C.), July 24, 1808, Roll 2, Dispatches from U.S. Consul at Havana, DNA.

35 J[ohn] H. D[ent], Captain, U.S. Navy (Hornet, at Havana) to James Anderson (Havana), March 26, 1809, Roll 2, Dispatches from U.S. Consul at Havana, DNA.

36   John H. Dent (Havana) to James Anderson (Havana), April 1, 1809, Roll 2, Dispatches from U.S. Consul at Havana, DNA.

37   *Washington Federalist* (Georgetown, D.C.), September 6, 1808.

38   Levett Harris (St. Petersburg) to Robert Smith (Washington), July 5/17, 1809, Roll 1, Dispatches from U.S. Consul at St. Petersburg, DNA.

39   Edward Gray, *William Gray*, 20.

40   *Salem Gazette* (Salem, MA), December 19, 1809.

41   For a sense of the extensive, sympathetic historiography related to Adams and U.S. foreign policy—which has overwhelmingly minimized Adams's commercial interests —see Samuel Flagg Bemis, *John Quincy Adams and the Foundations of American Foreign Policy* (New York: Knopf, 1949); William E. Weeks, *John Quincy Adams and American Global Empire* (Lexington: University Press of Kentucky, 1992), and James E. Lewis, Jr., *John Quincy Adams: Policymaker for the Union* (Wilmington, DE: Scholarly Resources, 2001).

42   New York Commercial Advertiser (New York), February 6, 1810; John Quincy Adams (St. Petersburg) to Thomas Boyston Adams, October 11, 1810, in *Writings of John Quincy Adams*, Vol. III, ed. Worthington Chauncey Ford, ed. (New York: MacMillan Company, 1913–17) [hereafter JQAW3], 521.

43   *Columbian Phenix* (Providence, RI), August 5, 1809.

44   *The Star* (Raleigh, NC), September 27, 1810.

45   William Gray (Boston) to John Quincy Adams (St. Petersburg), April 25, 1810, quoted in Edward Gray, *William Gray*, 52; John Quincy Adams (St. Petersburg) to William Gray (Boston), August 3, 1810, JQAW3, 465–6.

46   Alfred Crosby, Jr., *America, Russia, Hemp, and Napoleon*, 172–3; John Quincy Adams (St. Petersburg) to William Gray, October 20, 1810, JQAW3, 519–20; David W. McFadden, "John Quincy Adams, American Commercial Diplomacy, and Russia, 1809–1825," *New England Quarterly* 66, no. 4 (December 1993), 617–18; Greg G. Williams, *The French Assault on American Shipping, 1793–1813: A History and Comprehensive Record of Merchant Marine Losses*, (London: McFarland, 2009), 228, 70.

47   Francis Gregory, *Nathaniel Appleton*, 50; Alfred Crosby, Jr., *America, Russia, Hemp, and Napoleon*, 172–3.

48   Levett Harris (St. Petersburg) to Robert Smith (Washington), December 12/24, 1810, Roll 2, Dispatches From U.S. Consul at St. Petersburg, DNA.

49   Christopher Kingston, "Marine Insurance in Britain and America," 19; *Boston Gazette* (Boston, MA), June 3, 1811.

50   October–November 1809, pages 22, 26, 38, Folder "A.H. Everett Journal Narrative, Aug. 1809–Sep. 1811," Everett-Noble Papers, MHS.

51   Jerome Branche, *Colonialism and Race in Luso-Hispanic Literature* (Columbia, MO: University of Missouri Press, 2006), 128; David Murray, *Odious Commerce: Britain, Spain and the Abolition of the Cuban Slave Trade* (New York: Cambridge University Press, 2002), 167; Alexander Everett Diaries, February 24–May 31, 1840, Everett-Noble Papers; David McFadden, "John Quincy Adams, American Commercial Diplomacy, and Russia, 1809–1825," 621–2; Rufus Wilmot Griswold, *The Prose Writers of America* (New York: Garrett Press, 1969), 284–6; John Spear Smith Diary, Roll 5, Samuel Smith Family Papers, DNA; Stephen Cullen Carpenter, *Memoirs of the*

Honorable Thomas Jefferson (Printed for the Purchasers, 1809), 213–23; Samuel Flagg Bemis, *John Quincy Adams and the Foundations of American Foreign Policy*, 154.

52 John Spear Smith (St. Petersburg) to Samuel Smith (Baltimore), May 1, 1810, Roll 3, Samuel Smith Family Papers, DNA.

53 Thomas Hazard (New Bedford, MA) to Samuel Hazard (Archangel), March 31, 1812, April 9, 1812, Thomas Hazard Jr. Letter Book, 1811–1816, YALE.

54 Harvard University Porcellian Club, Catalogue of the Honorary and Immediate Members of the Library of the Porcellian Club of Harvard University (Boston: J.H. Eastburn, 1839), 21–5.

55 On Saabye, Alexander Everett noted: "Mr. Gray has long been connected with him and has assisted him very much." Alexander Everett, September 1809, page 12, Folder "A.H. Everett Journal Narrative, Aug. 1809–Sep. 1811," Everett-Noble Papers, MHS.

56 John M. Forbes (Copenhagen), undated [mid-January 1810], Copenhagen Letter-book, 1809–1810, Forbes Family Papers, HBS.

57 Harvard University Porcellian Club, Catalogue of the Porcellian Club of Harvard University, 21 5.

58 John Quincy Adams, February 27, 1811, in *Russian Memoirs*, 235; Edward Channing, *The Jeffersonian System, 1801–1811* (New York: Greenwood Press, 1969), 252–3.

59 Kenneth Wiggins Porter, *The Jacksons and the Lees: Two Generations of Massachusetts Merchants, 1765–1844* (Cambridge, MA: Harvard University Press, 1937), 106.

60 *Newburyport Herald* (Newburyport, MA), March 27, 1807; Charles Amburger & Co. (Archangel) to Nicholas Thorndike (St. Petersburg), May 31, 1812 ["care of Messrs. Mius, Fisher & Co."], Nicholas Thorndike Papers, 1810–1812, Fam.Mss. 1004, PEM; Alexander Everett, September 1809, page 8, Folder "A.H. Everett Journal Narrative, Aug. 1809–Sep. 1811," Everett-Noble Papers, MHS.

61 Alexander Everett, January 27, 1810, page 103, Folder "A.H. Everett Journal Narrative, Aug. 1809–Sep. 1811," Everett-Noble Papers, MHS.

62 Alexander Everett, February 5, 1810, page 110, Folder "A.H. Everett Journal Narrative, Aug. 1809–Sep. 1811," Everett-Noble Papers, MHS.

63 John Quincy Adams, February 4, 1814, *Russian Memoirs*, 575; Alfred Crosby, Jr., *America, Russia, Hemp, and Napoleon*, 176.

64 John Quincy Adams (St. Petersburg) to Robert Smith (Washington), November 1/13, 1810, JQAW3, 536.

65 John Quincy Adams in Charles Francis Adams, ed., *Memoirs of John Quincy Adams* VI (Philadelphia: J.B. Lippincott & Co., 1875), 32.

66 Alfred Crosby, Jr., America, Russia, Hemp, and Napoleon, 172–3; John Quincy Adams (St. Petersburg) to William Gray, October 20, 1810 in JQAW3, 519–20; David W. McFadden, "John Quincy Adams, American Commercial Diplomacy, and Russia, 1809–1825," 617–18; Greg G. Williams, *The French Assault on American Shipping*, 228, 70.

67 John Quincy Adams, December 20, 1810, *Russian Memiors*, 201–2; Alexander Everett, November 30, 1809, page 47, Folder "A.H. Everett Journal Narrative, Aug. 1809–Sep. 1811," Everett-Noble Papers, MHS.

68 Alexander Everett (St. Petersburg) to Oliver Everett (St. Petersburg), December 13/25, 1809, Misc. Vols./Notes on Russia [1809–1811], Everett-Noble, MHS.

69   John Spear Smith (St. Petersburg) to Samuel Smith (Baltimore), October 2, 1810, Roll 3, Samuel Smith Family Papers, DNA.

70   Alfred Crosby, Jr., *America, Russia, Hemp, and Napoleon*, 175–6.

71   Levett Harris (St. Petersburg) to Robert Smith (Washington), September 13/25, 1810, Roll 2, Dispatches from U.S. Consul at St. Petersburg, DNA.

72   Levett Harris (St. Petersburg) to Robert Smith (Washington), June 1/13, 1810, Roll 2, Dispatches from U.S. Consul at St. Petersburg, DNA.

73   Levett Harris (St. Petersburg) to Robert Smith (Washington), October 28/September 9, 1810, Roll 2, Dispatches from U.S. Consul at St. Petersburg, DNA.

74   Gautham Rao, "The Creation of the American State: Customhouses, Law, and Commerce in the Age of Revolution" (Ph.D. diss., University of Chicago, 2008).

75   John Spear Smith (Stockholm) to Samuel Smith (Baltimore), February 22, 1810, Roll 3, Samuel Smith Family Papers, LOC.

76   John Spear Smith (St. Petersburg) to Samuel Smith (Baltimore), October 1, 1810, Roll 3, Samuel Smith Family Papers, LOC.

77   Levett Harris (St. Petersburg) to Robert Smith (Washington), October 28/September 8, 1810, Roll 2, Dispatches from U.S. Consul at St. Petersburg, DNA.

78   Alexander Everett, November 1809, pages 24, 37, Folder "A.H. Everett Journal Narrative, Aug. 1809–Sep. 1811," Everett-Noble Papers, MHS.

79   John Spear Smith to Samuel Smith, October 1, 1810, Roll 3, Samuel Smith Family Papers, LOC.

80   "Account Notes"; John Spear Smith to Samuel Smith, April 2, 1810, Roll 3, Samuel Smith Family Papers, LOC.

81   John Spear Smith to Samuel Smith, October 4, 1810, Roll 3, Samuel Smith Family Papers, LOC.

82   Levett Harris (St. Petersburg) to Robert Smith (Washington), December 12/24, 1810, Roll 2, Dispatches from U.S. Consul at St. Petersburg, DNA.

83   John Quincy Adams, May 13, 1811, *Russian Memoirs*, 263.

84   John Quincy Adams (St. Petersburg) to James Monroe (Washington), July 22, 1811, *Writings*, Vol. IV, 149–50. Levett Harris submitted much lower estimates, however, and calculated that only 138 U.S. ships had reached St. Petersburg by October 1811. Levett Harris (St. Petersburg) to James Monroe (Washington), October 14/26, 1811, Roll 2, Dispatches from U.S. Consul at St. Petersburg, DNA.

85   *Boston Gazette* (Boston), December 9, 1811.

86   Alfred Crosby, Jr., *America, Russia, Hemp, and Napoleon*, 225; N.N. Bolkhovitinov, *The Beginnings of Russian–American Relations, 1775–1815* (Cambridge, MA: Harvard University Press, 1975), 222.

87   "When [Alexander I of Russia] was attacked by Napoleon in 1812, it was because he would not exclude American shipping from his ports." George Dangerfield, *The Era of Good Feelings* (Ivan R. Dee, Inc.: Chicago, 1989), 55.

88   N.N. Bolkhovitinov, *The Beginnings of Russian–American Relations*, 235–6.

89   John Quincy Adams, May 15, 1812, *Russian Memoirs*, 370–1.

90   Ibid.

4   Opportunists

1   J. J. Chauviteau (Havana) to John D'Wolf (Bristol), December 18, 1812, Box 7, Folder 37, D'Wolf Family Papers, BHS.

2   George A. Cushing (Boston) to Juan Hernandez (Havana), November 2, 1801, George A. Cushing Letterbook, 1799–1802, HBS.

3   Hernandez & Chauviteau (Havana) to John D'Wolf (Bristol), September 3, 1812, Box 7, Folder 37, D'Wolf Family Papers, BHS.

4   Nathaniel Ingraham (New York) to James Madison, February 18, 1811, in J. C. A. Stagg, ed., *The Papers of James Madison Digital Edition* (Charlottesville: University of Virginia Press, Rotunda, 2010) [hereafter JMPD]. In later decades, Ingraham's son of the same name (Nathaniel G. Ingraham, Jr., who was living in England in 1810) would also serve as U.S. consul in Mexico. Like many Americans in the Caribbean and Central American regions, however, Nathaniel Ingraham, Jr. did not last long in Mexico: shortly after receiving his commission he died at Tampico in April 1824. W. Taylor (Alvarado) to John Quincy Adams, March 29, 1824, Roll 1, Dispatches from U.S. Consul at Veracruz, DNA; James Hepburn (Pueblo Viejo de Tampico) to W. Taylor (Alvarado), May 8, 1824, Roll 1, Dispatches from U.S. Consul at Veracruz, DNA.

5   James D'Wolf's son, James D'Wolf, Jr., for example, operated the Manhattan branch of his Rhode Island commercial empire. Other New York merchants invested in the Cuba–Baltic trade were Baily & Willis and Minturn & Champlin. See, for example, "Account of sales," December 16, 1811, Baily & Willis (New York), Box 7, Folder 6, D'Wolf Family Papers, BHS.

6   William Shaler (Havana) to Robert Smith, October 24, 1810, Roll 2, Dispatches from U.S. Consul at Havana, DNA.

7   When writing to Secretary of State Robert Smith for advice on handling the Creole planters, for example, Shaler advised Smith to write "in cypher" before forwarding information to Vincent Gray, because of Gray's tendency to "suppress letters." William Shaler (Havana) to Robert Smith, October 24, 1810, Roll 2, Dispatches from U.S. Consul at Havana, DNA. Vincent Gray, for his part, appears to have had no significant ties of loyalty or affection to Fellowes. In subsequent years, Gray would even advise Fellowes's creditors in Massachusetts. Vincent Gray (Havana) to Jeremiah Neilson (Newburyport), August 25, 1815, Roll 3, Dispatches from U.S. Consul at Havana, DNA.

8   William Shaler, "Sketches," Roll 2, Dispatches from U.S. Consul at Havana, DNA. With the specter of Haiti and race war hanging over their plantations, Hernandez had recently completed a demographic study of the colony that seemed to indicate a movement in the "wrong direction": Whereas in Havana in 1790, for example, "whites" had constituted 53 percent of the population, by 1810 this number had fallen to 43 percent. They were now, in Hernandez's estimation, a minority throughout much of the island. Antonio del Hernandez, *Sucinta Noticia de la Situacion Presente de esta Colonia*, 1800 (Havana: Editorial de Ciencias Sociales, 1977), 12–16.

9   José Luciano Franco, *Las Conspiraciones de 1810 y 1812*, 9.

10 Matt Childs, *The 1812 Aponte Rebellion in Cuba* (Chapel Hill: University of North Carolina Press, 2006), 158–9.

11 William Shaler (Havana) to "Secretary of State," June 5, 1811, Roll 2, Dispatches from U.S. Consul at Havana, DNA.

12 William Shaler (Havana) to "Secretary of State," June 14, 1811, Roll 2, Dispatches from U.S. Consul at Havana, DNA.

13 William Shaler (Havana), July 8, 1811, Roll 2, Dispatches from U.S. Consul at Havana, DNA.

14 *Diario de la Habana* (Havana), August 9, 1811, UHL.

15 *Boston Gazette* (Boston), December 13, 1810.

16 William Shaler (Havana) to "Secretary of State," July 19, 1811, Roll 2, Dispatches from U.S. Consul at Havana, DNA. On Shaler's deep-rooted belief in Cuba's importance to the United States, see also J. C. A. Stagg, "The Political Essays of William Shaler," *William and Mary Quarterly* LVIV, Number 2 (2002).

17 William Shaler (Havana) to James Monroe (Washington), December 6, 1811, Roll 2, Dispatches from U.S. Consul at Havana, DNA.

18 "Nota. Las Cortes Espanoles convocadas en la Isla de Leon," December 1, 1811, Havana, Roll 2, Dispatches from U.S. Consul at Havana, DNA.

19 Thomas Jefferson to William C. C. Claiborne, October 29, 1808, in Paul Leicester Ford, ed., *The Works of Thomas Jefferson in Twelve Volumes*, Vol. IX (New York: G.P. Putnam, 1904–1905), 381.

20 Samuel Flagg Bemis, *John Quincy Adams and the Foundations of American Foreign Policy* (New York: Alfred A. Knopf, 1949), 373; Brian Loveman, *No Higher Law: American Foreign Policy and the Western Hemisphere since 1776* (Chapel Hill: University of North Carolina Press, 2010), 26–8.

21 Richard Hackley to James Monroe, September 10 and 27, 1811, JMPD; William Shaler to James Monroe, September 17, 1811, Roll 2, Dispatches from U.S. Consul at Havana, DNA.

22 *National Intelligencer* (Washington), October 31, 1811.

23 William Shaler, October 21, 1811, Roll 2, Dispatches from U.S. Consul at Havana, DNA; Richard Hackley to Monroe, September 10, 1811, JMPD.

24 James Madison (Washington) to Joel Barlow, November 11, 1817, RC (DLC), JMPD.

25 William Shaler (Fundador Estate) to James Monroe (Washington), October 21, 1811; William Shaler (Havana) to James Monroe (Washington), November 13, 1811, Roll 2, Dispatches from U.S. Consul at Havana, DNA.

26 William Shaler (Havana) to James Monroe (Washington), November 13, 1811, and "Shaler's Sketches," 1811, Roll 2, Dispatches from U.S. Consul at Havana, DNA.

27 William Shaler, "Sketches," Roll 2, Dispatches from U.S. Consul at Havana, DNA.

28 William Shaler (Havana) to James Monroe (Washington), November 13, 1811, Roll 2, Dispatches from U.S. Consul at Havana, DNA.

29 "Sobre recibo y pago de las facturas de varios libros en idioma Ynglés encargados al Norte de America," 1811, Real Consulado y Junta de Fomento, Negociado de cuentas, Legajo 22, Expediente 765, 1295, ANC.

30 William Shaler (Havana) to James Monroe (Washington), November 13, 1811, Roll 2, Dispatches from U.S. Consul at Havana, DNA.

31 Many of the approximately 18,000 French emigres in Cuba left in 1808–9, when at

least 9,000 moved to New Orleans, doubling that port's population. Matt Childs, *The 1812 Aponte Rebellion in Cuba*, 40. The exodus of French slaveowners to the United States led to temporary and specific remittances of the ban on the U.S. slave trade. American merchants often found themselves in the uncomfortable position of petitioning Congress on behalf of French passengers with slaves in tow. In December 1809, for example, Harry Caldwell (a native of New Jersey) and Amasa Jackson (from New York) submitted a petition in favor of "Madam Chazel, Madam Burreau, and Duvalles, with certain slaves and domestics belonging to them," who had recently left Cuba for Jamaica and now hoped to immigrate to New Orleans. See "Violation of the act prohibiting the importation of slaves. Communicated to the House of Representatives, December 22, 1809," American State Papers 038, Miscellaneous Vol. 2 10th Congress, 2nd Session Publication No. 269.

32 Matt Childs, *The 1812 Aponte Rebellion in Cuba*, 160–2.

33 Vincent Gray (Havana), April 14, 1812, Roll 2, Dispatches from U.S. Consul at Havana, DNA.

34 H. L. Howard (Havana) to Elizabeth (Matthew) Wainwright, January 7, 1810, Wainwright Papers, NYPL.

35 H. L. Howard (Havana) to Elizabeth (Matthew) Wainwright, February 26, 1810, Wainwright Papers, NYPL.

36 H. L. Howard (Havana) to Elizabeth (Matthew) Wainwright, March 17, 1810, Wainwright Papers, NYPL.

37 "An Act to prohibit the exportation of specie, goods, wares and merchandise, for a limited time," April 14, 1812, in Richard Peters, ed., *Public Statutes at Large of the United States of America*, Vol. 2 (Boston: Charles C. Little and James Brown, 1845), 707–8.

38 "The present situation of political affairs causes a stagnation in all commercial transactions," a commercial house in Moscow wrote to the American merchant Nicholas Thorndike in July 1812. "No Sales have been effected for this last fortnight." John Hippius & Adolph Arhusen (Moscow) to Nicholas Thorndike (St. Petersburg), July 22, 1812, Nicholas Thorndike Papers, 1810–1812, PEM.

39 See Matt Childs, *The 1812 Aponte Rebellion in Cuba*, and Daniel Rasmussen, *American Uprising: The Untold Story of America's Largest Slave Revolt* (New York: Harper, 2011).

40 Thomas Hazard to Thomas R. Hazard & Co, November 17, 1813, Letter Book, 1811–16, YALE.

41 For an overview of Federalist opposition and the Hartford Convention, see David Hackett Fischer, *The Revolution of American Conservatism: The Federalist Party in the Era of Jeffersonian Democracy* (New York: Harper and Row, 1965), and James M. Banner, Jr., *To the Hartford Convention: The Federalists and the Origins of Party Politics in Massachusetts, 1789–1815* (New York: Alfred A. Knopf, 1970).

42 John Corlis (Cranston) to Lebbeus Loomis, January 4, 1814, Box 1, Folder 4, Corliss-Respess Papers, FHS.

43 Vincent Gray (Havana) to John Graham, July 17, 1813, and Vincent Gray (Havana) to James Monroe (Washington, D.C.), September 13, 1813, Roll 3, Dispatches from U.S. Consul at Havana, DNA.

44 In 1811, for example, James D'Wolf and Bradford Hersy had lost the Andromache

to a French privateer en route from St. Petersburg to New York. They eventually collected almost $29 million for the capture in the treaty signed with France on July 4, 1831. Greg H. Williams, *The French Assault on American Shipping*, 58.

45 Thomas Hazard to Jacob Barker, January 23, 1813, Thomas Hazard Jr. Letter Book, 1811–16, YALE.

46 Thomas Hazard to William Gray, July 11, 1812, Thomas Hazard Jr. Letter Book, 1811–16, YALE.

47 "Authorizing the Issuing of Letters of Marque, Prizes and Prize Goods," June 26, 1812, in Richard Peters, ed., *Public Statutes at Large*, 759.

48 Of the 515 privateering commissions issued, 150 were to Massachusetts privateers, 18 to Rhode Islanders, 102 to New Yorkers, and 112 to Marylanders. Federalist New England actually commanded a much smaller share than in the Revolutionary period (as in the case of Salem, which went from 158 privateers in the Revolution to just forty in the War of 1812), in part because of opposition to the war. George Howe, Mount Hope, 169–70. Jose Luciano Franco similarly counts 517 privateering commissions issued by the United States and more than 1,300 by England and her allies. Jose Lucian Franco, *La Batalla por el Dominio del Caribe*, 121. See also Frank A. Cassell, *Merchant Congressman in the Young Republic: Samuel Smith of Maryland, 1752–1839* (Madison: University of Wisconsin Press, 1971). For an introduction to the nature of privateering and law in this period see Charles Fenwick, *The Neutrality Laws of the United States* (Washington: Carnegie Endowment for International Peace, 1913); Lewis Winkler Bealer, "The Privateers of Buenos Aires, 1815–1821: Their Activities in the Hispanic American Wars of Independence" (Ph.D. diss., University of California, Berkeley, 1935); Jerome Garitee, *The Republic's Private Navy: The American Privateering Business as Practiced by Baltimore During the War of 1812* (Middletown, CT: Wesleyan University Press, 1977); Donald Petrie, *The Prize Game: Lawful Looting on the High Seas in the Age of Fighting Sail* (New York: Berkley Books, 1999); David Head, "Sailing For Spanish America: The Atlantic Geopolitics of Foreign Privateering from the United States in the Early Republic" (Ph.D. diss., University of Buffalo, New York, 2009).

49 Oliver Wilson ("Off the South Point of Newfoundland") to James D'Wolf (Bristol), July 29, 1812, Reel 9, Part 2, D'Wolf Papers, Papers of the American Slave Trade, RIHS.

50 D'Wolf owned one-fourth, worth about $24,000 after the war. John D'Wolf (Boston) to James D'Wolf, February 13, 1816; John D'Wolf (Bristol) to James D'Wolf, February 29, 1816, Box 8, Folder 2, D'Wolf Family Papers, BHS; James D'Wolf (Bristol) to Honb. Wm Gray, April 22, 1817, and James D'Wolf (Bristol) to Wm B. Liviet[?] & Co., June 22, 1817; James D'Wolf Letterbook, 1817, D'Wolf Papers, Vol. 2, HBS; Edward Gray, *William Gray*, 33; George Howe, *Mount Hope*, 217.

51 Spanish authorities in Cuba limited the length of time British prize vessels could remain in port to forty-eight hours in an effort to curtail their involvement with U.S. privateering. Richard Bell (St. Jago) to James Monroe (D.C.), Nov. 21, 1812, Roll 1, Dispatches from U.S. Consul at Santiago, DNA.

52 Quoted in *American and Commercial Daily Advertiser* (Baltimore), September 7, 1812.

53 Stephen Kingston (Havana) to James Monroe, July 10, 1812, Roll 2, Dispatches from U.S. Consul at Havana, DNA.

54 On June 3, 1813, for example, John D'Wolf, in partnership with James L'Barron, insured the Arogancea from New York to Havana at a premium of just 4 percent. This was only a few points higher than the pre-war levels of 1.5 to 2.5 percent that had characterized the U.S.–Cuba trade. Bailey & Willis (New York), June 3, 1813, Box 7, Folder 8, D'Wolf Family Papers, BHS; Francis Gregory, *Nathaniel Appleton*, 33.

55 Packard & Gowen (Havana) to Brown & Ives (Providence), November 25, 1814, Records of Brown & Ives, JCB.

56 Richard Bell (St. Jago) to Monroe (D.C.), July 1, 1814, Roll 1, Dispatches from U.S. Consul at Santiago, DNA.

57 David Morgan (New Orleans), January 14, 1814, Roll 2, Dispatches from U.S. Consul at Havana, DNA.

58 José Luciano Franci, *La Batalla por el Dominio del Caribe*, 122.

59 Vincent Gray (Havana) to John Graham, July 17, 1813, Vincent Gray (Havana) to James Monroe (Washington, D.C.), September 13, 1813, Roll 3, Dispatches from U.S. Consul at Havana, DNA.

60 James Monroe (Washington), January 1, 1813, Senate Journals, 12A–A3, DNA.

61 "Forty years after the battle, in 1855, General Richard Keith revealed that James Innerarity (d. 1847) informed Call who in turn informed Jackson of the British plans. Innerarity himself was informed of the plans in 1814 by a letter from Vincent Gray, a native of Massachusetts, on business in Havana, Cuba." William Coker, "How General Jackson Learned of the British Plans Before the Battle of New Orleans," *Gulf Coast Historical Review* 1987 3(1): 84–95. See also Mary W. M. Hargreaves and James F. Hopkins, eds., *The Papers of Henry Clay*, Vol. VI, (Lexington, KY: University Press of Kentucky, 1981), 595.

62 William Coker, "How General Jackson Learned of the British Plans," 87–90; Lawrence A. Clayton, ed., *The Hispanic Experience in North America* (Columbus, OH: Ohio State University Press, 1992), 113.

63 Vincent Gray (Havana) to Jeremiah Neilson (Newbury Port), August 25, 1815, Roll 2, Dispatches from U.S. Consul at Havana, DNA.

64 J. J. Chauviteau (Havana) to John D'Wolf (Bristol, RI), December 20, 1814, Box 7, Folder 39, BHS.

65 John D'Wolf (Bristol, RI) to J. J. Chauviteau (Havana), April 1, 1815, Box 7, Folder 40, BHS.

5 Slavemongers

1 "Capt Benj M Bosworth" (Bristol) to Edward Spalding ["on board Brig Eliza Ann"] (Havana), December 24, 1816, Box 1, Folder 1, Edward Spalding Papers, RIHS.

2 Eliga Gould, "Zones of Law, Zones of Violence: The Legal Geography of the British Atlantic, circa 1772," *William & Mary Quarterly* 60 (2003): 471–510; Bernard

Bailyn, Christopher Tomlins and Brice H. Manns, eds., *The Many Legalities of Early America* (Chapel Hill, 2001).

3   Benjamin Bosworth (Fredericksburg) to Edward Spalding (Bristol), October 28, 1816, Box 1, Folder 1, Edward Spalding Papers, RIHS.

4   Benjamin Bosworth to Edward Spalding, September 1, 1816, Box 1, Folder 1, Edward Spalding Papers, RIHS.

5   Benjamin Bosworth (Fredericksburg) to Edward Spalding (Bristol), October 28, 1816, Box 1, Folder 6, Edward Spalding Papers, RIHS; "Jn Zeck[?]" [Benjamin Bosworth] ("Fredericksg") to "Sam" [Edward Spalding] (Bristol), November 5, 1820, Box 1, Folder 6, Edward Spalding Papers, RIHS.

6   Edward Baptist, "'Cuffy,' 'Fancy Maids,' and 'One-Eyed Men': Rape, Commodification, and the Domestic Slave Trade in the United States," American Historical Review 106 (December 2001): 1619–50.

7   "Prohibition of slavery in Missouri. Communicated to the Senate, January 12, 1820," American State Papers 038, Miscellaneous Vol. 2 16th Congress, 1st Session Publication No. 479.

8   Benjamin Bosworth (Bristol) to Edward Spalding, February 16, 1816, Box 1, Folder 1, Edward Spalding Papers, RIHS.

9   James Anderson, "Benjamin Bosworth, Master of the Schooner Concord of Bristol Rhode Island hath duly entered and cleared his vessel at my office according to law," February 9, 1808; Crew list pay for Schooner Concord, Benjamin Bosworth, Master [paid 20 doll/month], "Master, now bound from the Port of Bristol to Africa," undated; January 25, 1808—Mount Hope Insurance Policy, No. 376, Schooner Concord & Cargo, Havannah &c to United States $3000 Dolls, Box 1, Folder 2, Edward Spalding Papers, CHC.

10 "Capt Benj M Bosworth" (Bristol) to Edward Spalding ["on board Brig Eliza Ann"] (Havana), December 24, 1816, Box 1, Folder 1, Edward Spalding Papers, RIHS.

11 Still, after the disruptions that had plagued the U.S.–Cuba trade since 1797, Packard remained understandably cautious and wrote that it would be impossible to predict precisely how the market might change. Packard, Thomas, Gowen (Havana) to Brown & Ives (Providence), March 20, 1816, Papers of Brown & Ives, JCB.

12 Francisco Pérez de la Riva, *El Café: Historia de su Cultivo y Explotación en Cuba* (Havana: J. Montero, 1944), 48–9.

13 Advertisements in *El Aviso de la Habana* are a case in point and often featured the phrase "Excellent land for Coffee Plantations" ("Tierra excelente para cafetales") alongside advertisements for slaves, which might be "exchanged for coffee" ("cambiaba por Café"). Quoted in Francisco Pérez de la Riva, *El Café*, 50–1.

14 José A. Benitez, *Las Antillas: Colonización, Azúcar e Imperialismo* (Havana: Casa de las Americas, 1976), 199. See also Louis Pérez, "Cuba and the United States," 72.

15 See Roger Betancourt, "Why Cuba Remained a Colony while Latin America Became Independent," University of Maryland and Development Research Center, econweb.umd.edu.

16 Roland Ely, *La Economia Cubana*, 87; Ramon de la Sagra, *Historia económico-política y estadística de la isla de Cuba, ó sea de sus progresos en la población, la agricultura, el*

comercio y las rentas (Havana: 1831), 182–3; Robert Francis Jameson, *Letters from the Havana* (London: Printed for John Miller, 1821), 91.

17 John Mason (St. Jago) to John Quincy Adams (Washington), August 11, 1818, Roll 1, Dispatches from U.S. Consul at Santiago, DNA. That same year, three slave ships—the *Merino* (with nineteen slaves), the *Constitution* (eighty-two slaves), and the *Louisa* (six slaves), with a total of 107 enslaved Africans to supplement their cargoes of sugar—were seized by U.S. forces occupying West Florida under the command of Andrew Jackson. All were owned, at least in part, by Americans and destined for Havana, including to the consignment of U.S. "vice consul" Vincent Gray and Americans John Murdock and David Nagle, along with familiar Spanish slave trading houses, such as Antonio de Frias. The ships had been sailing north from Cuba to smuggle slaves through Pensacola and Mobile. "The Merino, The Constitution, The Louisa, Barrias, and others, Claimaints," in Henry Wheaton, *Reports of Cases Argued and Adjudged in the Supreme Court of the United States, February Term, 1824*, Vol. IX (New York: R. Donaldson, 1824), 391–408; "Message from the President of the United States [John Quincy Adams] In Relation to the Cargoes of Certain Slave Ships" (Washington: Gales & Seaton, March 8, 1826), 3–77.

18 Francisco Pérez de la Riva, *El Café*, 30, 49. The liberalization of trade in 1817 represented, in part, an acknowledgement of the informal economic activities that already characterized the economy and a consolidation of decades of piecemeal trade reforms. They were accompanied by a series of legal allowances for Spanish citizens in Cuba and a simultaneous curtailment of civil liberties and political rights for slaves.

19 José A. Benitez, *Las Antillas*, 92. From 1790 to 1820, between 225,474 and 369,300 enslaved Africans were brought to Cuba, and while the 1817 Anglo-Spanish treaty outlawing the trade in 1820 may have impacted slave prices, Africans continued to arrive in Cuba in bondage into the late 1860s and perhaps even until the early 1870s. In fact, estimates of the Cuban slave trade vary considerably: From 1790 to 1820, for example, American Vincent Gray's elite German guest, Alexander von Humboldt, estimated 225,474, whereas Louis Pérez placed the number much higher at 369,300 (Matt Childs, *The 1812 Aponte Rebellion*, 50). See also Vincent Gray (Havana) to James Madison, April 28, 1804, and Vincent Gray (Havana) to James Madison, May 8, 1804, Roll 1, Dispatches from U.S. Consul at Havana, DNA. For the scholarly debate on the ending of the Cuban slave trade, see Jorge Giovannetti and Camillia Cowling, "Hard Work with the Mare Magnum of the Past: Nineteenth-Century Cuban History and the Miscelánea de Expedientes Collection," *Cuban Studies* 39 (2008): 65; José Luciano Franco, *Comercio clandestino de esclavos* (Havana: Editorial de Ciencias Sociales, [1980] 1996), 164–5; Hugh Thomas, *Cuba: The Pursuit of Freedom* (London: Picador, [1971] 2001), 784, 1049–51; David Eltis, "The Nineteenth-Century Transatlantic Slave Trade," *Hispanic American Historical Review* 67, no. 1 (February 1987): 109–38; D.R. Murray, "Statistics of the Slave Trade to Cuba, 1790–1867," *Journal of Latin American Studies* 3, no. 2 (November 1971): 131–49; Pérez de la Riva, *El monto de la immigración forzada en el siglo XIX* (Havana: Editorial de Ciencias Sociales, 1979), 16. For a more detailed examination of evidence of official permission given to the slave trade in this period, see José Luciano Franco, *La Batalla por el Dominio del Caribe*, 81–4. In July and August of 1818, planters and merchants

from Santiago submitted petitions to address the "grave evil" that would be done to them by the end of the slave trade. Their investments in ships such as the *Yrene, La Santa Gertrudis, La Veloz* and *Keyt* were directly at risk: If these vessels were stopped, the leading merchants of Santiago would lose thousands of dollars and risk seizure on the open sea. On August 5, 1818, Spanish authorities agreed and began to issue a "Patente para Africa en Cuba" to allow the slave trade to legally continue to the equitorial line. "Expediente promovido por varios comerciantes de Cuba sobre patentes originales para continuar el tráfico de negros bozales," 1818, Real Consulado y Junta de Fomento de la Isla de Cuba, Negociado de Marina, Legajo 90, Expediente 3759, ANC.

20   "Suppression of the slave trade—conference of foreign governments on the subject. Communicated to the House of Rep, February 9, 1821," American State Papers 05, Foreign Relations Vol. 5 16th Congress, 2nd Session Publication No. 346.

21   Gerald Horne, *The Deepest South* (New York: New York University Press, 2007), 20.

22   Welcome Arnold Greene, December 26, 1819, The Journals of Welcome Arnold Greene, Vol. 1, 180.

23   Ibid.

24   *El Diario de la Habana* (Havana), December 14, 1820. See also "[illegible] Necesidad" consigned to "Gray & Hernandez," in December 17, 1820, UHL.

25   Moreover, earlier generations of scholars and archivists were well aware that the destruction of incriminating evidence was common practice after 1808. As George Howe suggests in *Mount Hope*, "it is hard to unearth the facts about the slave trade between 1808, when it was driven underground, and 1820, when it became a hanging crime. The few who continued did all they could to hide the fact by registering their ships under false name of foreign registry, and by destroying all papers that might incriminate them. When [Charles] Collins lost his Collectorship [in Bristol, RI] in 1820 he burned all his records." Howe goes on to suggest that "John [D'Wolf – James D'Wolf's brother and business partner] kept the records of the whole family, but destroyed those that connected it with contraband." George Howe, Mount Hope (New York: Viking Press, 1959), 205; Leonardo Marques, "Slave Trading in a New World: The Strategies of North American Slave Traders in the Age of Abolition," *Journal of the Early Republic* 32 (2012):256.

26   Edward Spalding (Trinidad, Cuba) to José Garcia Alvarez (Havana, Cuba), February 27, 1820, Edward Spalding Letterbook, 1820, Box 3, West Indies Collection, LSU. See also Spalding to Don Morice, Esq., February 26, 1820, Edward Spalding Letterbook, LSU. Note: Many of these letters are included in both the Edward Spalding Letterbook, 1820, held at the Louisiana & Lower Mississippi Valley Collections, Special Collections, Louisiana State University (Baton Rouge, LA) and in the Edward Spalding Papers at the Rhode Island Historical Society (Providence, RI). They differ, however, from the materials in the Edward Spalding papers held at the Cuban Heritage Collection, University of Miami (Miami, FL), the Spalding Papers that compose a portion of the D'Wolf Family Papers at the Bristol Historical Society (Bristol, RI), the D'Wolf Family Papers in the Papers of the American Slave Trade (RIHS), and the D'Wolf Papers at the Baker Library, Harvard Business School (Boston, MA). Alvarez wrote back anyway, noting the arrival of the "Span[ish] Fregatte [sp] Mariquita from

the coast of Africa with a cargoe [sp] of 290 Negroes" that had been consigned to "Messrs. Miro Du & Co." "I had no news from your house at Bristol," Alvarez fretted, and there were reports "that 4 English men of war have taken the number of 17 vessels at the coast of Africa." José Garcia Alvarez (Havana) to Edward Spalding (Trinidad), February 29, 1820, Box 1, Folder 3, Edward Spalding Papers, CHC.

27 John Thomas Noonan, *The Antelope: The Ordeal of the Recaptured Africans in the Administrations of James Monroe and John Quincy Adams* (Berkeley: University of California Press, 1977), 28, 84, 110.

28 *Rhode Island American and General Advertiser* (Providence), November 7, 1820.

29 Edward Spalding Memorandum Book, Box 1, Folder 7, Edward Spalding Papers, RIHS; Laird Bergad, *Cuban Slave Market, 1790–1880* (New York: Cambridge University Press, 1995), 48.

30 P. C. Greene (Bristol) to S. W. Payton (Matanzas), August 21, 1820, Box 1, Folder 3, Edward Spalding Papers, CHC; Edward Spalding (Trinidad, Cuba) to José Garcia Alvarez (Havana, Cuba), April 4, 1821, Roll 3, D'Wolf Papers, Papers of the American Slave Trade, RIHS. Juan Hernandez was a partner at the Cuban firm of Hernandez and Chauviteau, with which the D'Wolfs did a regular business.

31 Daniel Giraud (St. Jago) to JQA, November 22, 1822, Roll 1, Dispatches from U.S. Consul at Santiago, DNA.

32 James Wright (St. Jago) to JQA, July 6, 1824, Roll 1, Dispatches from U.S. Consul at Santiago, DNA.

33 Caleb Miller (Bristol) to Edward Spalding (Havana), April 8, 1817, Caleb Miller Letters, Mss 3326, LSU.

34 David Eltis and David Richardson, *Atlas of the Transatlantic Slave Trade* (New York: Yale University Press, 2010).

35 Thos Russell (St. Pears, Martinique) to Edward Spalding, December 18, 18[18], Box 1, Folder 3; Jos Rush Buck (Martinique) to Charles D'Wolf, Jr. (Bristol), December 6, 1818, Box 1, Folder 2, Edward Spalding Papers, CHC.

6 Assassins

1 *The Trial of Robert M. Goodwin on an indictment of manslaughter for killing James Stoughton, Esq.* (New York: G. L. Birch & Co., 1820); Robert Greenhalgh Albion, *The Rise of New York Port 1815–1860* (New York: C. Scribner's Sons, 1939), 172.

2 *Niles Weekly Register*, April 19, 1823.

3 The U.S. navy had been gradually expanded following the War of 1812, but it was not enough to stop Cuban pirates and South American privateers. On April 29, 1816, $1 million per year was appropriated to expand the size of the U.S. navy; on March 3, 1821, this was lowered to $500,000 per year. *Abridgment of the Debates of the Congress*, VII (New York: D. Appleton & Co., 1858), 306.

4 Packard & Gowen (Havana) to Brown & Ives (Providence), August 30, 1817, Papers of Brown & Ives, JCB.

5 "I cannot take leave of Cuba, without adverting to the scandalous system of piracy,

organized by the lawless banditti of Havana and Regla, and countenanced and protected by the subaltern authorities of the Island." Joel Poinsett, *Notes on Mexico Made
in the Autumn of 1822* (London: John Miller, 1825), 295–8.

6   David Long, *Nothing Too Daring: A Biography of Commodore David Porter, 1780–1843*
(Annapolis, MD: U.S. Naval Institute, 1970), 203; Joel Poinsett, *Notes on Mexico*,
295–8; José Luciano Franco, *La Batalla por el Dominio del Caribe* (Havana: Instituto
de Historia, Academia de Ciencias, 1964), 117–200.

7   "Sobre el armamento de buques, que se preparan en los E.U. contra nuestra bandera,"
1816, Real Consulado y Junta de Fomento, Legajo 89, Expediente 979, 3739.

8   In the eighteenth century, for example, the Maryland native William Bowles launched
three attacks (in 1788, 1791, and 1799–1800) against Spanish Florida in violation
of the 1794 Neutrality Act. J. Leitch Wright, Jr., *William Augustus Bowles: Director
General of the Creek Nation* (Athens, GA: University of Georgia Press, 1967), 1,
19–35, 55–86, 119–41, 169–71. For a sense of the extensive historiography relat-
ing to U.S. foreign policy in the wake of Spanish empire in North America see
Hubert H. Bancroft, *History of the North Mexican States and Texas*, Vols. I and II
(San Francisco: A.L. Bancroft, 1889); James Morton Callahan, *American Foreign
Policy in Mexican Relations* (New York: Macmillan Co., 1932); Philip Brooks,
Diplomacy and the Borderlands: The Adams–Onis Treaty of 1819 (Berkeley: University
of California Press, 1939); Harold A. Bierck, Jr., "Dr. John Hamilton Robinson,"
Louisana Historical Quarterly 25 (1942): 644–69; Odie B. Faulk, *The Last Years of
Spanish Texas, 1778–1821* (The Hague: Mouton, 1964); Charles Griffin, *The United
States and the Disruption of the Spanish Empire* (New York: Octagon Books, 1968);
Félix D. Almaráz Jr., *Tragic Cavalier: Governor Manuel Salcedo of Texas, 1808–1813*
(Austin, TX: University of Texas Press, 1971); T. Ray Shurbutt, ed., *United States–
Latin American Relations, 1800–1850* (Tuscaloosa: University of Alabama Press,
1991); Francisco Valdés-Ugalde, "Janus and the Northern Colossus: Perceptions of
the United States in the Building of the Mexican Nation," *Journal of American History*
86 (1999): 568–600.

9   Baltimore dominated the outfitting of American privateers, and many privateers
received letters of marque "without even visiting the countries whose flags they
flew." *The True-Blooded Yankee*, for example, was a New York ship sailing under a
Chilean flag without ever visiting Chile; it was captured by the Spanish near Haiti in
1817. Robert Greenhalgh Albion, *The Rise of New York Port*, 168–71; Samuel Eliot
Morrison, "Old Bruin": Commodore Matthew C. Perry, 1794–1858 (Boston: Little
and Brown, 1968), 77; Hans Vogel, "New Citizens for a New Nation: Naturalization
in Early Independent Argentina," *Hispanic American Historical Review* 71 (1991):
107–31.

10 For more on the role of privateers in U.S.–Spanish relations see Charles Carroll
Griffin, *The United States and the Disruption of the Spanish Empire, 1810–1822* (New
York: Columbia University Press, 1937); Arthur Preston Whitaker, *The United States
and the Independence of Latin America, 1800–1830* (New York: Russell and Russell,
1962 [1941]); Rafe Blaufarb, "The Western Question: The Geopolitics of Latin
American Independence," *American Historical Review* 112 (2007): 742–63; Samuel
Bemis, *John Quincy Adams and the Foundations of American Foreign Policy* (New

York: Alfred A. Knopf, 1949); William Weeks, *John Quincy Adams and American Global Empire* (Lexington: University Press of Kentucky, 1992); Frank Owsley and Gene Smith, *Filibusters and Expansionists: Jeffersonian Manifest Destiny, 1800–1821* (Tuscaloosa: University of Alabama Press, 1997); James Lewis, *The American Union and the Problem of Neighborhood: The United States and the Collapse of the Spanish Empire, 1783–1829* (Chapel Hill: University of North Carolina Press, 1998).

11 "Illegal armaments, and occupation of Amelia Island. Communicated to Congress, March 14, and to the House of Representatives, March 26, 1818," American State Papers 04, Foreign Relations Vol. 4 15th Congress, 1st Session Publication No. 300. In 1816–17, for example, Beverly Chew—the collector at New Orleans—recorded eleven revolutionary warships in port, six with Mexican commissions and five operating under Venezuelan papers. The ships were: (Mexican) *Bellona, Calibra, Diana, Esperanza, Mosquito,* and *Victory*; (Venezuelan) *General Arismanda, Guerera, Hidalgo, Josefina,* and *Eugenia*. "Suppression of piratical establishments. Reported on January 10, 1818," American State Papers 04, Foreign Relations Vol. 4 15th Congress, 1st Session Publication No. 290.

12 "Sobre el armamento de buques, que se preparan en los E.U. contra nuestra bandera," 1816, Real Consulado y Junta de Fomento, Legajo 89, Expediente 979, 3739, ANC. For a much more detailed account of the context of this expedition see José Luciano Franco, *La Batalla por el Dominio del Caribe*, 58–67.

13 Importantly, in his letter, printed more than forty years after it was written, General Jessup counciled President Monroe, "We have nothing to fear from Cuba in the feeble hands of Spain, but in the hands of Great Britain it must become so formidable as to menace the independence of our country … Cuba is not only capable of holding in check all the southern possessions of the United States, but the whole of Spanish North America also; and if we occupy it will secure the independence of that country, and throw into our hands its valuable commerce." Seizing Cuba now, General Jessup believed, would "save many future wars." *New York Herald* (New York, NY), December 26, 1858.

14 The *Daily National Intelligencer* estimated that the number of coffee plantations had risen from "only 8 or 14 coffee plantations" to "779 large coffee estates" in "the district of the Havana alone." *Daily National Intelligencer* (Washington, D.C.), October 10, 1821.

15 Levi Marrero, *Cuba: Economia y Sociedad, Azucar, Ilustracion y Conciencia, 1793–1868*, Vol. II (Madrid: Editorial Playor), 149–51; Moreno Fraginals, *El Ingenio: Complejo Economico Social Cubano del Azucar*, Vol. I (Havana: Editorial de Ciencias Sociales, 1978), 46–7, 67–71.

16 Richard Madden, *The Island of Cuba* (London: C. Gilpin, 1849), 83.

17 "Promovido por el D.D. Gerardo Pendergrast, para que se le permita la introducción de cinco mil cerdos de los E.U. libres de dinero de extrangeria," 1819, Real Consulado y Junta de Fomento de la Isla de Cuba, Negociado de derechos, Legajo 103, Expediente 1120, 4387, ANC.

18 "Commerce and navigation for the year ending September 30, 1821. Communicated to the Senate, January 24, 1822," American State Papers 015, Commerce and Navigation Vol. 2 17th Congress, 1st Session Publication No. 246, 539–540, 553.

19 "Commerce and navigation for the year ending September 30, 1821. Communicated to the Senate, January 24, 1822." These figures represent the share of total U.S. exports, not the share of total Cuban imports. American State Papers 015, Commerce and Navigation Vol. 2 17th Congress, 1st Session Publication No. 246, 552, 559, 561–3, 570, 572, 574.

20 Michael Hogan (Havana) to John Quincy Adams (Washington), December 19, 1819, Roll 3, Dispatches from the U.S. Consul in Havana, DNA.

21 Michael Hogan (Havana) to John Quincy Adams (Washington), March 2, 1820, Roll 3, Dispatches from U.S. Consul at Havana, DNA.

22 Michael Hogan (Havana) to John Quincy Adams (Washington), February 3, 1820, Roll 3, Dispatches from the U.S. Consul in Havana, DNA.

23 John Warner (Havana) to John Quincy Adams (Washington), May 28, 1820, Roll 3, Dispatches from U.S. Consul at Havana, DNA.

24 Michael Hogan (Havana) to John Quincy Adams (Washington), February 19, 1820, Roll 3, Dispatches from U.S. Consul at Havana, DNA.

25 Welcome Arnold Greene, December 16, 1819, Howard Greene and Alice Smith, eds., *Journals of Welcome Arnold Greene* (Madison: State Historical Society of Wisconsin, 1956–7), 179.

26 Edward Spalding Memorandum Book, 1820, Edward Spalding Papers, Folder 7, RIHS. Similarly, at Santiago, the U.S. commercial agent Thomas Willock wrote in December 1817 that "the Officers therefore take bribes to such an extent that often half a Cargo, or in some instance more is landed on the Kings Wharf without paying duty—the Officers being bribed with half the Duty." Thomas Willock ["U.S. Commerl Agent Office"] (St. Jago) to Richard Rush ["acting Secretary of State"] (D.C.), December 31, 1817, Roll 1, Dispatches from U.S. Consul at Santiago, DNA. Although there are numerous difficulties tracking undocumented or falsely documented trade practices, Spalding's correspondence is a remarkable exception. In his study of the Appleton shipping empire, for example, Francis Gregory reported that he could locate only one "recorded incident of illicit exporting." Francis Gregory, *Nathaniel Appleton*, 101.

27 Edward Spalding to [illegible], 1819, Roll 9, D'Wolf Papers, Papers of the American Slave Trade, Part 2, RIHS. Jay Coughtry similarly argues, "The port records them-selves are suspiciously suggestive and support the Spanish flag theory convincingly." Jay Coughtry, *The Notorious Triangle* (Philadelphia: Temple University Press, 1981), 235.

28 Welcome Arnold Greene, January 1, 1820, Journals of Welcome Arnold Greene, 182; "Commercial intercourse with foreign nations. Communicated to the House of Representatives, March 15, 1822," American State Papers 015, Commerce and Navigation Vol. 2 17th Congress, 1st Session Publication No. 256.

29 Welcome Arnold Greene, September 27, 1818, Journals of Welcome Arnold Greene, 109.

30 Dl Ns Morice (Bristol), January 7, 1822, "Instructions to Edward Spalding," Box 1, Folder 4, Edward Spalding Papers, CHC.

31 "Commerce and navigation for the year ending September 30, 1821. Communicated to the Senate, January 24, 1822," American State Papers 015, Commerce and Navigation Vol. 2 17th Congress, 1st Session Publication No. 246, 554.

32   "Commerce and navigation for the year ending September 30, 1821. Communicated to the Senate, January 24, 1822," American State Papers 015, Commerce and Navigation Vol. 2 17th Congress, 1st Session Publication No. 246.

33   Welcome Arnold Greene, January 1, 1820, *Journals of Welcome Arnold Greene*, 181. Of the 1,322 vessels to arrive in Havana in 1821, 655 were logged as American. *Niles Weekly Register*, March 30, 1822.

34   Alexander von Humboldt, trans. John S. Thrasher, *The Island of Cuba* (New York: Derby and Jackson, 1856), 301.

35   Based on a review of 2,588 entrances published in selected issues of *El Diario de la Habana (Havana), 1820–1823* [non-inclusive], held at the University of Havana, Rare Books Library (Havana, Cuba).

36   Welcome Arnold Greene, February 21, 1810, *Journals of Welcome Arnold Greene*, 185.

37   A circular printed by Latting, Adams & Stewart, which listed the U.S. vessels in port on February 7, 1824, is generally instructive: of the forty-four American ships at Matanzas, Latting, Adams & Stewart handled the consignments of twenty-two; Zacharia Atkins handled twelve; Simpson, Tiyon & Co. handled nine, and the remaining ship was handled by the Spanish merchant Felix Pujadas. Moreover, as in Havana, at Matanzas a disproportionate number (twenty-one of forty-four ships, or just under 50 percent) were bound to New England ports. "List of Foreign Vessels [all American] in the Port of Matanzas February 7th. 1824," Latting, Adams & Stewart, Roll 1, Jacob Babbitt Papers, Papers of the American Slave Trade, Part 2, RIHS.

38   Thomas Willock ["U.S. Comml Agent Office"] (St. Jago) to John Quincy Adams (Washington), March 1, 1818, Roll 1, Dispatches from U.S. Consul at Santiago, DNA.

39   "Oficio del ministro de S.M. en Estados Unidos, fecha Bristol 26 de agosto de 1818, al intendente sobre envío de once familias Islenas a Nuevitas," 1818, Intendencia Gral de Hacienda, Legajo 1125, No. Orden: 9, ANC.

40   "Copia certificada de la instancia de Dn Guillermo Koskins del Comercio de la Nva Orleans y Natural de Boston en los Estados Unidos de América para establecerse con su familia en la Isla de Cuba en virtud de la Real Cedula de 21 de Octubre de 1817," 1818, Intendencia General de Hacienda, Legajo 407, Expediente 45, ANC.

41   Louis Pérez, "Cuba and the United States: Origins and Antecedents of Relations, 1760s–1860s," in *Cuban Studies* 21 (1989): 77.

42   The Evening Post (New York), November 5, 1816; "D. Jayme DeWolf contra D. Jorge P. Stevenson sobre pesos procedentes de unos bocoyes de azúcar," 1818, Tribunal de Comercio, Legajo 158, Expediente 17, ANC; Thomas Jefferson (Monticello) to James Monroe, October 30, 1817 in Gerard Gawalt, ed., *Thomas Jefferson and James Monroe Correspondence* (Washington: Library of Congress); [George] P. Stevenson (Baltimore) to John Quincy Adams, December 15, 1817, Roll 3, Dispatches from U.S. Consul at Havana, DNA; *Portland Gazette* (Portland, ME), July 6, 1819. Yet, in the case of George Stevenson, D'Wolf's interest was as short-lived as its target: Stevenson died of yellow fever in Havana on June 11, 1819, at the age of twenty-nine, brought down— in the estimation of one of his friends—by "the very resolution which in any other profession might have preserved him." *Baltimore Patriot* (Baltimore), July 9, 1819.

43 "Testamentaria de D. Jacobo King de nación americana," 1806, Bienes de difuntos, Legajo 223, Expediente 3900, ANC.

44 In 1823, for example, the American agent John Morland—who had by this point resided in Havana for decades—served as an agent in Cuba for the elite Boston merchant-statesman Israel Thorndike in a suit related to a substantial debt and disputed slave sales with New Englanders Jacob Knight and Nathaniel Clark. As was the case for many U.S. merchants, Morland was employed by Thorndike due to his local influence and long-standing commercial connections in both Havana and Boston. Ultimately, with the aid of another Spanish attorney, Rafael Dias, Morland waged a continuous legal campaign on Thorndike's behalf in this case until at least 1827. Escribania de Galletti, Legajo 553, Expediente 9, ANC. Meanwhile, Jacob Knight, a native Bostonian, remained active in New England commercial circles and would be one of five merchants to lobby Secretary of State Henry Clay from Portland, Maine, about excessive port duties being charged by the Spanish consul at Boston. See "A. Mewhall, Philip Greely, Hez[ekiah] Winslow, Jacob Knight, and Charles Fox, Portland (Maine)" in James F. Hopkins, ed., *The Papers of Henry Clay*, Vol. 4 (Lexington: University Press of Kentucky, 1972), 921.

45 Henry Wysham Lanier, *A Century of Banking in New York, 1822–1922* (New York: George H. Doran, 1922), 105.

46 Henry Wysham Lanier, *A Century of Banking in New York*, 99. In 1822, the New York directors were Richard Harrison, James Magee, George Griswold, Benjamin Marshall, C.C. Cambreleng, James D'Wolf, Jr., Henry Wheaton, Gabriel L. Lewis, Henry Mactier, James M'Bride, A.H. Lawrence, Benjamin Bailey, Thomas Franklin, John Johnston, Thomas S. Townsend, Francis Saltus, William W. Russell, and Frederick A. Tracey. Non-Resident Directors: Southern District—James Tallmadge, Pottghkeepsie; Christian Schell, Rhinebeck; Middle District—William James, Albany; Eastern District—John L. Viele, Waterford; Western District—George Andrus, Adams, Jefferson Country; David White, Palmyra, Ontario Country; John T. Champlin, President; Archibald McIntyre, Secretary. Henry Wysham Lanier, *A Century of Banking in New York*, 187.

47 Henry Wysham Lanier, *A Century of Banking in New York*, 188–9. As Elizabeth Blackmar has demonstrated, this came on the eve of a series of judicial measures to ensure that such property held in trust was invested away from "real property" and into corporate and financial assets. Elizabeth Blackmar, "Inheriting Property and Debt: From Family Security to Corporate Accumulation" in Michael Zakim and Gary Kornblith, eds., *Capitalism Takes Command: The Social Transformation of Nineteenth-Century America* (Chicago: University of Chicago Press, 2012).

48 John Quincy Adams, June 6, 1812, in Charles Francis Adams, ed., *The Russian Memoirs of John Quincy Adams: His Diary from 1809 to 1814* (Philadelphia: J. B. Lippincott & Co., 1874), 396.

49 Thomas Hazard to Samuel Hazard (Archangel), March 31, 1812, Thomas Hazard Letterbook, YALE.

50 As Robert Dalzell has documented, for example, "The capital that created the Boston Company had been accumulated in foreign commerce." In fact, "all but a few of Boston's larger private fortunes [by the 1820s] had similar origins." Robert Dalzell,

Enterprising Elite: The Boston Associates and the World They Made (Cambridge, MA: Harvard University Press, 1987), 41.

51   James Fichter, *So Great A Profit*, 263; Robert Dalzell, *Enterprising Elite*, 108.

52   Henry Wysham Lanier, *A Century of Banking in New York*, 276–7; *New York Evening Post* (New York), August 6, 1822.

53   Henry Wysham Lanier, *A Century of Banking in New York*, 195, 284–6.

54   In March 1918, it joined the Federal Reserve, taking 3,800 shares of stock in the New York Reserve Bank. Henry Wysham Lanier, *A Century of Banking in New York*, 286. Four years later, in 1922, Edwin Atkins—one of the largest sugar producers in Cuba and a direct descendant of the Matanzas slave trader Zachariah Atkins—lobbied the U.S. Senate for a reduction in the tariff on Cuban sugar. Hugh Thomas, *Cuba: The Pursuit of Freedom* (New York: Harper and Row, 1971), 552.

7 Merchant-statesmen

1   The Collector was "destroyed by pirates" in the fall of 1821. James D'Wolf (Bristol) to Francis Diman (Cuba), October 15, 1821, Roll 3, D'Wolf Papers, Papers of the American Slave Trade, RIHS.

2   *Abridgment of the Debates of Congress*, Vol. VII, 154–5. The Seventeenth Congress met from December 3, 1821, to May 8, 1822, and from December 2, 1822, to March 3, 1823. The Eighteenth Congress met from December 1, 1823, to May 27, 1824, and from December 6, 1824, to March 3, 1825. The Nineteenth Congress met at a special session from March 4, 1825, to March 9, 1825, from December 5, 1825, to May 22, 1826, and from December 4, 1826 to March 3, 1827.

3   See Nathaniel Fellow[e]s (Havana) to Harrison Gray Otis, September 8, 1808, Roll 4; Rufus G. Amory (Boston) to Harrison Gray Otis, October 13, 1818, Roll 6; Nathaniel Fellow[e]s to Harrison Gray Otis, December 1, 1818, Roll 6; Harrison Gray Otis (Boston) to Nathaniel Fellow[e]s (Havana), August 2, 1819, Roll 7, Harrison Gray Otis Papers, MHS. That the bill gained ground was not due to D'Wolf's skills of oratory. He was a former slave ship captain and consummate businessman, not a public speaker, and, according to one contemporary observer of a debate later that year, it showed: "De Wolf ... rose at three different times and made a more bungling piece of work in delivering his sentiments than he used to in our state legislature. Many of the members could not forbear repeated smiles at the conjoined earnestness and awkwardness of his motley matter and manner. Could he be contented to sit still, to those who do not know his character, his grey locks might make him appear a respectable delegate." Welcome Arnold Greene, April 20, 1822, *Journals of Welcome Arnold Greene*, Vol. 2, 76.

4   Samuel Morrison, *"Old Bruin": Commodore Matthew C. Perry, 1794–1858* (London: Oxford University Press, 1968), 77.

5   Richard Peters, ed., *Public Statutes at Large of the United States of America*, Vol. 3 (Boston: Charles C. Little and James Brown, 1846), 510–14, 532–4; *Laws of the United States*, Vol. 6, 435–7; Samuel Burch, ed., *General Index to the Laws of the United States* (Washington: P. Force, 1828), 277.

6 Laws of the United States, Vol. 6, 529; *Index to the Laws of the United States*, 277; "An Act to protect the commerce of the United States, and punish the crime of piracy," *The National Register*, Vol. 7 (Washington, 1819), 184; Act of 1820, Statute I. May 15, 1820. abolition.nypl.org [accessed May 2, 2009].

7 Vincent Nolte, *Fifty Years in Both Hemispheres* (New York: Redfield, 1854), 189. And pirates did not stay confined to the water: They launched periodic inland raiding parties to capture Cuban slaves and resell them to planters. In 1823, for example, the wife of a New England planter near Matanzas wrote that they could not celebrate the Fourth of July with their neighbors because "armed vessels supposed to be Pirates" were nearby and other American planters "would not leave their families and Plantations while those suspicious vessels were about." S. Wilson (Camarioca) to John (Bristol), July 6, 1823, Box 16, Folder 7, D'Wolf Papers, BHS.

8 José A. Benitez, *Las Antillas: Colonización, azúcar e imperialism* (Havana: Casa de las Americas, 1977), 92; Laird Bergad, Fe Iglesias García and María del Carmen Barcia, *The Cuban Slave Market, 1790–1880* (New York: Cambridge University Press, 1995), 38–9, 51.

9 Daniel Giraud (St. Jago) to John Quincy Adams, May 25, 1821, Roll 1, Dispatches from U.S. Consul at Santiago, DNA.

10 Thomas Willock (St. Jago) to John Quincy Adams (Washington), May 27, 1818, Roll 1, Dispatches from U.S. Consul at Santiago, DNA.

11 John Mason (St. Jago) to John Quincy Adams (Washington), November 25, 1818. See also John Mason (St. Jago) to John Quincy Adams (Washington), June 12, 1818; John Mason (St. Jago) to John Quincy Adams (Washington), June 13, 1818; and John Mason (St. Jago) to John Quincy Adams (Washington), February 5, 1819, Roll 1, Dispatches from U.S. Consul at Santiago, DNA.

12 William Russell (Providence) to John Corliss (New York [care Colo. Lebbeus Loomis]), November 6, 1820, Box 2, Folder 10, Corliss-Respess Papers, FHS.

13 James Noonan, *The Antelope: The Ordeal of the Recaptured Africans in the Administrations of James Monroe and John Quincy Adams* (Berkeley: University of California Press, 1977), 84.

14 A slave trader, businessman and ruthless opportunist, D'Wolf remained determined throughout his Senate career to crush Bates. After four long years, D'Wolf eventually succeeded.James D'Wolf (Washington) to John D'Wolf (Bristol), April 19, 1824, Box 9, Folder 8, BHS. "There were now two subjects for consultations: the renomination of Bates as Collector at Bristol, Rhode Island, and the message on the compact with Georgia and the Cherokee titles. There were specific written charges against Bates by D'Wolf, the Senator from Rhode Island, and two bundles of papers for and against him." John Quincy Adams, March 29, 1824, in Charles Francis Adams, ed., *Memoirs of John Quincy Adams*, Volume VI (Philadelphia: J. B. Lippincott & Co., 1874–1877), 270–1. See also "George D'Wolf et al to James Monroe, January 10, 1824, Bristol, accuse Barnabas Bates of misconduct and call for his dismissal as collector of customs at Bristol, Rhode Island." Daniel Preston, ed., *A Comprehensive Catalogue of the Correspondence and Papers of James Monroe* (Westport, CT: Greenwood Press, 2002), 914. Much of the political correspondence held at the Bristol Historical Society between James D'Wolf and John D'Wolf, 1823–4, is

concerned with maneuvers—including claims that Bates was not legally a U.S. citizen and was, in fact, English—to destroy the political career of Barnabas Bates, who was supported by opponents of the slave trade. Box 9, Folders 1–8, D'Wolf Papers Bristol Historical Society (Bristol, RI). Although James D'Wolf gloated, "I now have an after game to play which is all easy & Plain sailing," the destruction of Bates's career had been, he later confessed, a "long & troublesome job." James D'Wolf (Washington) to John D'Wolf (Bristol), April 19, 1824, and James D'Wolf (Washington) to John D'Wolf (Bristol), May 17, 1824, Box 9, Folder 8, D'Wolf Papers, BHS.

15 In the same speech, James D'Wolf reflected on the importance of his constituents' interests and swore that should the "interests of the people of this state come into competition with mine, I shall consider myself bound to consult their Interests and not my own" and resign his position if compromised—which he did in October 1825. *Rhode Island American and General Advertiser*, November 7, 1820. Such "want of learning" in nationally elected public officials was, in fact, commonplace. As John Quincy Adams reflected in 1821 in reference to Henry Clay, for example, "He is, like almost all the eminent men of this country, only half educated." John Quincy Adams, March 9, 1821, quoted in Walter LaFeber, John Quincy Adams and American Continental Empire (Chicago: Quadrangle Books, 1965), 33.

16 *The Albany Advertiser* (Albany, NY), May 18, 1816; *New-Bedford Mercury* (New Bedford, MA), September 19, 1817; *Providence Gazette* (Providence, RI), September 28, 1822.

17 Vote tallies are based on a review of 246 Senate votes in which James D'Wolf participated, from January 24, 1822, to March 9, 1825, as published in the U.S. Senate Journals.

18 *Abridgment*, Vol. VII, 244–5.

19 John Warner (Havana) to Caesar Rodney, February 20, 1822, James Monroe Papers, LOC.

20 See, for example, the report from the Committee on Naval Affairs, submitted on March 2, 1822, which detailed the steps that had been taken "respecting the piracies committed in the Gulf of Mexico and the contiguous seas." "Additional number of small vessels to be employed for the suppression of piracy. Communicated to the House of Representatives, March 2, 1822," American State Papers 023, Naval Affairs Vol. 1 17th Congress, 1st Session Publication No. 207; *Abridgment*, VII, 266–7.

21 "What, however, I dread still more [than the threat from the Cuban slave population], and what in my opinion would be much more detrimental to our interests, is the occupation of this island by a great maritime power. Such an event would not only deprive us of this extensive and profitable branch of commerce, but in case of war with that nation ... might effectually blockade all the ports and shut up the outlets of our great western waters. Cuba is not only the key of the Gulph of Mexico, but of all the maritime frontier south of Savannah, and some of our highest interest, political and commercial, are involved in its fate." Joel Poinsett, *Notes on Mexico*, 294.

22 John Quincy Adams, April 7, 1822, *Memoirs*, Vol. V, 486.

23 "The trade to Havanna alone was now almost the only resource we had for procuring specie, and if it should be cut off it would greatly increase the embarrassments of our circulating medium." John Quincy Adams, *Memoirs*, Vol. IV, 205, quoted in Edward

Tatum, *The United States and Europe, 1815–1823: A Study in the Background of the Monroe Doctrine* (New York: Russell & Russell, 1936), 164.

24 John Quincy Adams, *Memoirs*, Vol. VI, 72–3, quoted in Samuel Flagg Bemis, John *Quincy Adams and the Foundations of American Foreign Policy* (New York: Alfred A. Knopf, 194, 372–3.

25 "Garnett of Virginia on recognition of South America. Annals of Congress, 17 Cong., 1 sess., House, April 10, 1822," quoted in Edward Tatum, *The United States and Europe, 1815–1823*, 168.

26 Quoted in Herminio Portell-Vilá, *La Historia de Cuba en Sus Relaciones con los Estados Unidos y España*, Vol. 1 (Miami, FL: Mnemosyne Publishing, 1969), 212–15.

27 Ibid., 216–17.

28 "The British squadron above mentioned arrived at Havana on the 24th ultimo. The commander immediately repaired to the house of the Governor-General of Cuba. A great sensation was felt at Havana from the appearance of this force, coming direct from England." This was noted, importantly, in the *Rhode Island Providence Patriot*, reprinted from the *Boston-Centinel*. *Providence Patriot, Columbian Phenix* (Providence), December 14, 1822.

29 As Joel Poinsett later noted, however, the captain-general had claimed that "he had no disposable force," when in fact he had "three corvettes, a gun brig, and four schooners" with "5,000 men in garrison."Register of the Debates in Congress, Vol. 1 (Washington: Gales & Seaton, 1825), 487–9.

30 *Niles Weekly Register* (Washington), March 30, 1822.

31 "Condition of the Navy, and its operations. Communicated to Congress, December 3, 1822," American State Papers 023, Naval Affairs Vol. 1 17th Congress, 2nd Session Publication No. 212.

32 Samuel Morrison, *Old Bruin*, 54; "Plantation Accounts, 1818–1852," D'Wolf Family Papers, Roll 11, Papers of the American Slave Trade, Part 2, RIHS.

33 "Expediente promovido por varios comerciantes de esta plaza en solicitud de practicos para la expedición Inglesa contra los piratas," 1822, Junta de Fomento de la Isla de Cuba, Negociado de Marina, Legajo 90, Expediente 3805, ANC.

34 *Abridgment*, Vol. VII, 382, 353–4, 384–9; Richard Peters, ed., *Public Statutes of the United States*, Vol. III (Boston: Charles C. Little and James Brown, 1846), 720. See also *Niles Weekly Register*, Vol. 29, October 8, 1825, 90.

35 In 1822, American papers reported that the British were briefly given "permission to make use of any part of [Cuba] in any expedition to suppress or punish the buccaneers" and had dispatched warships with marine soldiers for this purpose. *Louisville Public Advertiser* (Louisville, KY), December 28, 1822; "… the Spanish Cortes were in negociation with the British Ministry for the cession of the island of Cuba." *Providence Patriot, Columbian Phenix* (Providence, RI), December 14, 1822.

36 *Abridgment*, Vol. VII, 354, 384–9; Richard Peters, ed., *Public Statutes of the United States*, Vol. III (Boston: Charles C. Little and James Brown, 1846), 720. See also *Niles Weekly Register*, Vol. 29, October 8, 1825, 90.

37 *Abridgment*, Vol. VII, 409.

38 James D'Wolf (Washington) to John D'Wolf (Bristol), December 20, 1822, Box 8, Folder 32, D'Wolf Family Papers, BHS.

39 On January 4, 1823, when U.S. vice consul in Havana John Mountain wrote of "the recent tumult here," fears of anti–slave trade British warships were almost certainly what he had in mind. John Mountain (Havana) to John Quincy Adams, January 4, 1823, Roll 3, Dispatches from U.S. Consul at Havana, DNA.

40 By February 1823, American newspapers were arguing that although the British navy had been dispatched "it was supposed, in concert with the government of Cuba for the suppression of piracy," "now it would appear, that some other object was in view," which was likely "the cession of Cuba to Great Britain, as the price of her neutrality." *Maryland Gazette and Political Intelligencer* (Annapolis, MD), February 6, 1823. In early March 1823, these rumors increased: "It is evident that the ministerial papers of England are anxious to keep alive the pretensions of that government, for the *Courier*, and the *London Sun*, lately hazarded the suggestion, that the next advices from the West Indies will bring the important intelligence, that the Island of Cuba is a British possession." *Louisville Public Advertiser* (Louisville, KY), March 5, 1823. There had also been American fears of British acquisition of Cuba in the aftermath of the Florida treaty in 1819. See Edward Tatum, *The United States and Europe, 1815–1823*, 163, 170–1.

41 *Abridgment*, Vol. VII, 357; Peter Dalleo, "Thomas McKean Rodney: U.S. Consul in Cuba: The Havana Years, 1825–1829," *Delaware History* 22, No. 3 (1987), 207; John Warner (Havana) to John Quincy Adams (Washington, D.C.), January 27, 1823, Roll 3, Dispatches from U.S. Consul at Havana, DNA.

42 James D'Wolf (Washington) to John D'Wolf (Bristol), February 6, 1823, Box 9, Folder 2, D'Wolf Papers, BHS.

43 James D'Wolf (Washington) to John D'Wolf (Bristol), February 14, 1824, Box 9, Folder 6, D'Wolf Papers, BHS.

44 James D'Wolf (Washington) to John D'Wolf (Bristol), February 25, 1822, Box 8, Folder 28; James D'Wolf (Washington) to John D'Wolf (Bristol), March 14, 1824, Box 9, Folder 7, D'Wolf Papers, BHS.

45 James D'Wolf (Washington) to John D'Wolf (Bristol), March 19, 1824, Box 9, Folder 7, D'Wolf Papers, BHS.

46 James D'Wolf (Washington) to John D'Wolf (Bristol), March 19, 1824, Box 9, Folder 7, D'Wolf Papers, BHS.

47 Quoted in Herminio Portell-Vilá, *La Historia de Cuba*, 221.

48 Quoted in Louis Pérez, *Cuba in the American Imagination: Metaphor and the Imperial Ethos* (Chapel Hill: University of North Carolina Press, 2008), 30.

49 John Quincy Adams, Report Upon Weights and Measures, 1821; John Quincy Adams, Diary 31, January 1, 1819–March 20, 1821, November 10, 1824–December 6, 1824, in *The Diaries of John Quincy Adams: A Digital Collection* (Boston, MA: Massachusetts Historical Society, 2004), 529, masshist.org/jqadiaries.

50 Charles Mercer of Virginia delivered an extended speech to the House of Representatives on February 28, 1823, detailing how, even though the slave trade had been denounced as piracy "three years ago," "the African slave trade continues to spread its ravages over that much-injured continent." The House passed a resolution pressing for the right to search vessels and encouraging a universal declaration of the slave trade as piracy. *Abridgment*, Vol. VII, 456–9.

51 Laird Bergad, *Cuban Slave Market*, 52, 29, 31.
52 Zachariah Atkins and Thomas Wuturn (Matanzas), October 13, 1823; Case of Two Brothers, October 27, 1823; Frederick G. Wolbert (Lieutenant Commander for the U.S. Navy on the Wild Cat, Matanzas, October 15, 1823); Translation of Bill of Lading, Matanzas, October 10, 1823, in "Papers of David Porter, 1922," David Porter Papers, LOC.
53 Captain-General Vives (Havana) to David Porter, November 12, 1823, in "Papers of David Porter, 1922," David Porter Papers, LOC.
54 The summer recess between the Seventeenth Congress and the Eighteenth Congress lasted from March 3 to December 1, 1823.

8 Presidents

1 John Mountain (Havana) to John Quincy Adams, December 12, 1823; January 10, 1824, Dispatches from U.S. Consul to Havana, DNA.
2 Mark Gilderhus, "Monroe Doctrine: Meanings and Implications," *Presidential Studies Quarterly* 36 (2006): 8.
3 Edward Howland Tatum, *The United States and Europe, 1815–1823: A Study in the Background of the Monroe Doctrine* (New York: Russell & Russell, 1936).
4 See, for example, Gretchen Murphy, *Hemispheric Imaginings: The Monroe Doctrine and Narratives of U.S. Empire* (Durham: Duke University Press, 2005); Amy Kaplan, *The Anarchy of Empire in the Making of U.S. Culture* (Cambridge, MA: Harvard University Press, 2002).
5 For a sense of the exhaustive, largely early-twentieth-century historiography of this diplomatic initiative—which has tended to almost wholly overlook the importance of the Cuban slave trade—see Worthington C. Ford, "John Quincy Adams and the Monroe Doctrine," *American Historical Review* 7 (July 1902): 676–96; Hiram Bingham, *The Monroe Doctrine: An Obsolete Shibboleth* (New Haven: Yale University Press, 1913); William R. Manning, "Statements, Interpretations, and Applications of the Monroe Doctrine and of More or Less Allied Doctrines: From 1823–1845," *Proceedings of the American Society of International Law* 8 (1914): 34–58; Albert Bushnell Hart, *The Monroe Doctrine: An Interpretation* (Boston: Little, Brown, 1916); Dexter Perkins, "Europe, Spanish America, and the Monroe Doctrine," *American Historical Review* 27 (January 1922): 207–18; Alejandro Alvarez, *The Monroe Doctrine: Its Importance in the International Life of the States of the New World* (New York: Oxford University Press, 1924); Dexter Perkins, *The Monroe Doctrine, 1823–1826* (Cambridge, MA: Harvard University Press, 1927); W. R. Craven, Jr., "The Risk of the Monroe Doctrine," *Hispanic American Historical Review* 7 (August 1927): 320–33; Dexter Perkins, *The Monroe Doctrine, 1826–1867* (Baltimore: Johns Hopkins Press, 1933); Thomas R. Schellenberg, "Jeffersonian Origins of the Monroe Doctrine," *Hispanic American Historical Review* 14 (February 1934): 1–32; Edward Howland Tatum, *The United States and Europe, 1815–1823: A Study in the Background of the Monroe Doctrine* (New York: Russell & Russell, 1936); Thomas B. Davis, Jr., "Carlos de Alvear and James

Monroe: New Light on the Origin of the Monroe Doctrine," *Hispanic American Historical Review* 23 (November 1943): 632–49; Laura Bornholdt, "The Abbe de Pradt and the Monroe Doctrine," *Hispanic American Historical Review* 24 (May 1944): 201–21; Gale W. McGee, "The Monroe Doctrine—A Stopgap Measure," *Mississippi Valley Historical Review* 38 (September 1951): 233–50; Nikolai N. Bolkhovitinov, "Russia and the Declaration of the Noncolonization Principle: New Archival Evidence," *Oregon Historical Quarterly* 72 (June 1971): 101–26; Ernest R. May, *The Making of the Monroe Doctrine* (Cambridge, MA: Belknap Press of Harvard University Press, 1975); Edward P. Crapol, "John Quincy Adams and the Monroe Doctrine: Some New Evidence," *Pacific Historical Review* 48 (August 1979): 413–18; Timothy E. Anna, *Spain and the Loss of America* (Lincoln: University of Nebraska Press, 1983); Jay Sexton, *The Monroe Doctrine: Empire and Nation in Nineteenth-Century America* (New York: Hill and Wang, 2011).

6   See Edward Tatum, *The Monroe Doctrine*; Dexter Perkins, *The Monroe Doctrine*; Ernest May, *The Monroe Doctrine*.

7   See Louis Pérez, *Cuba and the United States: Ties of Singular Intimacy* (Athens: University of Georgia Press, 1990); Louis Pérez, *The War of 1898: The United States and Cuba in History and Historiography* (Chapel Hill: University of North Carolina Press, 1998); Richard Gott, *Cuba: A New History* (New Haven: Yale University Press, 2004); Louis Pérez, *Cuba in the American Imagination: Metaphor and the Imperial Ethos* (Chapel Hill: University of North Carolina Press, 2008).

8   See, for example, Kinley Brauer, "The Great American Desert Revisited: Recent Literature and Prospects for the Study of American Foreign Relations, 1815–1861," *Diplomatic History* 13 (Summer 1989): 395–418; William E. Weeks, "New Directions in the Study of Early American Foreign Relations," *Diplomatic History* 17 (Winter 1993): 73–96; Kinley Brauer, "The Need for a Synthesis of American Foreign Relations, 1815–1861," *Journal of the Early Republic*, 14 (1994): 467–76; Bradford Perkins, "Early American Foreign Relations: Opportunities and Challenges," *Diplomatic History* 22 (1998): 115–20; Peter P. Hill, "The Early National Period, 1775–1815," in Robert D. Schulzinger, ed., *A Companion to American Foreign Relations* (Malden, MA: Blackwell Publishing, 2003), 48–63; Mark T. Gilderhus, "Forming An Informal Empire Without Colonies: U.S.–Latin American Relations," *Latin American Research Review* 40, No. 3 (2005): 312–25; Michael Hogan and Thomas G. Paterson, eds., *Explaining the History of American Foreign Relations* (New York: Cambridge University Press, 2004).

9   See, for example, J. C. A. Stagg, "The Madison Administration and Mexico: Reinterpreting the Gutiérrez-Magee Raid of 1812–1813, *William and Mary Quarterly* 49 (2002): 449–80; J. C. A. Stagg, "James Madison and George Mathews: The East Florida Revolution of 1812 Reconsidered," *Diplomatic History* 30 (2006): 23–55; Rafe Blaufarb, "The Western Question: The Geopolitics of Latin American Independence," *American Historical Review* 112 (2007): 742–63; James E. Lewis, Jr., *The American Union and the Problem of Neighborhood: The United States and the Collapse of the Spanish Empire, 1783–1829* (Chapel Hill: University of North Carolina Press, 1998); James E. Lewis, Jr., *John Quincy Adams: Policymaker for the Union* (Wilmington, DE: Scholarly Resources, 2001); Peter J. Kastor, *The Nation's Crucible: The Louisiana*

Purchase and the Creation of America (New Haven: Yale University Press, 2004); J. C. A. Stagg, *Borderlines in Borderlands: James Madison and the Spanish–American Frontier, 1776–1821* (New Haven: Yale University Press, 2009).

10   See Robert Kagan, *Dangerous Nation* (New York: Alfred A. Knopf, 2006); Richard Kluger, *Seizing Destiny: How America Grew from Sea to Shining Sea* (New York: Alfred A. Knopf, 2007); George C. Herring, *From Colony to Superpower: U.S. Foreign Relations since 1776* (Oxford: Oxford University Press, 2008); Walter Nugent, *Habits of Empire: A History of American Expansion* (New York: Alfred A. Knopf, 2008).

11   See Herminio Portell-Vilá, *La Historia de Cuba*, Vol. 1, 221–45; Herminio Portell-Vilá, "La Doctrina de Monroe, Su Historia y Su Actual Status," 1962 [typed manuscript, Spanish with English notes], Box 10, unprocessed papers of Herminio Portell-Vilá, CHC.

12   N. N. Bolkhovitinov, Dokrtina Monro (Proiskhozdenie I Kharakter) [The Monroe Doctrine (Origin and Character)] (Moscow: Publishing House of Institute of International Relations, 1959).

13   Andrei V. Grinev, "The Plans for Russian Expansion in the New World," 16. Although Ernest May rightly drew attention to pressure on Adams from merchants such as James Lloyd and Charles Jared Ingersoll to "take a bold stand on the northwest coast question," he provides no evidence that these missives found their way into cabinet meetings. "Although there is no evidence on the point," Ernest May writes, "it seems probable that Adams showed these lines to Monroe" before suggesting that this prompted Adams's communications with the Russian minister. Ernest May, *The Monroe Doctrine*, 211–14.

14   N. N. Bolkovitinov, "Kontinental'naya kolonizatsiya ..." [Continental Colonization of Siberia and Maritime Colonization of Alaska: Similarity and Difference], *Acta Slavica Iaponica* 20 (2003); Yu A. Petrov, *Obrazovanie Rossiisko-Amerikanskoi kompanii* [Formation of the Russian-American Company] (Moscow: Nauka, 2000); V. V. Alekseev, E. V. Alekseeva, K. I. Zubkov, I. V. Poberezhnikov, *Aziatskaya Rossiya...* [Asiatic Russia in the Geopolitical and Civilizational Dynamic of the Sixteenth to Twentieth Century] (Moscow: Nauka, 2004); Andrei V. Grinev, "The Plans for Russian Expansion in the New World and the North Pacific in the Eighteenth and Nineteenth Centuries," *European Journal of American Studies*, Special Issue (2010): 1–25.

15   See Dexter Perkins, *The Monroe Doctrine, 1823–1826*, 75–80. I disagree with Tatum's interpretation of the relative importance of Cuba vis-à-vis other European threats in 1822–3. In discussing Canning–Rush negotiations, for example, he writes that Canning's "purpose in those interviews was a double one. He wished to limit the action of the United States with regard to Cuba, but he also wished to secure the support of the American government against the possible aggression of France. In the evolution of the Monroe Doctrine, it is obviously the second of these purposes which is the more important." Such a premise is by no means "clear," and the French machinations, including naval buildups in Europe and Haiti, were of immediate concern precisely because they might target Cuba. Edward Tatum, *The Monroe Doctrine*, 62. For a concise chronology of the administration's discussions and negotiations, see Ernest May, *The Making of the Monroe Doctrine* (Cambridge, MA: Harvard University Press, 1975).

16   Brian Loveman, *No Higher Law: American Foreign Policy and the Western Hemisphere since 1776* (Chapel Hill: University of North Carolina Press, 2010), 40–2.

17   Thomas Jefferson to James Monroe, October 24, 1823, in Gerard W. Gawalt, ed., Thomas Jefferson and James Monroe Correspondence, LOC.

18   James Monroe (Washington) to Thomas Jefferson, June 30, 1823, in Gerard W. Gawalt, ed., Thomas Jefferson and James Monroe Correspondence, LOC.

19   John Quincy Adams, quoted in Herminio Portell-Vilá, *La Historia de Cuba*, 244. During the period from 1820 to 1823, when representatives from the Creole elite in Cuba pressed for U.S. annexation, there was simultaneously a second Cortes de Cádiz in Spain, in which members of the Cuban delegation even considered the abolition of Cuban slavery. Spanish absolutism in 1823 put an end to these efforts.

20   James Monroe (Washington) to Thomas Jefferson, June 30, 1823, in Gerard W. Gawalt, ed., Thomas Jefferson and James Monroe Correspondence, LOC.

21   See Thomas G. Patterson, J. Garry Clifford and Kenneth J. Hagan, *American Foreign Relations: A History to 1920*, 5th ed (Boston: Houghton Mifflin, 2000), 101–3; Dexter Perkins, *A History of the Monroe Doctrine*, rev. ed. (Boston: Little, Brown, 1963); Edward Tatum, *The United States and Europe, 1815–1823* (New York: Russell & Russell, 1936), 258.

22   John Johnson, *A Hemisphere Apart: The Foundations of United States Policy Toward Latin America* (Baltimore: Johns Hopkins University Press, 1990), 80–1.

23   Ernest Obadele-Starks, *Freebooters and Smugglers: The Foreign Slave Trade in the United States* (Fayetteville: University of Arkansas Press, 2007), 71.

24   John Noonan, *The Antelope: The Ordeal of the Recaptured Africans in the Administrations of James Monroe and John Quincy Adams* (Berkeley: University of California Press, 1977), 85.

25   "Message of the President of the U.S., at the commencement of the first session of the Eighteenth Congress. Comm to the Senate, Dec 2, 1823," American State Papers 05, Foreign Relations Vol. 5 18th Congress, 1st Session Publication No. 360.

26   John Quincy Adams to S. Smith, May 30, 1823, quoted in Ernest May, *Monroe Doctrine*, 183.

27   *Abridgment*, Vol. VII, 466–71. For a further breakdown, see Mark Gilderhus, "Monroe Doctrine: Meanings and Implications," 5–16.

28   As early as 1793, for example, he had been master of the *Hannah*, which provided supplies to the French government at Saint Domingue. Greg H. Williams, *The French Assault on American Shipping, 1793–1813*, 169. During the War of 1812, Parrott had invested in trade ventures with Boston merchant Thomas Amory—the same man who challenged Nathaniel Fellowes, Jr. for control of his uncle's Cuban estate—and in recent years, John Parrott's brother William had remained a prominent New England–Cuba merchant. In 1819, for example, William had written to John from Boston about "the African ships from the Havanna" and the profits traders accumulated in "the purchase of their slaves." "Merchants," William wrote, "will forever find some expedient or other to get clear of advalorem duties" and described complex schemes, including counterfeit bills, to avoid tariffs. There was no way around it, William said: "When this is stopped some other mode equally ingenious will be found out." See John Parrott (Portsmouth) to Peter Coffin (Boston), November 4, 1812, Box 1, Folder

1, Letterbook, 1811–1819, John Parrott Papers, NHHS; William Parrott (Boston) to John Parrott (Washington), January 6, 1819, Box 1, Folder 8, John Parrott Papers, NHHS. On Parrott's cousin see Kenneth Scott, "Bonaparte Toscan and the Cuban Pirates," *The American Neptune*, Vol. VI, No. 2 (1946); John Parrott Papers, 1925–2, Finding Aid, New Hampshire Historical Society. A decade earlier, John Parrott may have even employed the *Gossypium* in the Baltic trade. In an 1812 letter to William Pearce and Sons of Gloucester, Massachusetts, for example, Parrott referred to the difficulty of having "insurance effected on Brig Gossypium to the North of Europe." John Parrott (Portsmouth, NH) to William Pearce and Sons (Gloucester, MA), April 7, 1812, Box 1, Folder 1, Letterbook 1811–1819, John Parrott Papers, NHHS.

29 J. Mason to John Parrott (Washington), undated [answered January 7, 1822], Box 2, Folder 3, John Parrott Papers, NHHS.

30 At the time of James Monroe's December 1823 address, twenty-one U.S. naval vessels already patrolled the West Indies, fifteen of which had been "specifically equipped for the suppression of piracy." The other six "vessels of war" had been drawn from the total U.S. fleet of sixteen warships, leaving just ten other warships for such locales as the "Pacific" and the "Mediterranean." Tallied by the number of guns per vessel (as a better measure of relative tonnage/cost than sheer number of ships) in 1823, 48 percent of commissioned U.S. naval forces were already deployed in the Caribbean, primarily on behalf of the U.S.–Cuba trade. I have calculated a rough total of 426 guns deployed on U.S. naval vessels. As the United States was listed as "Preparing to relieve the Franklin" in the Pacific, the Franklin's guns have not been included. For barges, I estimated two guns. I estimated one gun for both the steam galliot Sea Gull and transport ship, Decoy. The total guns therefore deployed in the West India Squadron were 108; another 98 guns were deployed on the six warships listed as dispatched to the "West Indies" for a total of 206 guns deployed in the Caribbean. This does not include ships on the Great Lakes that were overwhelmingly in poor condition or out of service or other vessels under repair or awaiting deployment. "Condition and disposition of the Navy," December 1823, American State Papers 023, Naval Affairs Vol. 1 18th Congress, 1st Session Pub No. 258.

31 The senator from Maine, Chandler, who had urged "promptitude" in handling the previous naval bills, now wondered if the "increased [would be] beyond what the circumstances of the country require." Five ships would be sufficient, he said, not ten. He was answered by the Massachusetts senator who had led the earlier naval push, Lloyd, who "read a letter from the Secretary of the Navy to the Committee on Naval Affairs," which argued for "an addition of as many as ten vessels." Unfortunately, the secretary of the navy wrote, "the small number of naval yards on our seacoast, rendered it probable that not more than five or six of the vessels would be built in the present year." So, Lloyd said, "if the act passed in its present shape ... not more than $400,000 or $500,000 of the money would be wanted within the year." Of course, as was quickly pointed out, this sum alone would exceed the amount annually appropriated for the expansion of the navy. Parrott had effectively moved to double the naval expansion centered on Cuba. When discussion resumed on January 27, 1824, "the clause respecting the sum to be appropriated" was struck out. A few objections were raised, but discussion continued on February 6, 1824, when the "blank for the

appropriation" was filled in: $425,000 was to be spent annually for two years for a total of $850,000 to purchase ten additional warships. The bill was defended by senators who suggested that this total, when combined with the $500,000 annual appropriation for the expansion of the navy, would still lag behind the $1 million per year that had been allocated from 1816 to 1821. But this time more senators voiced concern. However, "on the ground that in peace we ought to prepare for war, Mr. L[owrie] was willing to vote for the whole number of vessels proposed by this bill." The bill was amended to fund the navy at $250,000 the first year and $200,000 for each of the three following years. *Abridgment*, Vol. VII, 491–2, 494, 504–8.

32   M. C. Perry (New York) to Thomas Breese, March 3, 1824, quoted in Samuel Morrison, *Old Bruin*, 69–84.

33   John Noonan, *The Antelope*, 86.

34   Based on a review of debates and votes in *Journal of the Senate, 1789–1873*, 446–53; *Journal of the Executive Proceedings of the Senate, 1815–1829*, 380–7. Further review of senators' motivations in siding with D'Wolf and Chandler to oppose specific provisions of the treaty is out of the scope of this study, but demands further examination.

35   *Abridgment*, Vol. VII, 587.

36   Since at least the peak years of the Cuba–Baltic trade in 1810–11, Bayard had invested in Cuba as a member of the commercial house of LeRoy, Bayard & McEvers, where he continued to work. *Memorial of Sundry Merchants (and others) ... The Subject of Piracies* (Washington, December 13, 1824); Baily & Willis (New York), December 16, 1811, Box 7, Folder 6, D'Wolf Papers, BHS; John M. Forbes to J. A. Hambrock (Hamburg), January 8, 1810, Copenhagen Letterbook, 1809–1810, Forbes Papers, HBS. Bayard was also involved—along with the New York–Cuba merchants G.G. & S. Howland—in the building of vessels of the Greek government. A well-connected member of the Manhattan commercial elite, Bayard had even opened his doors to Alexander Hamilton after the Hamilton–Burr duel. Henry Wysham Lanier, *A Century of Banking in New York*, 94. The house would eventually fail in 1827. See *Papers of Henry Clay*, Vol. 4, 383.

37   Like the merchants in New York, the Portland investors requested "that the class of small cruisers" that had been dispatched to fight pirates "should be increased." The merchants who signed the Portland petition as members of the committee were Ezekiel Whitman, Asa Clapp, Albert Newhall, William Swann, and Charles Fox. *Memorial of a Committee Selected by the Merchants of Portland in the State of Maine on the Subject of Piracies* (Washington, December 16, 1824).

38   "Philadelphia ... piracy," December 20, 1824, Sen 18A–G5, DNA.

39   The Bristol petition included a roster of fifty of the leading Rhode Island investors in the Cuba trade, packed with virtually every member of the D'Wolf commercial empire in Rhode Island and their allies. The full roster listed a who's who in the D'Wolf commercial network: George D'Wolf, John Howe, Thomas Warren, John D'Wolf, Jr., Hersey Bradford, John D'Wolf, Samuel Smith, N. Bullock, Hy. D'Wolf, Lemuel Briggs, L. Drury, Golden Dearth, Greenwood Reynolds, B. Potter Dimond, Joseph Torrey, Hezekiah Brown, John Peckman, Joshua Gladding, Giles Luther, Milton French, Samuel Bosworth, William D'Wolf, Edw. Church, Benj. Norris, John Wardwell, Jacob Babitt, Wm Munscher[?], Richmond, Tho. Church, N. Peck,

Nicholas Peck, Jr., John Howland, Benjamin Tilley, Hw. Norris, Geo. B. Monro, Byron Diman, S. S. Asher, Jo. Diman, B. Browning, Geo Coggeshall, Ephraim Monro, Saml. Wardwell, Norton Watson, Wm Throop[?], Leonard Waldon II, Benjm. Waldron, Henry Dearth, Simon Davis, and Heze. Wardwall. "Rhode Island … piracy," December 29, 1824, Sen 18A–G5, DNA.

40   "Boston … piracy … Cuba," December 27, 1824, Sen 18A–G5, DNA.

41   *Abridgment of the Debates of Congress*, Vol. VIII, 150.

42   Thomas Amory Coffin to Robert Hazlchurst & Co., July 16, 1797, Letterbook 1, 1797–1798, Thomas Amory Coffin Papers, HBS; Francis Gregory, Nathan Appleton, 125.

43   Robert Greenhalgh Albion, *The Rise of New York Port 1815–1860* (New York: C. Scribner's Sons, 1939), 412. Prior to the West India Squadron's arrival, the Rhode Island merchant Jacob Babbitt insured his ship *Sally* on June 27, 1816, from Bristol, Rhode Island, to Havana, Cuba, at a rate of 2.5 percent. Similarly, on October 12, 1818, he insured the *Cashier* from Bristol to Trinidad, Cuba, at 2 percent, and on July 18, 1820, this same ship was insured for an identical voyage at 2.5 percent. Commercial Insurance Company policy to Jacob Babbitt & Co., *Sally* from Bristol, Rhode Island, to Havana, Cuba, June 27, 1816, for $2,000 at 2.5 percent; Invoice, *Cashier* to Trinidad de Cuba for Jacob Babbitt & Co., October 12, 1818, for $2,732.29 at 2 percent; Invoice, *Cashier* to Trinidad de Cuba for Jacob Babbitt & Co., July 18, 1820, $563.75 at 2.5 percent; Jacob Babbitt Papers, Roll 1, Papers of American Slave Trade, Part 2, RIHS.

44   Robert Greenhalgh Albion, *The Rise of New York Port*, 193.

45   Junta de Fomento de la Isla de Cuba, Negociado de harina, Legajo 90, Expediente 3785, ANC.

46   Robert Beale, ed., *A Report of the Trial of Commodore David Porter* (Washington: The United States Navy, 1825), 38–9, 51, 54–5, 142.

47   *Niles Weekly Register*, Vol. 29, 90–6.

48   Quoted in David Dixon Porter, *Memoirs of Commodore David Porter*, 286.

49   The specie transport totals recorded in the questioning of naval officers were: Gallagher (*Shark*): $127,000; Dallas (*John Adams*): $104,000; Stephen Cassin (*Peacock*): $140,000; Francis H. Gregory (*Grampus*): $7,000; Thomas H. Stevens (*Jackall, Shark*): $163,500; Charles W. Skinner (*Wild Cat*): $148,532; John P. Zantinger (*Weasel*): $197,000; John T. Ritchie (*Ferret, Fox*): $60,000; Charles Boarman (*Weasel*): $65,000. Robert Beale, ed., *A Report of the Trial of Commodore David Porter*, 50, 56, 62, 64, 68, 71, 74, 79–80. For precedents see the *Ontario* in Robert Greenhalgh Albion, *The Rise of New York Port*, 170.

50   See Robert Beale, ed., *A Report of the Trial of Commodore David Porter*, 56, 68; William Charles Redfield, ed., *Genealogical History of the Redfield Family in the United States* (Albany: Munsell & Rowland, 1860), 61.

51   *Register of Debates in Congress*, Vol. II, 56–8; John Mountain (Havana) to John Warner (Baltimore), October 30, 1824, Roll 3, Dispatches from U.S. Consul at Havana, DNA.

52   See David F. Long, *Nothing Too Daring: A Biography of Commodore David Porter, 1780–1843* (Annapolis, MD: United States Naval Institute, 1970), 256–83.

53 James D'Wolf (Washington) to John D'Wolf (Bristol), February 9, 1825, Box 9, Folder 9, D'Wolf Papers, BHS.

54 With other New Englanders and a local Kentuckian, D'Wolf had purchased 107 acres in downtown Louisville at a total cost of $10,720, where he and his partners invested $100,000 in the Hope Distillery Company. James D'Wolf (Bristol) to Henry Clay, September 5, 1821, in James F. Hopkins, ed., *The Papers of Henry Clay*, Vol. 3, 109–11; James De Wolf (Bristol) to Henry Clay, July 5, 1823, in James F. Hopkins, ed., *The Papers of Henry Clay*, Vol. 3, 453–4.

55 *Appendix to Register*, Vol. 1, 117; Richard Peters, ed., *The Public Statutes at Large of the United States of America* (Boston: Little, Brown, 1856), 131. As Delaware congressman Louis McLane noted on January 26, 1826, the additional $500,000 was combined with the naval appropriations in 1825: "Five hundred thousand for the regular annual sum, and five hundred thousand more for building ten sloops of war." *Register of Debates in Congress*, Vol. II, 1208.

9 Speculators

1 Jos W. Torrey (Bristol) to E Spalding (Matanzas), January 12, 1823, Box 1, Folder 5, Edward Spalding Papers, CHC.

2 Joseph Torrey (Bristol) to E Spalding (Matanzas), December 31, 1823, Box 1, Folder 6, Edward Spalding Papers, CHC.

3 Jacob Babbitt (Bristol) to Edward Spalding (Matanzas), March 25, 1823, Box 2, Folder 1, Edward Spalding Papers, RIHS; Benjamin Parker (Salem) to Edward Spalding (Matanzas), November 19, 1823, Box 2, Folder 2, Edward Spalding Papers, RIHS. Samuel Bosworth also died in December 1823. See Golden Dearth (Bristol) to Edward Spalding (Matanzas), December 19, 1823, Box 2, Folder 2, Edward Spalding Papers, RIHS.

4 Ibid.

5 Joseph Torrey (Bristol) to E Spalding (Matanzas), March 26, 1824, Box 1, Folder 7, Edward Spalding Papers, CHC.

6 John S. Gilkeson, Jr., *Middle-Class Providence, 1820–1940* (Princeton, 1986), 19. See also Mark S. Schantz, *Piety in Providence: Class Dimensions of Religious Experience in Antebellum Rhode Island* (Ithaca: Cornell University Press, 2000); Louis P. Masur, *Rites of Execution: Capital Punishment and the Transformation of American Culture* (New York: Oxford University Press, 1989), 101; Stuart Blumin, "Middle-Class Formation in Nineteenth Century America: A Critique and Some Proposals," *American Historical Review* 90 (1985): 338. For a detailed analysis of issues of political suffrage and related activism in this context, see Patrick T. Conley, *Democracy in Decline: Rhode Island's Constitutional Development, 1776–1841* (Providence: Rhode Island Historical Society, 1977), 217–89.

7 Edward Baptist, "Toxic Debt, Liar Loans, Collateralized and Securitized Human Beings, and the Panic of 1837," in Michael Zakim and Gary Kornblith, eds., *Capitalism Takes Command: The Social Transformation of Nineteenth-Century America*

(Chicago: University of Chicago Press, 2012), 76; Larry Neal, "The Financial Crisis of 1825 and the Restructuring of the British Financial System," *Federal Reserve Bank of St. Louis Review* 80 (May–June 1998): 53–76.

8   This partnership had briefly been Latting, Adams & Tracy, when John Latting partnered with another well-connected American, the Newbury merchant John Tracy, in 1821. Tracy didn't last long, however, and he died in Matanzas on August 28, 1822. See Moses Tryon (Hartford) to Edward Spalding (Bristol), October 1, 1821, Box 1, Folder 8, Edward Spalding Papers, RIHS; "Latting & Tracy Account with the Brig Mount Pleasant, Matanzas April 19th," 1822, Box 1, Folder 9, Edward Spalding Papers, RIHS; James Edward Greenleaf, *Genealogy of the Greenleaf Family* (Boston: F. Wood, 1896), 31; John James Currier, *"Ould Newbury": Historical and Biographical Sketches* (Boston: Damrell and Upham, 1896), 579; Robert Rogers, Jr. (Bristol) to Edward Spalding (Matanzas), January 12, 182[4], Box 2, Folder 3, Edward Spalding Papers, RIHS.

9   Newton would later become an anti-Jackson U.S. congressman in the late 1820s and early 1830s. *Virginia Magazine of History and Biography*, Vol. 9 (Richmond: Virginia Historical Society, 1901), 200; "Thomas Newton, Jr. (1768–1847)," Congressional Biographical Directory, bioguide.congress.gov [accessed June 1, 2010].

10   Allan Nevins, *James Truslow Adams: Historian of the American Dream* (Urbana: University of Illinois Press, 1968), 4. Adams's tenure in Cuba was also short-lived, however, and he died on May 1, 1825, at the age of thirty-two. After Adams was buried on his Cuban estate, Adams's brother-in-law, the Virginia–Cuba merchant Albert O. Newton, unsuccessfully lobbied Henry Clay from Matanzas to replace him. Albert O. Newton (Matanzas) to Henry Clay, May 4, 1825, in James F. Hopkins, ed., *The Papers of Henry Clay*, Vol. 4, 326; *Commercial Advertiser* (New York), May 18, 1825. Francis Adams's allies at the New York commercial house of Gardiner, Greene & Howland—which had grown to include Joseph Howland's brother Samuel Shaw in 1816—also lobbied Secretary of State Henry Clay in 1825 for Howland to become the U.S. commercial agent at Matanzas. James F. Hopkins, ed., *The Papers of Henry Clay*, Vol. 4, 395.

11   See James F. Hopkins, ed., *The Papers of Henry Clay*, Vol. 4, 552–3.

12   Francis Adams (New York) to Edward Spalding (Bristol), August 16, 1824, Box 1, Folder 7, Edward Spalding Papers, CHC.

13   Brothers Cramers, quoted in John D'Wolf (Boston) to Edward Spalding (Matanzas), February 4, 1825, Box 1, Folder 8, Edward Spalding Papers, CHC.

14   John D'Wolf (Boston) to Edward Spalding (Matanzas), February 4, 1825 and John D'Wolf (Boston) to Edward Spalding (Matanzas), February 25, 1825, Box 1, Folder 8, Edward Spalding Papers, CHC.

15   Edward Spalding (Matanzas) to John D'Wolf (Bristol), February 19, 1825, Box 7, Folder 29, D'Wolf Family Papers, BHS.

16   William Savage (Boston) to Edward Spalding (Matanzas), March 15, 1825 and Thomas Savage (Havana) to E Spalding (Mat), March 15, 1825, Box 1, Folder 8, Edward Spalding Papers, CHC.

17   "I never saw such miserable sugars," John Morland wrote from Havana on January 5, 1825, "Geo' crops will be short on the Nueva Esperanza." John Morland (Havana) to

Edward Spalding (Matanzas), January 5, 1825. See also G[eorge] D'Wolf to Edward Spalding, January 10, 1825, Box 1, Folder 2, Edward Spalding Papers, RIHS.

18   John Morland (Havana) to Edward Spalding (Matanzas), February 22, 1825, Box 1, Folder 4, Edward Spalding Papers, RIHS.

19   Robert Trueman, Jr. (Boston) to James D'Wolf (Bristol), March 30, 1825, Box 1, Folder 8, Edward Spalding Papers, CHC.

20   Joseph "José" O. Wilson (Sn Juan, Camarioca) to Edward Spalding (Matanzas), April 20, 1825, Box 1, Folder 8, Edward Spalding Papers, CHC.

21   John Morland (Havana) to Edward Spalding (Matanzas), March 11, 1825, Box 1, Folder 8, Edward Spalding Papers, CHC.

22   See George Howe, *Mount Hope*, 229–36.

23   Francis Gregory, *Nathan Appleton*, 128.

24   Daniel Webster, April 1–2, 1824, quoted in Edwin Percy Whipple, ed., *The Great Speeches and Orations of Daniel Webster* (Boston: Little, Brown, 1879), 96.

25   "Gold in the form of bullion or Spanish doubloons was purchased in Lisbon or Havana, being cheaper there than in Boston or London." Francis Gregory, *Nathan Appleton*, 134.

26   This same report estimated the value of U.S. exports to China and the East Indies at $12 million, and the value of Chinese and Indian imports at $5 million, employing more than three thousand mariners. "Coins, foreign and domestic. Communicated to the House of Representatives, January 26, 1819," American State Papers 011, Finance Vol. 3 15th Congress, 2nd Session Publication No. 551.

27   James Fichter, *So Great A Profit: How the East Indies Trade Transformed Anglo-American Capitalism* (Cambridge, MA: Harvard University Press, 2010), 4; Jacques A. Barbier, "The United States Balance of Payments with Spanish America and the Philippine Islands, 1790–1819: Estimates and Analysis of Principal Components," in Allan J. Kuethe, ed., *The North American Role in the Spanish Imperial Economy, 1760–1819* (Manchester: Manchester University Press, 1984), 29–49. Notably, contemporaries were almost universally explicit in linking specie flows with national economic prosperity and power. Specie was of paramount importance, both in reality and in its influence on the course of economic activity based on the actions of individuals who believed it to be essential.

28   For an introduction to elite, early-nineteenth-century American trade with Asia, see Samuel Eliot Morison, *The Maritime History of Massachusetts* (Boston, 1921), 247, 273–4; James Phillips, *Salem and the Indies: The Story of the Great Commercial Era of the City* (Boston: Houghton Mifflin, 1947), 92–100, 333–4; Ernest May and John Fairbank, eds., *America's China Trade in Historical Perspective: The Chinese and American Performances* (Cambridge, MA: Harvard University Press, 1986), 12–23.

29   Daniel Webster (Boston), September 28, 1825, quoted in James F. Hopkins, ed., *The Papers of Henry Clay*, Vol. 4, 695–8.

30   *The National Gazette* (Philadelphia), December 16, 1825. As the Spanish would soon learn, by dispatching a spy via an American ship, these rumors turned out to be greatly exaggerated.

31   Alexander Burton (Cadiz, Spain), June 30, 1825, and Andrew Armstrong (Port au

Prince, Haiti), July 10, 1825, in James F. Hopkins, ed., *The Papers of Henry Clay*, Vol. 4, 493, 524.

32 James Wright (Santiago de Cuba), July 31, 1825; Joel Poinsett (Mexico), August 21, 1825; Joel R. Poinsett (Mexico), September 13, 1825, in James F. Hopkins, ed., *The Papers of Henry Clay*, Vol. 4, 63, 584, 640–1.

33 Rufus King (Cheltenham), August 11, 1825, and Thomas Rodney (Wilmington), August 12, 1825, in James F. Hopkins, ed., *The Papers of Henry Clay*, Vol. 4, 574–5.

34 Henry Clay (Washington) to John Quincy Adams, October 3, 1825; Henry Clay to James Brown (Paris), October 25, 1825; Joel Poinsett (Mexico), October 29, 1825, in James F. Hopkins, ed., *The Papers of Henry Clay*, Vol. 4, 711–12, 762, 777.

10 Executioners

1 Abiel Abbot, *Letters Written in the Interior of Cuba* (Boston: Bowles and Dearborn, 1829), 231.

2 On Northerners' presence in the U.S. South, see Dennis C. Rousey, "Friends and Foes of Slavery: Foreigners and Northerners in the Old South," *Journal of Social History* 35 (Winter, 2001): 373–96. See also Charles G. Hoffmann & Tess Hoffmann, *North by South: The Two Lives of Richard James Arnold* (Athens: University of Georgia Press, 1988), and Fletcher Green, *The Role of the Yankee in the Old South* (Athens: University of Georgia Press, 1972).

3 The following account is primarily based on the work of Manuel Barcia Paz and the correspondence of Sarah Wilson, Joseph "Jose" O. Wilson, and contacts of Ebenezer William Sage. S. Wilson (Camarioca) to John D'W (Bristol), June 26, 1825, Box 16, Folder 9, D'Wolf Papers, BHS; [Joseph] "Jose" O. Wilson (Sn Juan, Camarioca) to Edward Spalding (Matanzas), June 19, 1825, Box 2, "Correspondence a Plan Cuban Slave," unprocessed, Edward Spalding Papers, Cuban Heritage Collection, University of Miami (Miami, Florida); Ebenezer William Sage Papers, Box 2, Folder 1825, MHS (Boston, MA); Stephen "Esteban" Fales (Sumedero, Cuba) to Lydia French [Fales] (Bristol, RI), June 21, 1825, unprocessed, Fales Family Papers.

4 Cuban dogs were so well known that in 1803 the Spanish sold three hundred of them, along with one hundred horses, to the French for use in Haiti. The horses had "cost from 70 to 100 Dollars per Head and the Dogs from 20 to 50" dollars. Vincent Gray (Havana) to James Madison (Washington), May 26, 1803, Reel 1, Dispatches from the United States Consuls in Havana, U.S. National Archives (Washington, D.C.). Generations later, Cuban dogs would also be used by the Confederacy during the U.S. Civil War to hunt runaways. Matt Childs, *The 1812 Aponte Rebellion* (Chapel Hill: University of North Carolina Press, 2006), 42. For more detailed information on the breeding and uses of particular types of Cuban dogs, see Barcia Paz, *Seeds of Insurrection*, 58–9. On the dragoons' involvement, see S. Wilson (Camarioca) to John D'W (Bristol), June 26, 1825, Box 16, Folder 9, D'Wolf Papers, BHS. Two decades later, Gangá would be executed for his alleged participation in the La Escalera conspiracy in 1844. On the Africans' ethnicities and the plantations affected, see

Barcia Paz, *Seeds of Insurrection*, 34–5, and Barcia Paz, *The Great African Slave Revolt of 1825*.

5   Mary Fales (Bristol, RI) to Lydia S. Fales (Hartford, CT), June 12, 1806, and July 18, 1806, Fales family letters, 1806–1840, Hay Library, Brown University.

6   Welcome Arnold Greene, February 21, 1810, *Journals of Welcome Arnold Greene* (Madison: State Historical Society of Wisconsin, 1956), 185. See, for example, Joyce E. Chaplin, *An Anxious Pursuit: Agricultural Innovation and Modernity in the Lower South, 1730–1815* (Chapel Hill: University of North Carolina Press, 1993); Mark Smith, *Mastered by the Clock: Time, Slavery and Freedom in the American South* (Chapel Hill: University of North Carolina Press, 1995); Richard Follett, *The Sugar Masters: Planters and Slaves in Louisiana's Cane World, 1820–1860* (Baton Rouge: Louisiana State University Press, 2005); B. W. Higman, *Plantation Jamaica, 1750–1850: Capital and Control in a Colonial Economy* (Kingston, Jamaica: University of the West Indies Press, 2008).

7   "Inventory of Negroes, Stock …" D'Wolf Papers Part III, Reel 11, Papers of the American Slave Trade; James D'Wolf (Bristol) to George Munro, November 2, 1818, D'Wolf Papers, Reel 9, Part 2, Papers of the American Slave Trade; Byron Diman (New Counting Room, Bristol) to George Munro (Saint Marcos, Cuba), January 24, 1819, and Byron Diman (Bristol) to James D'Wolf (Havana), February 13, 1819, Reel 9, Part 2, Papers of the American Slave Trade. Munro did not get on well: In 1821, like many foreigners in the Caribbean, he died of illness. For years following his death, his allies in Rhode Island would try to collect from Cuba on debts for his wife and "young family of orphan children." Byron Diman (Bristol) to Edward Spalding (Havana), February 7, 1823, Edward Spalding Papers, Box 1, Folder 9, RIHS and Nathaniel Bullock (Bristol) to Edward Spalding (Matanzas), March 14, 1824, Edward Spalding Papers, Box 2, Folder 3, RIHS.

8   James D'Wolf to George Munro, February 14, 1820, D'Wolf Papers Part I, Reel 9, Papers of the American Slave Trade, RIHS. As Richard Follett notes, in Cuba "planters imported free contract laborers to toil alongside slaves in the cane economy … where new technology was deemed too complex for slaves, sugar planters recruited waged (mainly male) Spanish and [later] Chinese workers to labor alongside bondspeople." Richard Follett, *The Sugar Masters* (Baton Rouge, LA: Louisiana State University Press, 2005), 84–5.

9   John D'Wolf (Bristol) to Stephen Fales, April 5, 1817, and James (Bristol) to Francis M. Dimond, May 20, 1821, Reel 9, Part 2, Papers of the American Slave Trade; W[illia]m Fales (Madruga, Cuba) to Lydia S. [Fales] French (Bristol), November 7, 1818, and Stephen Fales (Madruga) to [Lydia S. Fales French] (Bristol), July 21, 1820, Fales Letters, John Hay Library, Brown University (Providence, Rhode Island); "Dn. Jorge Bertlett, natural de Boston … en Dic de 1819," April 23, 1827, Legajo 405, Intendencia Gral de Hacienda, Cartas de naturalizacion, Archivo Nacional de Havana (Havana, Cuba); Stephen Fales (Sumedero, Cuba) to Lydia S. [Fales] French (Bristol), June 24, 1822, Fales Letters; Stephen "Esteban" Fales (Sumedero, Cuba) to Lydia French [Fales] (Bristol, RI), June 21, 1825, unprocessed, Fales Family Papers; Stephen Fales (Sumedero) to Lydia S. [Fales] French (Bristol), April 4, 1824, Fales Family Papers. Fales also likely had ties to Philadelphia, where George Fales actively worked

with James D'Wolf in 1817–18 (with the commercial house Cheever & Fales). See Box 7, Folder 21: Fales, George (Philadelphia), Samuel, 1817, 1818, D'Wolf Papers, BHS.

10   James D'Wolf (Bristol) to Stephen Fales, August 8, 1817, 1817 Letterbook, D'Wolf Papers, Baker Library, HBS; James D'Wolf (Bristol) to Stephen Fales, October 20, 1817, 1817 Letterbook, D'Wolf Papers, Baker Library; "Dn. James D'Wolf contra Dn. Guillermo B. Bowen por pesos," March 11, 1816, Legajo 575, Expediente 6631, Escribania de Salinas, ANC.

11   Stephen Fales (Sumedero) to Lydia S. [Fales] French (Bristol), June 24, 1822, Fales Letters; Stephen Fales (Sumedero) to Lydia S. [Fales] French (Bristol), August 22, 1822, Fales Family Papers. Fales was granted a leave, for example, in May 1821 and temporarily replaced with Francis Dimond. James D'Wolf (Bristol) to Francis M. Dimond, May 20, 1821, Reel 9, Part 2, D'Wolf Papers, Papers of the American Slave Trade.

12   "List of the Names of the Negros belonging to the Ingenio Nuevo Esperanza," Reel 11, D'Wolf Papers, Papers of the American Slave Trade, Part 2.

13   April 14, 1821, Joseph Goodwin Diary, Manuscript Collections Relating to Slavery, NYHS, nyhistory.org/slaverycollections; September 28, 1821, Joseph Goodwin Diary; May 20, 1821, Joseph Goodwin Diary. Enslaved *ingenio* workers typically worked from three in the morning until noon, and after a brief break, continued to work until sunset or later; during harvest these hours might last from four in the morning until midnight, with a single one-hour break. Matt Childs, *The 1812 Aponte Rebellion*, 61, 57. See also Jose A. Benitez, *Las Antillas: Colonización, Azúcar e Imperialismo* (Havana Casa de las Americas, 1976), 88.

14   See January 19, 1823, and January 20, 1823, Joseph Goodwin Diary.

15   For typical labor tasks and wall-building, see January 7, 1822, February 1, 1822, and March 13, 1822. For the persistence of runaways, see, for example, April 1, 1826, April 9, 1826, June 25, 1826, June 27, 1826, Joseph Goodwin Diary. For wall-building, see also May 31, 1822, Joseph Goodwin Diary; Theresa Singleton, "Slavery and Spacial Dialectics in Cuban Coffee Plantations," *World Archaeology* 33, no. 1 (2001): 103. On Goodwin's relationship with the overseer and personal field management, see March 31, 1823, April 8, 1823, and April 27, 1823, Joseph Goodwin Diary. For sample feast days, the Sabbath and Christmas, see June 8, 1823, June 24, 1823, and December 25, 1824, Joseph Goodwin Diary.

16   For Goodwin's socializing with Spanish and Creole planters, see July 25, 1821, Joseph Goodwin Diary. For Americans' relations with Spanish merchants and elites more generally, see, for example, J. J. Latting (Camarioca, Cuba) to Edward Spalding (Matanzas), February 20, 1824, Box 1, Folder 8, Edward Spalding Papers, CHC. On a tour through New England in 1817, for example, President James Monroe had visited Bristol and "dined at Geo. DWolf's house, stayed about one hour [and] was very affable." John D'Wolf (Bristol) to James D'Wolf, July 1, 1817, D'Wolf Papers, Box 8, Folder 11, BHS. On George D'Wolf's relationship with Captain-General Francisco Dionisio Vives, see George Howe, *Mount Hope: A New England Chronicle* (New York: Viking Press, 1959), 235.

17   April 24, 1825, Joseph Goodwin Diary; Page 1, Joseph Goodwin Diary; November

25, 1821, Joseph Goodwin Diary; May 1, 1825, and May 3, 1825, Joseph Goodwin Diary; May 4, 1825, Joseph Goodwin Diary. Two years later, after a similar visit, Goodwin also noted that George D'Wolf left with "his son George & Charles two Negroes & a wench." February 22, 1827, Joseph Goodwin Diary. From August 1825 to June 1826, Goodwin purchased a total of eighteen slaves, some from the estate, and others which had no doubt recently arrived in the illegal African trade. See "Account of Speculation in negroes, 1825," Joseph Goodwin Diary.

18 Joseph "Jose" O. Wilson (Sn Juan Plantation) to Edward Spalding (Matanzas), May 25, 1825, Box 1, Folder 8, Edward Spalding Papers, CHC. See Asa Anthony (Mount Hope) to E Spalding (Matanzas), May 5, 1825, and Asa Anthony (Mount Hope) to E Spalding (Mat), June 8, 1825, Box 1, Folder 8, Edward Spalding Papers, CHC; S. Wilson (Camarioca) to John D'W (Bristol), June 26, 1825, Box 16, Folder 9, D'Wolf Papers, BHS.

19 S. Wilson (St. Juans Plantation, Camarioca) to John D'Wolf (Bristol, RI), July 11, 1818, Box 16, Folder 2, D'Wolf Papers, BHS; S. Wilson to John D'Wolf, February 10, 1819, Box 16, Folder 3 and S. Wilson (Camarioca) to John D'Wolf, May 18, 1820, Box 16, Folder 4, D'Wolf Papers, BHS; S. Wilson (Camarioca) to John D'Wolf (Bristol), March 19, 1823, Box 16, Folder 7, D'Wolf Papers, BHS; S. Wilson (Camarioca) to John D'Wolf (Bristol), July 6, 1823, Box 16, Folder 7, D'Wolf Papers, BHS. On the frequency of Americans riding armed in Cuba, see Karen Robert, *New Year in Cuba: Mary Gardner Lowell's Travel Diary, 1831–1832* (Boston: Massachusetts Historical Society: Northern University Press, 2003), 79.

20 Invoice, *Cashier* for Trinidad de Cuba, April 14, 1819, Jacob Babbitt Papers, Reel 1, Papers of the American Slave Trade, Part 2; S. Wilson (Camarioca) to John D'W (Bristol), June 26, 1825, Box 16, Folder 9, D'Wolf Papers, BHS; *El Diario de la Habana*, Rare Books and Manuscript Library, University of Havana (Havana, Cuba).

21 [Joseph] Jose O. Wilson (Sn Juan, Camarioca) to Edward Spalding (Matanzas), June 19, 1825, Box 2: "Correspondence a Plan Cuban Slave," Edward Spalding Papers, CHC; [Joseph] Jose O. Wilson (Sn Juan, Camarioca) to Edward Spalding (Matanzas), June 26, 1825, Box 2: "Correspondence a Plan Cuban Slave," Edward Spalding Papers, CHC.

22 Stephen "Esteban" Fales (Sumedero, Cuba) to Lydia French [Fales] (Bristol, RI), June 21, 1825, unprocessed, Fales Family Papers.

23 S. A. Rainey (Santa [La] Carolina) to Ebenezer William Sage (Boston), June 18, 1825; S.A. Rainey (Santa Ana) to N. Talcott (New York), June 19, 1825; Ephron William Webster (Ontario) to Ebenezer William Sage (Boston), November 13, 1825; S. A. Rainey (Santa Ana) to Ebenezer William Sage (Boston), September 9, 1825, Box 2, Folder 1825, Sage Papers.

24 Translation quoted in Theresa Singleton, "Slavery and Spacial Dialectics on Cuban Coffee Plantations," 103; S. A. Rainey (Santa Ana) to Ebenezer W. Sage (Boston), June 8, 1826, Box 2, Folder 1826–1830, Sage Papers; Stephen "Esteban" Fales (Sumedero, Cuba) to Lydia French [Fales] (Bristol, RI), January 28, 1826, unprocessed, Fales Family Papers; S. Wilson (Camarioca) to Susan D'Wolf (Bristol), April 3, 1826, Box 16, Folder 9, D'Wolf Papers, BHS. See S. Wilson (Camarioca) to [unknown], November 26, 1826, Box 16, Folder 9 and Box 16, Folder 11, D'Wolf Papers, BHS.

25 Abiel Abbot, *Letters Written in the Interior of Cuba* (Boston: Bowles and Dearborn, 1829), 21.

26 Ibid., 12–13, 54, 144, 13, 41.

27 Ibid., 50, 55. On Abbot's sense of restraint, see also S. Everett, ed., *Sermons by the Late Rev. Abiel Abbot* (Boston: Wait, Greene & Co., 1831), ix.

28 Abiel Abbot, *Letters Written in the Interior of Cuba*, 127.

29 Robert Paquette, *Sugar Is Made with Blood* (Middletown, CT: Wesleyan University Press), 72; Karen Robert, *New Year in Cuba*, 16. For perhaps the most comprehensive study of African resistance in this period, see Manuel Barcia Paz, *Seeds of Insurrection*.

30 Karen Robert, *New Year in Cuba*, 79. For more on the walls and security measures at the *Santa Ana* in this period, see the loose pages of Baconais's "Plantation Journal," 1832, Box 2, Folder 1831–1833, Sage Papers. See also Megan Marshall, *The Peabody Sisters: Three Women Who Ignited American Romanticism* (Boston: Houghton Mifflin, 2005), 275.

31 John Quincy Adams, *Amistad Argument* (Whitefish, MT: Kessinger Publishing, LLC 2004), 20; October 29, 1822, Joseph Goodwin Diary; Sarah S. Wilson (Camarioca) to John D'Wolf (Bristol), October 26, 1823, Box 16, Folder 8, D'Wolf Papers, BHS.

Conclusion

1 Laurie Robertson-Lorant, *Melville: A Biography* (New York: Clarkson Potter, 1996), 40.

2 Wilson L. Heflin, Mary K. Bercaw Edwards, and Thomas Farel Heffernan, *Herman Melville's Whaling Years* (Nashville: Vanderbilt University Press, 2004).

3 Henry Clay to Alexander Everett (Washington), April 27, 1825, in James F. Hopkins, ed., *The Papers of Henry Clay*, Vol. 4 (Lexington: University Press of Kentucky, 1972), 292–300. In 1825–6, Everett routinely received correspondence from his commercial contacts in New England through the office of the secretary of state, and in January 1826, Henry Clay forwarded Everett a protest from merchants in Maine against excessive fees being charged by Spanish officials in Cuba. Charles Stewart Davies (Portland, ME), January 2, 1826; Henry Clay to Alexander Everett, January 6, 1826, in James F. Hopkins, ed., *The Papers of Henry Clay*, Vol. 5, 2, 13.

4 Alexander Everett Diary, 1809–1811; Alexander Everett Diaries (Cuba), April 6, 1840, Everett-Noble Papers, MHS; Karen Robert, *New Year in Cuba: Mary Gardner Lowell's Travel Diary, 1831–1832* (Boston: Massachusetts Historical Society: Northeastern University Press, 2003), 180.

5 James G. Forbes (Washington), May 17, 1825, in James F. Hopkins, ed., *The Papers of Henry Clay*, Vol. 4, 380–1.

6 *New York Mirror* (New York), May 4, 1833.

7 "Papeles relativos al despacho de cartas de naturaleza a los pobladores extranjeros desde el año 1818 a 1855," 1818–1855, Cartas de naturalización, Legajo 405, No Orden 22, ANC.

8   Jos[eph] R. Corlis (["On board the Angelina, Lake Ponchetrain"]) to John Corlis (Paris, KY), January 6, 1825, Box 8, Folder 58, Corliss-Respess Papers, FHS. Joseph Corlis was well versed in both Spanish–American trade and the prospects of Western expansion: His family had invested in trade with South America for years, before one branch—led by John Corlis—had resettled in Bourbon County, Kentucky. In the early 1820s, Joseph's brother, fellow Rhode Islander John Corlis, regularly contended with the daily realities of exploitation and resistance on Kentucky plantations. In December 1820, for example, he not only fretted over the flight of an enslaved man named Ezekiel, but described how his neighbors' barn had burned down, destroying "all his grain." This was, John Corlis wrote, "the work of some of his negroes." JR Corliss (Bourbon County, KY) to John Corlis (New York), December 8, 1820, Box 2, Folder 10, Corliss-Respess Papers, FHS.

9   "Papeles relativos al despacho de cartas de naturaleza a los pobladores extranjeros desde el año 1818 a 1855," 1818–1855, Cartas de naturalización, Legajo 405, No Orden 22, ANC.

10   Auguste Pierre Chouteau and Jules de Mun (St. Louis) to Henry Clay [to John Quincy Adams], May 3, 1825, in James F. Hopkins, ed., *The Papers of Henry Clay*, Vol. 4, 322–3.

11   James Wright (St. Jago) to John Quincy Adams, July 6, 1824, Roll 1, Dispatches from U.S. Consul at Santiago, DNA.

12   "Report of the Committee of the Moa Land Company to the Board of Directors," April 17, 1826, JCB.

13   This material is taken from "El Consul de New York remite lista de los colonos que vienen a avecinarse en Baracoa. A la Junta de Poblacion," 1826, Real Consulado y Junta de Fomento, Legajo 184, Expediente 8335, ANC.

14   See David Roediger, *Wages of Whiteness* (New York: Verso, 1991), 133–56.

15   "El Consul de New York remite lista de los colonos que vienen a avecinarse en Baracoa. A la Junta de Poblacion," 1826, Real Consulado y junta de Fomento, Legajo 184, Expediente 8335, ANC.

16   *Saturday Evening Chronicle* (Cincinnati, OH), April 28, 1827.

17   "… delicadísimo si la grande empresa de establecimiento de extrangeros en Moa tiene o no su elemento en algún proyecto ambicioso del gobierno americano y un plan serio y muy combinado para engrandecer los Estados Unidos con la preciosa joya de la Isla de Cuba," El Comandante Militar de Matriculas de la Provincia de Cuba (Havana), August 22, 1827, in "El Consul de New York remite lista de los colonos que vienen a avecinarse en Baracoa. A la Junta de Poblacion," 1826, Real Consulado y junta de Fomento, Legajo 184, Expediente 8335, ANC.

18   "El Consul de New York remite lista de los colonos que vienen a avecinarse en Baracoa. A la Junta de Poblacion," 1826, Real Consulado y junta de Fomento, Legajo 184, Expediente 8335, ANC.

19   This was not the same James Anderson who had served as the U.S. consul to Santiago: that James Anderson died in March 1824. *City Gazette and Commercial Advertiser* (Charleston, SC), March 23, 1824; "Papeles relativos al despacho de cartas de naturaleza a los pobladores extranjeros desde el año 1818 a 1855," 1818–1855, Cartas de naturalización, Legajo 405, No Orden 22, ANC.

20   "El Consul de New York remite lista de los colonos que vienen a avecinarse en Baracoa. A la Junta de Poblacion," 1826, Real Consulado y junta de Fomento, Legajo 184, Expediente 8335, ANC.

21   Karen Robert, *New Year in Cuba*, 16.

22   The region of Moa was never entirely depopulated, however, and it would later become a site of intensive nickel mining, which—after the decline of sugar in the twentieth century—would become the island's chief export.

23   Edward E. Baptist, *The Half Has Never Been Told: Slavery and the Making of American Capitalism* (New York: Basic Books, 2014); Mark Smith, *Mastered By the Clock: Time, Slavery, and Freedom in the American South* (Chapel Hill: University of North Carolina Press, 1997).

24   David Eltis, *Economic Growth and the Ending of the Transatlantic Slave Trade* (New York: Oxford University Press, 1987), 190–3, 228. See also Dale Tomich, *Through the Prism of Slavery: Lsbor, Capital, and World Economy* (Lanham, MD: Rowman and Littlefield, 2004), 76–7.

25   Santamaría García and Alejandro García Alvarez, *Economia y colonia: la economía cubana y la relación con España, 1765–1902* (Madrid: CSIC, Instituto de Historia, Departamento de Historia de América, 2004), 74; Matt Childs, *The 1812 Aponte Rebellion*, 61.

26   Although sugar would ultimately determine the price structures of the slave trade and define the course of Cuba's plantation development, there was "a prolonged struggle with coffee planters, and for a time [sugar coexisted] with a coffee economy which also prospered on the basis of slave labor until the 1840s." Laird Bergad, Fe Iglesias García, and María del Carmen Barcia, *The Cuban Slave Market, 1790–1880* (New York: Cambridge University Press, 1995), 26.

27   See Louis Pérez, *Winds of Change: Hurricanes and the Transformation of Nineteenth-Century Cuba* (Chapel Hill: University of North Carolina Press, 2001).

28   Dale Tomich, *Through the Prism of Slavery*, 81, 86.

29   Louis Pérez, ed., *Impressions of Cuba in the Nineteenth Century: The Travel Diary of Joseph J. Dimock* (Wilmington, DE: Scholarly Resources, 1998), xiii, xi–xii.

30   Peter Dalleo, "Thomas McKean Rodney: U.S. Consul in Cuba: The Havana Years, 1825–1829," *Delaware History* 22 (1987): 211.

31   Robert Greenhalgh Albion, *The Rise of New York Port, 1815–1860* (New York: C. Scribner's Sons, 1939), 394–7.

32   See Roland T. Ely, *La Economia Cubana entre las Dos Isabeles, 1492–1832*, 3rd ed. (Bogota: Aedita Editores, 1962); Roland Ely, *Comerciantes Cubanos del Siglo XIX* (Bogota: Aedita Editores, 1961); Roland Ely, "From Counting House to Cane Field: Moses Taylor and the Cuban Sugar Plantations in the Reign of Isabel II, 1833–1868" (Ph.D. diss., Harvard University, 1959).

33   For a sampling of the English-language portion of nineteenth-century Cuba travel literature, see Robert Francis Jameson, *Letters from the Havana, during the Year 1820* (London, 1821); Abiel Abbot, *Letters Written in the Interior of Cuba* (Boston, 1829); George Hallam, *Narrative of a Voyage from the Montego Bay...* (London, 1831); James Edward Alexander, *Transatlantic Sketches, Comprising Visits to the Most Interesting Scenes in North and South America* (London, 1833); Henry Tudor, *Narrative of a Tour in*

North America (London, 1834); Charles Augustus Murray, *Travels in North America during the Years 1834, 1835, and 1836...* (London: James Duncan, 1839); David Turnbull, *Travels in the West, Cuba, with Notices of Porto Rico and the Slave Trade* (London: Longman, Orne, Brown, Green, and Longmans, 1840); Carlos Barinetti, *A Voyage to Mexico and Havana* (New York, 1841); J. G. F. Wurdermann, *Notes on Cuba* (Boston, 1844); Richard Madden, *The Island of Cuba* (London: Gilpin, 1849); Richard Burleigh, *Cuba and the Cubans* (New York: Samuel Hueston, 1850); John Glanville Taylor, *The United States and Cuba: Eight Years of Change and Travel* (London: Richard Bentley, 1851); Richard Henry Dana, *To Cuba and Back* (London: Smith, Elder & Co., 1859); Demoticus Philalethes (pseudonym), *Yankee Travels Through the Island of Cuba* (New York: D. Appleton & Co., 1859); Julia Ward Howe, *A Trip to Cuba* (Boston: Ticknor and Fields, 1860); Carlton Rogers, *Incidents of Travels in the Southern States and Cuba* (New York: R. Craighead, 1862); Anthony Trollope, *The West Indies and the Spanish Main*, 5th ed. (London, 1862); George William, *Sketches of Travel in the Old and the New World* (Charleston, SC, 1871); Samuel Hazard, *Cuba with Pen and Pencil* (London, 1873); William Howell Reed, *Reminiscences of Elisha Atkins* (Cambridge, MA, 1890); Edwin Atkins, *Sixty Years in Cuba* (Cambridge, MA: Riverside Press, 1926).

34 Julia Ward Howe, *A Trip to Cuba* (Boston, 1860); Samuel Hazard, *Cuba with Pen and Pencil* (London, 1873).

35 Louis Pérez, "Cuba and the United States: Origins and Antecedents of Relations, 1760s–1860s," in Louis Pérez, ed., *Cuban Studies 21* (Pittsburgh, PA: University of Pittsburgh Press, 1989), 71.

36 *New York Times* (New York), June 13, 1911.

37 Roland Ely, *La Economia Cubana entre las Dos Isabeles, 1492–1832*, 3rd ed. (Bogotá: Aedita Editores, 1962), 87.

38 When the Anglo-American gasworks engineer John Jeffrey—who had overseen the building of gasworks in numerous cities throughout North America—was hired to supervise the Havana gasworks in 1850–1, for example, he deplored the state of the primitive gasworks that had been prematurely build years earlier as "the most miserable wrecks, you can imagine." Though his business was focused in the United States, Jeffrey had also recently lobbied (unsuccessfully) to build gasworks throughout Mexico in 1849–50. John Jeffrey (Havana) to Alexander Jeffrey (Cleveland), October 16, 1851, Box 1, Folder 8 and related correspondence, Box 1, Folder 7–8, Alexander Jeffrey Papers, FHS.

39 Zanetti Lecuona and Garcia Alvarez, *Sugar and Railroads: A Cuban History, 1837–1959* (Chapel Hill: University of North Carolina Press, 1998), 6, 61–2; Rebecca Scott, *Slave Emancipation in Cuba: The Transition to Free Labor, 1860–1899* (Princeton: Princeton University Press, 1985), 87.

40 Louis Pérez, "Cuba and the United States," 72.

41 Matt Childs, *The 1812 Aponte Rebellion*, 49.

42 Dale Tomich, *Through the Prism of Slavery*, 84–5.

43 Robert Dalzell, *Enterprising Elite: The Boston Associates and the World They Made* (Cambridge, MA: Harvard University Press, 1987), 230.

44 Edward Gray, *William Gray* (Boston: Houghton Mifflin Company, 1914), 83–5.

45 Frank Cassell, *Merchant Statesman in the Young Republic: Samuel Smith of Maryland,*
    1752–1839 (Madison: University of Wisconsin Press, 1971), 263.
46 George Howe, *Mount Hope* (New York: Viking Press, 1959), 197.

Index

On the Typeface

This book is set in Adobe Garamond Pro, a typeface originally designed by Robert Slimbach in 1989 and named after the sixteenth-century French punchcutter Claude Garamont.

Although several typefaces named after Garamont appeared in the early twentieth century, a 1926 exposé by the type scholar Beatrice Warde revealed that the more popular Garamont "revivals" were in fact based on the typefaces of the seventeenth-century French printer Jean Jannon. In contrast, Slimbach's Garamond is based on actual Claude Garamont types and specimens held by the Plantin-Moretus Museum in Antwerp, Belgium.

Adobe Garamond exhibits traits characteristic of the old-style form: long extenders, tall capitals, an oblique axis and bracketed serifs. Yet its terminals are more blunt than those of similar faces, and the edges have few hard angles. The heavy weight of the roman also produces a stronger color than commonly found in digitized revivals of metal typefaces. The italics, based on the designs of Garamont's contemporary Robert Granjon, feature an extreme slope.

VersoBooks.com

facebook.com/   @versobooks   versobooks.   @versobooks
versobks   tumblr.com